ISBN 0-8373-3109-9

C-3109   CAREER EXAMINATION S

This is your PASSBOOK® for...

Standards Compliance Analyst

Test Preparation Study Guide

Questions & Answers

NATIONAL LEARNING CORPORATION

Copyright © 2012 by

National Learning Corporation

212 Michael Drive, Syosset, New York 11791

All rights reserved, including the right of reproduction in whole or in part, in any form or by any means, electronic or mechanical, including photocopying, recording, or by any information storage and retrieval system, without permission in writing from the Publisher.

(516) 921-8888
(800) 645-6337
FAX: (516) 921-8743
www.passbooks.com
sales @ passbooks.com
info @ passbooks.com

PRINTED IN THE UNITED STATES OF AMERICA

PASSBOOK®
NOTICE

This book is SOLELY intended for, is sold ONLY to, and its use is RESTRICTED to *individual*, bona fide applicants or candidates who qualify by virtue of having seriously filed applications for appropriate license, certificate, professional and/or promotional advancement, higher school matriculation, scholarship, or other legitimate requirements of educational and/or governmental authorities.

This book is NOT intended for use, class instruction, tutoring, training, duplication, copying, reprinting, excerption, or adaptation, etc., by:

(1) Other publishers

(2) Proprietors and/or Instructors of "Coaching" and/or Preparatory Courses

(3) Personnel and/or Training Divisions of commercial, industrial, and governmental organizations

(4) Schools, colleges, or universities and/or their departments and staffs, including teachers and other personnel

(5) Testing Agencies or Bureaus

(6) Study groups which seek by the purchase of a single volume to copy and/or duplicate and/or adapt this material for use by the group as a whole without having purchased individual volumes for each of the members of the group

(7) Et al.

Such persons would be in violation of appropriate Federal and State statutes.

PROVISION OF LICENSING AGREEMENTS. — Recognized educational commercial, industrial, and governmental institutions and organizations, and others legitimately engaged in educational pursuits, including training, testing, and measurement activities, may address a request for a licensing agreement to the copyright owners, who will determine whether, and under what conditions, including fees and charges, the materials in this book may be used by them. In other words, a licensing facility exists for the legitimate use of the material in this book on other than an individual basis. However, it is asseverated and affirmed here that the material in this book *CANNOT* be used without the receipt of the express permission of such a licensing agreement from the Publishers.

NATIONAL LEARNING CORPORATION
212 Michael Drive
Syosset, New York 11791

Inquiries re licensing agreements should be addressed to:
The President
National Learning Corporation
212 Michael Drive
Syosset, New York 11791

PASSBOOK® SERIES

THE *PASSBOOK® SERIES* has been created to prepare applicants and candidates for the ultimate academic battlefield — the examination room.

At some time in our lives, each and every one of us may be required to take an examination — for validation, matriculation, admission, qualification, registration, certification, or licensure.

Based on the assumption that every applicant or candidate has met the basic formal educational standards, has taken the required number of courses, and read the necessary texts, the *PASSBOOK® SERIES* furnishes the one special preparation which may assure passing with confidence, instead of failing with insecurity. Examination questions — together with answers — are furnished as the basic vehicle for study so that the mysteries of the examination and its compounding difficulties may be eliminated or diminished by a sure method.

This book is meant to help you pass your examination provided that you qualify and are serious in your objective.

The entire field is reviewed through the huge store of content information which is succinctly presented through a provocative and challenging approach — the question-and-answer method.

A climate of success is established by furnishing the correct answers at the end of each test.

You soon learn to recognize types of questions, forms of questions, and patterns of questioning. You may even begin to anticipate expected outcomes.

You perceive that many questions are repeated or adapted so that you can gain acute insights, which may enable you to score many sure points.

You learn how to confront new questions, or types of questions, and to attack them confidently and work out the correct answers.

You note objectives and emphases, and recognize pitfalls and dangers, so that you may make positive educational adjustments.

Moreover, you are kept fully informed in relation to new concepts, methods, practices, and directions in the field.

You discover that you are actually taking the examination all the time: you are preparing for the examination by "taking" an examination, not by reading extraneous and/or supererogatory textbooks.

In short, this PASSBOOK®, used directedly, should be an important factor in helping you to pass your test.

STANDARDS COMPLIANCE ANALYST

DUTIES

As a Standards Compliance Analyst, you would review operating certificate applications for public and private facilities. You would also serve on-site inspection teams; assist applicants in interpreting established regulatory requirements, policies and standards; participate in certification survey activities; and write reports on the results of review and inspection activities. As a Standards Compliance Analyst 2, you would be required to handle more complex issues and to exercise more independent judgment in performing those duties, and you may also supervise Standards Compliance Analysts.

Standards Compliance Analysts 2 (Mental Health) evaluate mental health programs against established standards, laws, rules and regulations. Program evaluations may include on-site inspections including review of treatment/service plans, program spaces, staff, services, program practices, etc. Other duties may include operating certificates; participating in quality management activities; providing technical assistance; and reviewing Prior Approval Review (PAR) applications.

Standards Compliance Analysts 2 (Developmental Disabilities) supervise and lead a team of staff engaged in quality improvement, on-site/field inspection, survey, and/or certification activities for developmental disabilities treatment, service and care providers funded and regulated by the federal government and/or New York State. Incumbents serve as the lead team member and technical expert in programs, rules and regulations by providing guidance, direction and supervision to subordinate staff; serving as the agency's representative on certification, quality improvement and on-site/field inspection and survey matters; resolving technical issues; assisting treatment, service and care providers in developing plans for remediation and corrective action; and assisting higher-level staff in the development of strategic plans, initiatives and projects.

SCOPE OF THE EXAMINATION

The written test will cover knowledge, skills and abilities in such areas as:

1. Evaluating information and evidence;
2. Interpersonal communications;
3. Interviewing;
4. Preparing written material;
5. Understanding and interpreting written material;
6. Mental health concepts, trends and facilities; and
7. Supervision.

HOW TO TAKE A TEST

I. YOU MUST PASS AN EXAMINATION

A. WHAT EVERY CANDIDATE SHOULD KNOW

Examination applicants often ask us for help in preparing for the written test. What can I study in advance? What kinds of questions will be asked? How will the test be given? How will the papers be graded?

As an applicant for a civil service examination, you may be wondering about some of these things. Our purpose here is to suggest effective methods of advance study and to describe civil service examinations.

Your chances for success on this examination can be increased if you know how to prepare. Those "pre-examination jitters" can be reduced if you know what to expect. You can even experience an adventure in good citizenship if you know why civil service exams are given.

B. WHY ARE CIVIL SERVICE EXAMINATIONS GIVEN?

Civil service examinations are important to you in two ways. As a citizen, you want public jobs filled by employees who know how to do their work. As a job seeker, you want a fair chance to compete for that job on an equal footing with other candidates. The best-known means of accomplishing this two-fold goal is the competitive examination.

Exams are widely publicized throughout the nation. They may be administered for jobs in federal, state, city, municipal, town or village governments or agencies.

Any citizen may apply, with some limitations, such as the age or residence of applicants. Your experience and education may be reviewed to see whether you meet the requirements for the particular examination. When these requirements exist, they are reasonable and applied consistently to all applicants. Thus, a competitive examination may cause you some uneasiness now, but it is your privilege and safeguard.

C. HOW ARE CIVIL SERVICE EXAMS DEVELOPED?

Examinations are carefully written by trained technicians who are specialists in the field known as "psychological measurement," in consultation with recognized authorities in the field of work that the test will cover. These experts recommend the subject matter areas or skills to be tested; only those knowledges or skills important to your success on the job are included. The most reliable books and source materials available are used as references. Together, the experts and technicians judge the difficulty level of the questions.

Test technicians know how to phrase questions so that the problem is clearly stated. Their ethics do not permit "trick" or "catch" questions. Questions may have been tried out on sample groups, or subjected to statistical analysis, to determine their usefulness.

Written tests are often used in combination with performance tests, ratings of training and experience, and oral interviews. All of these measures combine to form the best-known means of finding the right person for the right job.

II. HOW TO PASS THE WRITTEN TEST

A. NATURE OF THE EXAMINATION

To prepare intelligently for civil service examinations, you should know how they differ from school examinations you have taken. In school you were assigned certain definite pages to read or subjects to cover. The examination questions were quite detailed and usually emphasized memory. Civil service exams, on the other hand, try to discover your present ability to perform the duties of a position, plus your potentiality to learn these duties. In other words, a civil service exam attempts to predict how successful you will be. Questions cover such a broad area that they cannot be as minute and detailed as school exam questions.

In the public service similar kinds of work, or positions, are grouped together in one "class." This process is known as *position-classification*. All the positions in a class are paid according to the salary range for that class. One class title covers all of these positions, and they are all tested by the same examination.

B. FOUR BASIC STEPS

1) Study the announcement

How, then, can you know what subjects to study? Our best answer is: "Learn as much as possible about the class of positions for which you've applied." The exam will test the knowledge, skills and abilities needed to do the work.

Your most valuable source of information about the position you want is the official exam announcement. This announcement lists the training and experience qualifications. Check these standards and apply only if you come reasonably close to meeting them.

The brief description of the position in the examination announcement offers some clues to the subjects which will be tested. Think about the job itself. Review the duties in your mind. Can you perform them, or are there some in which you are rusty? Fill in the blank spots in your preparation.

Many jurisdictions preview the written test in the exam announcement by including a section called "Knowledge and Abilities Required," "Scope of the Examination," or some similar heading. Here you will find out specifically what fields will be tested.

2) Review your own background

Once you learn in general what the position is all about, and what you need to know to do the work, ask yourself which subjects you already know fairly well and which need improvement. You may wonder whether to concentrate on improving your strong areas or on building some background in your fields of weakness. When the announcement has specified "some knowledge" or "considerable knowledge," or has used adjectives like "beginning principles of…" or "advanced … methods," you can get a clue as to the number and difficulty of questions to be asked in any given field. More questions, and hence broader coverage, would be included for those subjects which are more important in the work. Now weigh your strengths and weaknesses against the job requirements and prepare accordingly.

3) Determine the level of the position

Another way to tell how intensively you should prepare is to understand the level of the job for which you are applying. Is it the entering level? In other words, is this the position in which beginners in a field of work are hired? Or is it an intermediate or advanced level? Sometimes this is indicated by such words as "Junior" or "Senior" in the class title. Other jurisdictions use Roman numerals to designate the level – Clerk I, Clerk II, for example. The word "Supervisor" sometimes appears in the title. If the level is not indicated by the title, check the description of duties. Will you be working under very close supervision, or will you have responsibility for independent decisions in this work?

4) Choose appropriate study materials

Now that you know the subjects to be examined and the relative amount of each subject to be covered, you can choose suitable study materials. For beginning level jobs, or even advanced ones, if you have a pronounced weakness in some aspect of your training, read a modern, standard textbook in that field. Be sure it is up to date and has general coverage. Such books are normally available at your library, and the librarian will be glad to help you locate one. For entry-level positions, questions of appropriate difficulty are chosen – neither highly advanced questions, nor those too simple. Such questions require careful thought but not advanced training.

If the position for which you are applying is technical or advanced, you will read more advanced, specialized material. If you are already familiar with the basic principles of your field, elementary textbooks would waste your time. Concentrate on advanced textbooks and technical periodicals. Think through the concepts and review difficult problems in your field.

These are all general sources. You can get more ideas on your own initiative, following these leads. For example, training manuals and publications of the government agency which employs workers in your field can be useful, particularly for technical and professional positions. A letter or visit to the government department involved may result in more specific study suggestions, and certainly will provide you with a more definite idea of the exact nature of the position you are seeking.

III. KINDS OF TESTS

Tests are used for purposes other than measuring knowledge and ability to perform specified duties. For some positions, it is equally important to test ability to make adjustments to new situations or to profit from training. In others, basic mental abilities not dependent on information are essential. Questions which test these things may not appear as pertinent to the duties of the position as those which test for knowledge and information. Yet they are often highly important parts of a fair examination. For very general questions, it is almost impossible to help you direct your study efforts. What we can do is to point out some of the more common of these general abilities needed in public service positions and describe some typical questions.

1) General information

Broad, general information has been found useful for predicting job success in some kinds of work. This is tested in a variety of ways, from vocabulary lists to questions about current events. Basic background in some field of work, such as sociology or economics, may be sampled in a group of questions. Often these are principles which have become familiar to most persons through exposure rather than through formal training. It is difficult to advise you how to study for these questions; being alert to the world around you is our best suggestion.

2) Verbal ability

An example of an ability needed in many positions is verbal or language ability. Verbal ability is, in brief, the ability to use and understand words. Vocabulary and grammar tests are typical measures of this ability. Reading comprehension or paragraph interpretation questions are common in many kinds of civil service tests. You are given a paragraph of written material and asked to find its central meaning.

3) Numerical ability

Number skills can be tested by the familiar arithmetic problem, by checking paired lists of numbers to see which are alike and which are different, or by interpreting charts and graphs. In the latter test, a graph may be printed in the test booklet which you are asked to use as the basis for answering questions.

4) Observation

A popular test for law-enforcement positions is the observation test. A picture is shown to you for several minutes, then taken away. Questions about the picture test your ability to observe both details and larger elements.

5) Following directions

In many positions in the public service, the employee must be able to carry out written instructions dependably and accurately. You may be given a chart with several columns, each column listing a variety of information. The questions require you to carry out directions involving the information given in the chart.

6) Skills and aptitudes

Performance tests effectively measure some manual skills and aptitudes. When the skill is one in which you are trained, such as typing or shorthand, you can practice. These tests are often very much like those given in business school or high school courses. For many of the other skills and aptitudes, however, no short-time preparation can be made. Skills and abilities natural to you or that you have developed throughout your lifetime are being tested.

Many of the general questions just described provide all the data needed to answer the questions and ask you to use your reasoning ability to find the answers. Your best preparation for these tests, as well as for tests of facts and ideas, is to be at your physical and mental best. You, no doubt, have your own methods of getting into an exam-taking mood and keeping "in shape." The next section lists some ideas on this subject.

IV. KINDS OF QUESTIONS

Only rarely is the "essay" question, which you answer in narrative form, used in civil service tests. Civil service tests are usually of the short-answer type. Full instructions for answering these questions will be given to you at the examination. But in case this is your first experience with short-answer questions and separate answer sheets, here is what you need to know:

1) Multiple-choice Questions

Most popular of the short-answer questions is the "multiple choice" or "best answer" question. It can be used, for example, to test for factual knowledge, ability to solve problems or judgment in meeting situations found at work.

A multiple-choice question is normally one of three types—

- It can begin with an incomplete statement followed by several possible endings. You are to find the one ending which *best* completes the statement, although some of the others may not be entirely wrong.
- It can also be a complete statement in the form of a question which is answered by choosing one of the statements listed.
- It can be in the form of a problem – again you select the best answer.

Here is an example of a multiple-choice question with a discussion which should give you some clues as to the method for choosing the right answer:

When an employee has a complaint about his assignment, the action which will *best* help him overcome his difficulty is to
- A. discuss his difficulty with his coworkers
- B. take the problem to the head of the organization
- C. take the problem to the person who gave him the assignment
- D. say nothing to anyone about his complaint

In answering this question, you should study each of the choices to find which is best. Consider choice "A" – Certainly an employee may discuss his complaint with fellow employees, but no change or improvement can result, and the complaint remains unresolved. Choice "B" is a poor choice since the head of the organization probably does not know what assignment you have been given, and taking your problem to him is known as "going over the head" of the supervisor. The supervisor, or person who made the assignment, is the person who can clarify it or correct any injustice. Choice "C" is, therefore, correct. To say nothing, as in choice "D," is unwise. Supervisors have and interest in knowing the problems employees are facing, and the employee is seeking a solution to his problem.

2) True/False Questions

The "true/false" or "right/wrong" form of question is sometimes used. Here a complete statement is given. Your job is to decide whether the statement is right or wrong.

SAMPLE: A person-to-person long-distance telephone call costs less than a station-to-station call to the same city.

This statement is wrong, or false, since person-to-person calls are more expensive.

This is not a complete list of all possible question forms, although most of the others are variations of these common types. You will always get complete directions for answering questions. Be sure you understand *how* to mark your answers – ask questions until you do.

V. RECORDING YOUR ANSWERS

For an examination with very few applicants, you may be told to record your answers in the test booklet itself. Separate answer sheets are much more common. If this separate answer sheet is to be scored by machine – and this is often the case – it is highly important that you mark your answers correctly in order to get credit.

An electric scoring machine is often used in civil service offices because of the speed with which papers can be scored. Machine-scored answer sheets must be marked with a pencil, which will be given to you. This pencil has a high graphite content which responds to the electric scoring machine. As a matter of fact, stray dots may register as answers, so do not let your pencil rest on the answer sheet while you are pondering the correct answer. Also, if your pencil lead breaks or is otherwise defective, ask for another.

Since the answer sheet will be dropped in a slot in the scoring machine, be careful not to bend the corners or get the paper crumpled.

The answer sheet normally has five vertical columns of numbers, with 30 numbers to a column. These numbers correspond to the question numbers in your test booklet. After each number, going across the page are four or five pairs of dotted lines. These short dotted lines have small letters or numbers above them. The first two pairs may also have a "T" or "F" above the letters. This indicates that the first two pairs only are to be used if the questions are of the true-false type. If the questions are multiple choice, disregard the "T" and "F" and pay attention only to the small letters or numbers.

Answer your questions in the manner of the sample that follows:

32. The largest city in the United States is
    A. Washington, D.C.
    B. New York City
    C. Chicago
    D. Detroit
    E. San Francisco

1) Choose the answer you think is best. (New York City is the largest, so "B" is correct.)
2) Find the row of dotted lines numbered the same as the question you are answering. (Find row number 32)
3) Find the pair of dotted lines corresponding to the answer. (Find the pair of lines under the mark "B.")
4) Make a solid black mark between the dotted lines.

VI. BEFORE THE TEST

Common sense will help you find procedures to follow to get ready for an examination. Too many of us, however, overlook these sensible measures. Indeed, nervousness and fatigue have been found to be the most serious reasons why applicants fail to do their best on civil service tests. Here is a list of reminders:

- Begin your preparation early – Don't wait until the last minute to go scurrying around for books and materials or to find out what the position is all about.
- Prepare continuously – An hour a night for a week is better than an all-night cram session. This has been definitely established. What is more, a night a

week for a month will return better dividends than crowding your study into a shorter period of time.
- Locate the place of the exam – You have been sent a notice telling you when and where to report for the examination. If the location is in a different town or otherwise unfamiliar to you, it would be well to inquire the best route and learn something about the building.
- Relax the night before the test – Allow your mind to rest. Do not study at all that night. Plan some mild recreation or diversion; then go to bed early and get a good night's sleep.
- Get up early enough to make a leisurely trip to the place for the test – This way unforeseen events, traffic snarls, unfamiliar buildings, etc. will not upset you.
- Dress comfortably – A written test is not a fashion show. You will be known by number and not by name, so wear something comfortable.
- Leave excess paraphernalia at home – Shopping bags and odd bundles will get in your way. You need bring only the items mentioned in the official notice you received; usually everything you need is provided. Do not bring reference books to the exam. They will only confuse those last minutes and be taken away from you when in the test room.
- Arrive somewhat ahead of time – If because of transportation schedules you must get there very early, bring a newspaper or magazine to take your mind off yourself while waiting.
- Locate the examination room – When you have found the proper room, you will be directed to the seat or part of the room where you will sit. Sometimes you are given a sheet of instructions to read while you are waiting. Do not fill out any forms until you are told to do so; just read them and be prepared.
- Relax and prepare to listen to the instructions
- If you have any physical problem that may keep you from doing your best, be sure to tell the test administrator. If you are sick or in poor health, you really cannot do your best on the exam. You can come back and take the test some other time.

VII. AT THE TEST

The day of the test is here and you have the test booklet in your hand. The temptation to get going is very strong. Caution! There is more to success than knowing the right answers. You must know how to identify your papers and understand variations in the type of short-answer question used in this particular examination. Follow these suggestions for maximum results from your efforts:

1) Cooperate with the monitor

The test administrator has a duty to create a situation in which you can be as much at ease as possible. He will give instructions, tell you when to begin, check to see that you are marking your answer sheet correctly, and so on. He is not there to guard you, although he will see that your competitors do not take unfair advantage. He wants to help you do your best.

2) Listen to all instructions

Don't jump the gun! Wait until you understand all directions. In most civil service tests you get more time than you need to answer the questions. So don't be in a hurry.

Read each word of instructions until you clearly understand the meaning. Study the examples, listen to all announcements and follow directions. Ask questions if you do not understand what to do.

3) Identify your papers

Civil service exams are usually identified by number only. You will be assigned a number; you must not put your name on your test papers. Be sure to copy your number correctly. Since more than one exam may be given, copy your exact examination title.

4) Plan your time

Unless you are told that a test is a "speed" or "rate of work" test, speed itself is usually not important. Time enough to answer all the questions will be provided, but this does not mean that you have all day. An overall time limit has been set. Divide the total time (in minutes) by the number of questions to determine the approximate time you have for each question.

5) Do not linger over difficult questions

If you come across a difficult question, mark it with a paper clip (useful to have along) and come back to it when you have been through the booklet. One caution if you do this – be sure to skip a number on your answer sheet as well. Check often to be sure that you have not lost your place and that you are marking in the row numbered the same as the question you are answering.

6) Read the questions

Be sure you know what the question asks! Many capable people are unsuccessful because they failed to *read* the questions correctly.

7) Answer all questions

Unless you have been instructed that a penalty will be deducted for incorrect answers, it is better to guess than to omit a question.

8) Speed tests

It is often better NOT to guess on speed tests. It has been found that on timed tests people are tempted to spend the last few seconds before time is called in marking answers at random – without even reading them – in the hope of picking up a few extra points. To discourage this practice, the instructions may warn you that your score will be "corrected" for guessing. That is, a penalty will be applied. The incorrect answers will be deducted from the correct ones, or some other penalty formula will be used.

9) Review your answers

If you finish before time is called, go back to the questions you guessed or omitted to give them further thought. Review other answers if you have time.

10) Return your test materials

If you are ready to leave before others have finished or time is called, take ALL your materials to the monitor and leave quietly. Never take any test material with you. The monitor can discover whose papers are not complete, and taking a test booklet may be grounds for disqualification.

VIII. EXAMINATION TECHNIQUES

1) Read the general instructions carefully. These are usually printed on the first page of the exam booklet. As a rule, these instructions refer to the timing of the examination; the fact that you should not start work until the signal and must stop work at a signal, etc. If there are any *special* instructions, such as a choice of questions to be answered, make sure that you note this instruction carefully.

2) When you are ready to start work on the examination, that is as soon as the signal has been given, read the instructions to each question booklet, underline any key words or phrases, such as *least, best, outline, describe* and the like. In this way you will tend to answer as requested rather than discover on reviewing your paper that you *listed without describing*, that you selected the *worst* choice rather than the *best* choice, etc.

3) If the examination is of the objective or multiple-choice type – that is, each question will also give a series of possible answers: A, B, C or D, and you are called upon to select the best answer and write the letter next to that answer on your answer paper – it is advisable to start answering each question in turn. There may be anywhere from 50 to 100 such questions in the three or four hours allotted and you can see how much time would be taken if you read through all the questions before beginning to answer any. Furthermore, if you come across a question or group of questions which you know would be difficult to answer, it would undoubtedly affect your handling of all the other questions.

4) If the examination is of the essay type and contains but a few questions, it is a moot point as to whether you should read all the questions before starting to answer any one. Of course, if you are given a choice – say five out of seven and the like – then it is essential to read all the questions so you can eliminate the two that are most difficult. If, however, you are asked to answer all the questions, there may be danger in trying to answer the easiest one first because you may find that you will spend too much time on it. The best technique is to answer the first question, then proceed to the second, etc.

5) Time your answers. Before the exam begins, write down the time it started, then add the time allowed for the examination and write down the time it must be completed, then divide the time available somewhat as follows:
    - If 3-1/2 hours are allowed, that would be 210 minutes. If you have 80 objective-type questions, that would be an average of 2-1/2 minutes per question. Allow yourself no more than 2 minutes per question, or a total of 160 minutes, which will permit about 50 minutes to review.
    - If for the time allotment of 210 minutes there are 7 essay questions to answer, that would average about 30 minutes a question. Give yourself only 25 minutes per question so that you have about 35 minutes to review.

6) The most important instruction is to *read each question* and make sure you know what is wanted. The second most important instruction is to *time yourself properly* so that you answer every question. The third most

important instruction is to *answer every question.* Guess if you have to but include something for each question. Remember that you will receive no credit for a blank and will probably receive some credit if you write something in answer to an essay question. If you guess a letter – say "B" for a multiple-choice question – you may have guessed right. If you leave a blank as an answer to a multiple-choice question, the examiners may respect your feelings but it will not add a point to your score. Some exams may penalize you for wrong answers, so in such cases *only*, you may not want to guess unless you have some basis for your answer.

7) Suggestions
   a. Objective-type questions
      1. Examine the question booklet for proper sequence of pages and questions
      2. Read all instructions carefully
      3. Skip any question which seems too difficult; return to it after all other questions have been answered
      4. Apportion your time properly; do not spend too much time on any single question or group of questions
      5. Note and underline key words – *all, most, fewest, least, best, worst, same, opposite,* etc.
      6. Pay particular attention to negatives
      7. Note unusual option, e.g., unduly long, short, complex, different or similar in content to the body of the question
      8. Observe the use of "hedging" words – *probably, may, most likely,* etc.
      9. Make sure that your answer is put next to the same number as the question
      10. Do not second-guess unless you have good reason to believe the second answer is definitely more correct
      11. Cross out original answer if you decide another answer is more accurate; do not erase until you are ready to hand your paper in
      12. Answer all questions; guess unless instructed otherwise
      13. Leave time for review

   b. Essay questions
      1. Read each question carefully
      2. Determine exactly what is wanted. Underline key words or phrases.
      3. Decide on outline or paragraph answer
      4. Include many different points and elements unless asked to develop any one or two points or elements
      5. Show impartiality by giving pros and cons unless directed to select one side only
      6. Make and write down any assumptions you find necessary to answer the questions
      7. Watch your English, grammar, punctuation and choice of words
      8. Time your answers; don't crowd material

8) Answering the essay question

Most essay questions can be answered by framing the specific response around several key words or ideas. Here are a few such key words or ideas:

M's: manpower, materials, methods, money, management
P's: purpose, program, policy, plan, procedure, practice, problems, pitfalls, personnel, public relations

   a. Six basic steps in handling problems:
      1. Preliminary plan and background development
      2. Collect information, data and facts
      3. Analyze and interpret information, data and facts
      4. Analyze and develop solutions as well as make recommendations
      5. Prepare report and sell recommendations
      6. Install recommendations and follow up effectiveness

   b. Pitfalls to avoid
      1. *Taking things for granted* – A statement of the situation does not necessarily imply that each of the elements is necessarily true; for example, a complaint may be invalid and biased so that all that can be taken for granted is that a complaint has been registered
      2. *Considering only one side of a situation* – Wherever possible, indicate several alternatives and then point out the reasons you selected the best one
      3. *Failing to indicate follow up* – Whenever your answer indicates action on your part, make certain that you will take proper follow-up action to see how successful your recommendations, procedures or actions turn out to be
      4. *Taking too long in answering any single question* – Remember to time your answers properly

IX. AFTER THE TEST

Scoring procedures differ in detail among civil service jurisdictions although the general principles are the same. Whether the papers are hand-scored or graded by machine we have described, they are nearly always graded by number. That is, the person who marks the paper knows only the number – never the name – of the applicant. Not until all the papers have been graded will they be matched with names. If other tests, such as training and experience or oral interview ratings have been given, scores will be combined. Different parts of the examination usually have different weights. For example, the written test might count 60 percent of the final grade, and a rating of training and experience 40 percent. In many jurisdictions, veterans will have a certain number of points added to their grades.

After the final grade has been determined, the names are placed in grade order and an eligible list is established. There are various methods for resolving ties between those who get the same final grade – probably the most common is to place first the name of the person whose application was received first. Job offers are made from the eligible list in the order the names appear on it. You will be notified of your grade and your rank as soon as all these computations have been made. This will be done as rapidly as possible.

People who are found to meet the requirements in the announcement are called "eligibles." Their names are put on a list of eligible candidates. An eligible's chances of getting a job depend on how high he stands on this list and how fast agencies are filling jobs from the list.

When a job is to be filled from a list of eligibles, the agency asks for the names of people on the list of eligibles for that job. When the civil service commission receives this request, it sends to the agency the names of the three people highest on this list. Or, if the job to be filled has specialized requirements, the office sends the agency the names of the top three persons who meet these requirements from the general list.

The appointing officer makes a choice from among the three people whose names were sent to him. If the selected person accepts the appointment, the names of the others are put back on the list to be considered for future openings.

That is the rule in hiring from all kinds of eligible lists, whether they are for typist, carpenter, chemist, or something else. For every vacancy, the appointing officer has his choice of any one of the top three eligibles on the list. This explains why the person whose name is on top of the list sometimes does not get an appointment when some of the persons lower on the list do. If the appointing officer chooses the second or third eligible, the No. 1 eligible does not get a job at once, but stays on the list until he is appointed or the list is terminated.

X. HOW TO PASS THE INTERVIEW TEST

The examination for which you applied requires an oral interview test. You have already taken the written test and you are now being called for the interview test – the final part of the formal examination.

You may think that it is not possible to prepare for an interview test and that there are no procedures to follow during an interview. Our purpose is to point out some things you can do in advance that will help you and some good rules to follow and pitfalls to avoid while you are being interviewed.

What is an interview supposed to test?

The written examination is designed to test the technical knowledge and competence of the candidate; the oral is designed to evaluate intangible qualities, not readily measured otherwise, and to establish a list showing the relative fitness of each candidate – as measured against his competitors – for the position sought. Scoring is not on the basis of "right" and "wrong," but on a sliding scale of values ranging from "not passable" to "outstanding." As a matter of fact, it is possible to achieve a relatively low score without a single "incorrect" answer because of evident weakness in the qualities being measured.

Occasionally, an examination may consist entirely of an oral test – either an individual or a group oral. In such cases, information is sought concerning the technical knowledges and abilities of the candidate, since there has been no written examination for this purpose. More commonly, however, an oral test is used to supplement a written examination.

Who conducts interviews?

The composition of oral boards varies among different jurisdictions. In nearly all, a representative of the personnel department serves as chairman. One of the members of the board may be a representative of the department in which the candidate would work. In some cases, "outside experts" are used, and, frequently, a businessman or some other representative of the general public is asked to serve. Labor and management or other special groups may be represented. The aim is to secure the services of experts in the appropriate field.

However the board is composed, it is a good idea (and not at all improper or unethical) to ascertain in advance of the interview who the members are and what groups they represent. When you are introduced to them, you will have some idea of their backgrounds and interests, and at least you will not stutter and stammer over their names.

What should be done before the interview?

While knowledge about the board members is useful and takes some of the surprise element out of the interview, there is other preparation which is more substantive. It *is* possible to prepare for an oral interview – in several ways:

1) Keep a copy of your application and review it carefully before the interview

This may be the only document before the oral board, and the starting point of the interview. Know what education and experience you have listed there, and the sequence and dates of all of it. Sometimes the board will ask you to review the highlights of your experience for them; you should not have to hem and haw doing it.

2) Study the class specification and the examination announcement

Usually, the oral board has one or both of these to guide them. The qualities, characteristics or knowledges required by the position sought are stated in these documents. They offer valuable clues as to the nature of the oral interview. For example, if the job involves supervisory responsibilities, the announcement will usually indicate that knowledge of modern supervisory methods and the qualifications of the candidate as a supervisor will be tested. If so, you can expect such questions, frequently in the form of a hypothetical situation which you are expected to solve. NEVER go into an oral without knowledge of the duties and responsibilities of the job you seek.

3) Think through each qualification required

Try to visualize the kind of questions you would ask if you were a board member. How well could you answer them? Try especially to appraise your own knowledge and background in each area, *measured against the job sought*, and identify any areas in which you are weak. Be critical and realistic – do not flatter yourself.

4) Do some general reading in areas in which you feel you may be weak

For example, if the job involves supervision and your past experience has NOT, some general reading in supervisory methods and practices, particularly in the field of human relations, might be useful. Do NOT study agency procedures or detailed manuals. The oral board will be testing your understanding and capacity, not your memory.

5) Get a good night's sleep and watch your general health and mental attitude

You will want a clear head at the interview. Take care of a cold or any other minor ailment, and of course, no hangovers.

What should be done on the day of the interview?

Now comes the day of the interview itself. Give yourself plenty of time to get there. Plan to arrive somewhat ahead of the scheduled time, particularly if your appointment is in the fore part of the day. If a previous candidate fails to appear, the board might be ready for you a bit early. By early afternoon an oral board is almost invariably behind schedule if there are many candidates, and you may have to wait.

Take along a book or magazine to read, or your application to review, but leave any extraneous material in the waiting room when you go in for your interview. In any event, relax and compose yourself.

The matter of dress is important. The board is forming impressions about you – from your experience, your manners, your attitude, and your appearance. Give your personal appearance careful attention. Dress your best, but not your flashiest. Choose conservative, appropriate clothing, and be sure it is immaculate. This is a business interview, and your appearance should indicate that you regard it as such. Besides, being well groomed and properly dressed will help boost your confidence.

Sooner or later, someone will call your name and escort you into the interview room. *This is it.* From here on you are on your own. It is too late for any more preparation. But remember, you asked for this opportunity to prove your fitness, and you are here because your request was granted.

What happens when you go in?

The usual sequence of events will be as follows: The clerk (who is often the board stenographer) will introduce you to the chairman of the oral board, who will introduce you to the other members of the board. Acknowledge the introductions before you sit down. Do not be surprised if you find a microphone facing you or a stenotypist sitting by. Oral interviews are usually recorded in the event of an appeal or other review.

Usually the chairman of the board will open the interview by reviewing the highlights of your education and work experience from your application – primarily for the benefit of the other members of the board, as well as to get the material into the record. Do not interrupt or comment unless there is an error or significant misinterpretation; if that is the case, do not hesitate. But do not quibble about insignificant matters. Also, he will usually ask you some question about your education, experience or your present job – partly to get you to start talking and to establish the interviewing "rapport." He may start the actual questioning, or turn it over to one of the other members. Frequently, each member undertakes the questioning on a particular area, one in which he is perhaps most competent, so you can expect each member to participate in the examination. Because time is limited, you may also expect some rather abrupt switches in the direction the questioning takes, so do not be upset by it. Normally, a board member will not pursue a single line of questioning unless he discovers a particular strength or weakness.

After each member has participated, the chairman will usually ask whether any member has any further questions, then will ask you if you have anything you wish to add. Unless you are expecting this question, it may floor you. Worse, it may start you off on an extended, extemporaneous speech. The board is not usually seeking more information. The question is principally to offer you a last opportunity to present further qualifications or to indicate that you have nothing to add. So, if you feel that a significant qualification or characteristic has been overlooked, it is proper to point it out in a sentence or so. Do not compliment the board on the thoroughness of their examination – they have been sketchy, and you know it. If you wish, merely say, "No thank you, I have nothing further to add." This is a point where you can "talk yourself out" of a good impression or fail to present an important bit of information. Remember, *you close the interview yourself.*

The chairman will then say, "That is all, Mr. _____, thank you." Do not be startled; the interview is over, and quicker than you think. Thank him, gather your belongings and take your leave. Save your sigh of relief for the other side of the door.

How to put your best foot forward

Throughout this entire process, you may feel that the board individually and collectively is trying to pierce your defenses, seek out your hidden weaknesses and embarrass and confuse you. Actually, this is not true. They are obliged to make an appraisal of your qualifications for the job you are seeking, and they want to see you in your best light. Remember, they must interview all candidates and a non-cooperative candidate may become a failure in spite of their best efforts to bring out his qualifications. Here are 15 suggestions that will help you:

1) Be natural – Keep your attitude confident, not cocky

If you are not confident that you can do the job, do not expect the board to be. Do not apologize for your weaknesses, try to bring out your strong points. The board is interested in a positive, not negative, presentation. Cockiness will antagonize any board member and make him wonder if you are covering up a weakness by a false show of strength.

2) Get comfortable, but don't lounge or sprawl

Sit erectly but not stiffly. A careless posture may lead the board to conclude that you are careless in other things, or at least that you are not impressed by the importance of the occasion. Either conclusion is natural, even if incorrect. Do not fuss with your clothing, a pencil or an ashtray. Your hands may occasionally be useful to emphasize a point; do not let them become a point of distraction.

3) Do not wisecrack or make small talk

This is a serious situation, and your attitude should show that you consider it as such. Further, the time of the board is limited – they do not want to waste it, and neither should you.

4) Do not exaggerate your experience or abilities

In the first place, from information in the application or other interviews and sources, the board may know more about you than you think. Secondly, you probably will not get away with it. An experienced board is rather adept at spotting such a situation, so do not take the chance.

5) If you know a board member, do not make a point of it, yet do not hide it

Certainly you are not fooling him, and probably not the other members of the board. Do not try to take advantage of your acquaintanceship – it will probably do you little good.

6) Do not dominate the interview

Let the board do that. They will give you the clues – do not assume that you have to do all the talking. Realize that the board has a number of questions to ask you, and do not try to take up all the interview time by showing off your extensive knowledge of the answer to the first one.

7) Be attentive

You only have 20 minutes or so, and you should keep your attention at its sharpest throughout. When a member is addressing a problem or question to you, give him your undivided attention. Address your reply principally to him, but do not exclude the other board members.

8) Do not interrupt

A board member may be stating a problem for you to analyze. He will ask you a question when the time comes. Let him state the problem, and wait for the question.

9) Make sure you understand the question

Do not try to answer until you are sure what the question is. If it is not clear, restate it in your own words or ask the board member to clarify it for you. However, do not haggle about minor elements.

10) Reply promptly but not hastily

A common entry on oral board rating sheets is "candidate responded readily," or "candidate hesitated in replies." Respond as promptly and quickly as you can, but do not jump to a hasty, ill-considered answer.

11) Do not be peremptory in your answers

A brief answer is proper – but do not fire your answer back. That is a losing game from your point of view. The board member can probably ask questions much faster than you can answer them.

12) Do not try to create the answer you think the board member wants

He is interested in what kind of mind you have and how it works – not in playing games. Furthermore, he can usually spot this practice and will actually grade you down on it.

13) Do not switch sides in your reply merely to agree with a board member

Frequently, a member will take a contrary position merely to draw you out and to see if you are willing and able to defend your point of view. Do not start a debate, yet do not surrender a good position. If a position is worth taking, it is worth defending.

14) Do not be afraid to admit an error in judgment if you are shown to be wrong

The board knows that you are forced to reply without any opportunity for careful consideration. Your answer may be demonstrably wrong. If so, admit it and get on with the interview.

15) Do not dwell at length on your present job

The opening question may relate to your present assignment. Answer the question but do not go into an extended discussion. You are being examined for a *new* job, not your present one. As a matter of fact, try to phrase ALL your answers in terms of the job for which you are being examined.

Basis of Rating

Probably you will forget most of these "do's" and "don'ts" when you walk into the oral interview room. Even remembering them all will not ensure you a passing grade. Perhaps you did not have the qualifications in the first place. But remembering them will help you to put your best foot forward, without treading on the toes of the board members.

Rumor and popular opinion to the contrary notwithstanding, an oral board wants you to make the best appearance possible. They know you are under pressure – but they also want to see how you respond to it as a guide to what your reaction would be under the pressures of the job you seek. They will be influenced by the degree of poise you display, the personal traits you show and the manner in which you respond.

EXAMINATION SECTION

EXAMINATION SECTION
TEST 1

DIRECTIONS: Each question or incomplete statement is followed by several suggested answers or completions. Select the one the BEST answers the question or completes the statement PRINT THE LETTER OF THE CORRECT ANSWER IN THE SPACE AT THE RIGHT.

1. Each of the following is a disadvantage associated with the use of functional definitions in relation to service delivery and program design, except 1._____

    A. lack of refinement in the key elements of definitions
    B. inattention to the assets of individual persons
    C. general lack of clarity
    D. increased likelihood that a person needing assistance may not be classified as disabled

2. Which of the following is a factor which contributes directly to a person's capacity for self-direction? 2._____

    A. Vocational skills
    B. Grooming
    C. Socialization
    D. Academic skills

3. The principle of normalization defines five accomplishments that define effective habilitation services. These include each of the following, except 3._____

    A. community presence
    B. status improvement
    C. competence development
    D. economic self-sufficiency

4. When determining a specific intervention strategy for a client, which of the following steps is usually performed first? 4._____

    A. Prioritizing interventions on the basis of the person's need to feel safe and successful
    B. Determining what skills will be needed and what challenges will be addressed
    C. Using person-environment assessment information to determine mismatches
    D. Determining whether behavioral skill training, prosthetics, or environmental accommodation will be used

5. Which of the following classifiers would be used in an ecological description of a person's environment? 5._____

    A. Physical design
    B. Procedures
    C. Demographics
    D. Personal development

6. Which of the following type of seizures is defined as an episode of inappropriate or purposeless behavior, with subsequent amnesia regarding the episode?

   A. Tourette's
   B. Petit mal
   C. Psychomotor
   D. Grand mal

7. Most experience with disabled learners supports the proposition that teaching the _____ function of language will enhance the acquisition of a broader vocabulary.

   A. receptive
   B. instrumental
   C. emotional
   D. symbolic

8. Which of the following factors may produce cerebral palsy?
   I. Congenital factors
   II. Injury
   III. Disease

   A. I only
   B. I and II
   C. I and III
   D. I, II, and III

9. Typically, a behavioral objective written for a client will first list

   A. a qualitative description of the desired behavior
   B. the criterion for success
   C. the observable outcome
   D. the target date for the trainee's accomplishment of the outcome.

10. A habilitation program involves a training regimen for teaching spinal cord-injured clients to do wheelchair push-ups in order to prevent pressure sores: a 30-second alarm sounds if the client has not done a 4-second push-up during a 10-minute interval. The alarm could be postponed at any time during the 10-minute interval by doing a push-up. This is an example of

    A. aversive control
    B. extinction
    C. fixed rate reinforcement
    D. stimulus control

11. To teach an autistic client to respond to questions, a habilitation program begins by helping the client answer yes/no questions. Typically, the instructor and the client would then focus on _____ questions.

    A. why
    B. who
    C. how
    D. where

12. Which of the following is a behavior that would typically require only intermittent reinforcement?   12.____

    A. A mentally retarded client drinking from a cup
    B. A retarded client dressing appropriately each morning
    C. A client with cerebral palsy climbing into a swing on the playground
    D. A client with cerebral palsy turning on a stereo

13. Which of the following developmental disabilities generally involves the greatest risk for obesity?   13.____

    A. Cerebral palsy
    B. Spina bifida
    C. Down syndrome
    D. Muscular dystrophy

14. Under federal law, if a program receives money from the government, it is required to allow individuals with disabilities to participate. This is a provision of section 504 of the   14.____

    A. Americans with Disabilities Act (ADA)
    B. Developmental Disabilities Assistance and Bill of Rights Act
    C. Individuals with Disabilities Education Act (IDEA)
    D. Rehabilitation Act

15. An autistic child is constantly picking up objects and putting them in his mouth. In order to reduce this behavior, the habilitation staff began a program of oral hygiene training in which the child brushed his gums with oral antiseptic and wiped his lips with a washcloth soaked in antiseptic. The frequency of this training reduced in measure with the child's placement of objects in his mouth. This is an example of the use of the behavior reduction technique known as   15.____

    A. extinction
    B. response contingent stimulation
    C. differential reinforcement of low rates of behavior
    D. overcorrection

16. In establishing an expressive speech system in a mentally retarded client, the first phase of a habilitation program usually involves   16.____

    A. imitation training
    B. instruction-followed behaviors
    C. reading aloud
    D. pronoun use

17. Which of the following is categorized as a psychosis?   17.____

    A. Conversion reaction
    B. Antisocial personality
    C. Adjustment disorder
    D. Schizophrenia

18. Which of the following is not a general guideline that should be followed when adapting recreation/leisure activities as part of a habilitation plan?

    A. Procedural adaptations should be tried before any other
    B. Any adaptation should be considered temporary
    C. Inexpensive and portable adaptations should be tried first
    D. No adaptation should be attempted until task assessment and instruction indicate that the person cannot learn the activity through conventional teaching strategies

19. The determinant in an interval schedule of behavior reinforcement is

    A. the likeness of the behavior to its established target
    B. the quantity of the behavior
    C. the passage of time since the last reinforcer was delivered
    D. the rate of performance of the behavior

20. Habilitation professionals propose that a person's quality of life increases as one's access to culturally typical activities and settings increases. This is known as the principle of

    A. the least-restrictive environment
    B. normalization
    C. autonomy
    D. Gestalt

21. Signs of intoxication of the major anticonvulsants include
    I. irritability
    II. dysarthria (poorly articulated speech)
    III. ataxia
    IV. aphasia

    A. I only
    B. I, II and III
    C. III and IV
    D. I, II, III and IV

22. In relation to community living programs, the focus of a residential living decision should generally be directed to each of the following, except

    A. presence of friends in the neighborhood
    B. personal preference for living situation
    C. preparation for normal adult living
    D. proximity to family

23. In general, high rates of _____ behavior occupy a disproportionate status in the repertoires of autistic and other severely impaired clients.

    A. aggressive
    B. self-destructive
    C. oversexualized
    D. self-stimulatory

24. According to D'Zurilla and Nezu, the problem-solving process begins with

   A. verification of the problem
   B. the generation of alternatives
   C. problem definition and formulation
   D. general orientation

25. Developmentally disabled clients frequently exhibit repetitious movements that occur at a high rate and have no apparent adaptive function. These behaviors are described as

   A. inconsequential
   B. stereotyped
   C. rumination
   D. ritualistic

KEY (CORRECT ANSWERS)

1.	B	11.	B
2.	C	12.	B
3.	D	13.	B
4.	B	14.	D
5.	A	15.	D
6.	C	16.	A
7.	B	17.	D
8.	B	18.	A
9.	C	19.	C
10.	A	20.	B

21.	B
22.	C
23.	D
24.	D
25.	B

TEST 2

DIRECTIONS: Each question or incomplete statement is followed by several suggested answers or completions. Select the one the BEST answers the question or completes the statement. *PRINT THE LETTER OF THE CORRECT ANSWER IN THE SPACE AT THE RIGHT.*

1. Definitions used in the field of habilitation are used for
    I. planning
    II. policy development
    III. establishing eligibility

    A. I and II
    B. I and III
    C. III only
    D. I, II and III

    1._

2. In _____% of mentally retarded individuals with an IQ of less than 50, there is an absence or near absence of speech.

    A. 15-35
    B. 35-45
    C. 55-65
    D. 75-85

    2._

3. In a typical habilitation plan documentation format, which of the following elements appears last?

    A. Service plan
    B. Current life-aim goals
    C. Discussions with the client and family
    D. Interdisciplinary recommendations

    3._

4. Which of the following is not considered to be an element of a person's psychosocial climate?

    A. Relationship
    B. Physical location
    C. Systems maintenance/change
    D. Personal development

    4._

5. All discrimination training begins with the

    A. formulation of behavioral objectives
    B. initiation of full-sequence training
    C. establishment of a predictable relationship between a cue and a response
    D. initiation of discrimination training

    5._

6. The primary visual cortex of the human brain is located in the _____ lobe.

    A. frontal
    B. parietal
    C. temporal
    D. occipital

    6._

7. The first step in a typical behavioral assessment is a(n)

   A. list of behavior parameters
   B. contingency survey
   C. detailed history
   D. ecological analysis

8. Approximately what percentage of people with cerebral palsy have a normal intelligence?

   A. 20
   B. 40
   C. 60
   D. 80

9. Which of the following statements about Duchenne muscular dystrophy is false?

   A. It involves a longer life expectancy than other forms of MD
   B. It is usually not apparent until a child begins to walk
   C. It eventually ends in wheelchair confinement
   D. It affects only males

10. The goals of an individual habilitation plan include motivation and participation fluency. Which of the following instructional techniques will be most helpful?

    A. Developing a stimulus-response chain
    B. Presenting multiple training examples within individual sessions
    C. Prompting and reinforcing targeted social interactions and sequences
    D. Using an effective balance of demand and reward

11. In evaluating a habilitation program, which of the following provides objective person-referenced data sets reflecting changes in the person's living skills, employment efforts, and community integration?

    A. Process analysis
    B. Outcome analysis
    C. Impact analysis
    D. Cost/benefit analysis

12. Which of the following is an objective measure of a client's quality of life?

    A. Friendships
    B. Relations with other people
    C. Recreation
    D. Appearance/physical condition

13. The most common speech disorder among clients with neurological impairments is

    A. dysfluency (stuttering)
    B. echolalia
    C. cri-du-chat
    D. aphasia

14. Disadvantages associated with the traditional pre-employment assessment of clients include
    I. assessments all take place in isolation from a true work environment
    II. results that tend to limit rather than expand the client's opportunities
    III. evaluations don't include an inquiry into client's interest
    IV. an inability to measure specific sets of skills

    A. I, II and III
    B. II and IV
    C. III only
    D. I, II, III and IV

15. An adult client with mild mental retardation is doing a set of math problems. The instructor, on average, praises the client after every fifth completed item sometimes after four items or nine items. This schedule, which produces a stable and high rate of behavior, is known as _____ reinforcement.

    A. variable interval
    B. fixed interval
    C. variable ratio
    D. fixed ratio

16. For teaching self-help skills to autistic or dual-diagnosis clients, the best approach is probably to use a combination of

    A. backward chaining and faded guidance
    B. extinction and positive reinforcement
    C. differential reinforcement of other behaviors (DRO) and response contingent stimulation
    D. faded guidance and overcorrection

17. In the teaching of attention and listening skills, "attention" is often defined as one or more of the following, except

    A. on-task behavior
    B. posture
    C. silence
    D. eye contact

18. In athetoid cerebral palsy,

    A. muscle tone is constantly changing
    B. a person has severe balance and coordination but is usually ambulatory
    C. only one side of the body is affected
    D. joints are consistently stiffened

19. A worker is attempting to teach a client to cross an uncontrolled intersection. The worker begins with a verbal prompt to walk to the curb and stop, but the trainee fails to do this. The worker than says, "Watch me, I'm going to walk to the curb and stop." This is an example of

    A. physical prompting
    B. task analysis

C. graduated guidance
D. summative assessment

20. Each of the following types of behaviors are generally included in the professional definition of "emotional disturbance," except those that

    A. markedly deviate from age-appropriate expectations
    B. interfere with positive personal and interpersonal development
    C. are considered socially unacceptable
    D. are culturally specific

20.____

21. In accordance with the principle of the least restrictive environment for a disabled client in treatment, one of the first types of strategies that should be attempted in a behavior reduction program is

    A. overcorrection
    B. response contingent stimulation
    C. response cost
    D. differential reinforcement

21.____

22. Which of the following is an instructional strategy that make use of task analysis?

    A. Response cost
    B. Extinction
    C. Overcorrection
    D. Backward chaining

22.____

23. The principles to be instituted in a community living program include
    I. guidance by personal reference outcomes
    II. the teaching of functional skills
    III. a regeneration of the community
    IV. a focus on behavior control

    A. I and II
    B. I, II and III
    C. III and IV
    D. I, II, III and IV

23.____

24. Clients with hemiplegia could generally perform well at each of the following occupations, except

    A. dispatcher
    B. shipping clerk
    C. small engine repair
    D. receptionist

24.____

25. The factor which distinguishes overcorrection from other behavior reduction techniques is that it

    A. can be administered in a nonemotional manner
    B. teaches alternate desirable behaviors
    C. is used to suppress self-injurious behaviors
    D. inflicts a form of punishment on the client

25.____

KEY (CORRECT ANSWERS)

1.	D	11.	B
2.	D	12.	D
3.	C	13.	D
4.	B	14.	A
5.	C	15.	C
6.	D	16.	A
7.	C	17.	C
8.	B	18.	A
9.	A	19.	C
10.	D	20.	D

21. D
22. D
23. B
24. C
25. B

EXAMINATION SECTION
TEST 1

DIRECTIONS: Each question or incomplete statement is followed by several suggested answers or completions. Select the one the BEST answers the question or completes the statement. *PRINT THE LETTER OF THE CORRECT ANSWER IN THE SPACE AT THE RIGHT.*

1. Mental retardation is primarily a(n) _____ concept.

    A. pharmaceutical
    B. psychological
    C. medical
    D. behavioral

    1._____

2. Trends which currently impact service delivery in habilitation programs include each of the following, except a focus on

    A. outcomes and accountability
    B. the natural environment
    C. independent living in separate housing
    D. rights and empowerment of persons to make choices and decisions

    2._____

3. In general, individual habilitation plans should be reviewed

    A. monthly
    B. every 6 months
    C. annually
    D. every 2 years

    3._____

4. Which of the following is a diagnostic condition that is most likely to result in physical impairment?

    A. Down's syndrome
    B. Metabolic/immune deficiency disorder
    C. Arthrogryposis
    D. Bilateral blindness

    4._____

5. A typical behavioral assessment concludes with a(n)

    A. ecological analysis
    B. contingency survey
    C. list of behavior parameters
    D. discussion of behavior change responsibility

    5._____

6. Providing a client with work that is interesting, rewarding, and worthwhile is most likely to contribute to the _____ factors that foster well-being.

    A. physical
    B. material
    C. cognitive
    D. social

    6._____

7. Of the following, probably the most significant trend affecting services for adults with disabilities is

   A. evolving knowledge about particular medical or psychological conditions
   B. the involvement of family and friends
   C. the rise of the treatment/medical model
   D. the need for person-referenced outcomes

8. A 4-year-old autistic child who had just undergone cataract surgery needed to wear glasses for nearly all of his waking hours, but consistently refused to do so, throwing them aside whenever they were placed on his face. The habilitation staff decided to reinforce the child's behavior in steps, rewarding him first for picking up his glasses, holding, or carrying them; and then for wearing them for a few seconds at a time. Eventually, the boy began to wear his glasses for 12 hours a day. The behavioral modification program used by the staff in this case is an example of

   A. extinction
   B. shaping
   C. response priming
   D. negative reinforcement

9. Which of the following statements about transitional employment is <u>false</u>?

   A. Ongoing job-related supports are required by the disabled worker to maintain employment
   B. Extent of supports is flexible
   C. The work is in an environment where most people do not have disabilities
   D. Wages may be less than the prevailing or minimum rate

10. To teach an autistic client to use three-word utterances to label pictures or events, a habilitation program should begin by helping the client to use _____.

    A. verb-adjective-noun
    B. negation in three words
    C. agent-action-object
    D. noun-verb-adverb

11. The two prime instructional strategies used in any behavior shaping program are

    A. discrimination and full-sequence training
    B. generalization and single-sequence training
    C. descriptive validation and response cost
    D. task analysis and instructional programming

12. Which of the following behavior reduction techniques generally involves the most punitive strategies?

    A. overcorrection
    B. response contingent stimulation
    C. response cost
    D. differential reinforcement

13. Which of the following approaches would be most useful in assessing the behavior and characteristics of an inhabitant in a particular environment?   13.____

    A. Space coding
    B. Social ecology
    C. Organizational evaluation
    D. Person-environmental analysis

14. Approximately what percentage of all disabled U.S. adults are unemployed?   14.____

    A. 35
    B. 50
    C. 65
    D. 80

15. Sometimes, during the expressive language training of a mentally retarded adult, imitative verbal responses are not learned through modeling alone; often, imitation must be   15.____

    A. generalized across major response domains
    B. shaped with physical prompts
    C. taught after functional or spontaneous speech is acquired
    D. placed into the demand/response mode

16. Generally, the training of receptive language skills in mentally retarded clients has emphasized   16.____

    A. responses to sounds other than speech
    B. syntax
    C. verbal control of motor behavior
    D. reading aloud

17. Signs of tethering in a client with spina bifida include   17.____
    I. Back pain
    II. Pigeon-toed walk
    III. Progressive foot deformity
    IV. Spasticity

    A. I only
    B. I, III and IV
    C. II and IV
    D. I, II, III and IV

18. The use of intermittent reinforcement produces behavior that is   18.____

    A. easily produced upon demand
    B. more likely to produce satiation
    C. tends to be performed self-consciously
    D. more resistant to extinction

19. What is the term for a person's sense of where his/her body and limbs are in space?   19.____

    A. Kinesthesia
    B. Coordination

C. Proprioception
D. Dexterity

20. The federal law which states that all children with special needs should be placed in least restrictive environment possible is the

    A. Americans with Disabilities Act (ADA)
    B. Developmental Disabilities Assistance and Bill of Rights Act
    C. Individuals with Disabilities Education Act (IDEA)
    D. Rehabilitation Act

21. A person's _____ originates with the fluid in the canals of the inner ear.

    A. auricular
    B. proprioceptive
    C. tactile
    D. vestibular

22. When using the technique of a time-out from positive reinforcement in order to reduce a certain behavior, the most crucial consideration is

    A. the type of behavior (language and posture) used by the professional to
    B. direct the client to the time-out area
    C. whether the client loses access to an environment that is reinforcing
    D. the frequency of the imposition of the time-out period
    E. the duration of the time-out period

23. In evaluating a habilitation program, which of the following contrasts a service's outcomes with those of a comparison group to determine whether the service made a difference?

    A. Process analysis
    B. Outcome analysis
    C. Impact analysis
    D. Cost/benefit analysis

24. Which of the following is not common to all behavior modification techniques that are applied to meet the needs of disabled adults?

    A. The ability to reproduce responses at will
    B. Reinforcement contingencies to alter the frequency of responses
    C. The identification of observable responses
    D. The measurement of responses over time

25. An individual habilitation plan should
    I. identify which agency will provide each listed service
    II. have objectives stated in terms of emotional satisfaction
    III. always be in writing
    IV. include a statement of both short-term and long-term goals

A. I and II
B. I, III and IV
C. III and IV
D. I, II, III and IV

KEY (CORRECT ANSWERS)

1.	D	11.	D
2.	C	12.	B
3.	C	13.	D
4.	C	14.	C
5.	D	15.	B
6.	C	16.	C
7.	D	17.	B
8.	B	18.	D
9.	A	19.	A
10.	C	20.	C

21. D
22. B
23. C
24. A
25. B

TEST 2

DIRECTIONS: Each question or incomplete statement is followed by several suggested answers or completions. Select the one the BEST answers the question or completes the statement. *PRINT THE LETTER OF THE CORRECT ANSWER IN THE SPACE AT THE RIGHT.*

1. Each of the following statements about the social reinforcement of desired behaviors is true, except that it

    A. is naturally occurring
    B. is automatically reinforcing
    C. doesn't interrupt the performance of the behavior
    D. is very easy to administer

2. In the currently evolving mindset among habilitation professionals, the one common element seems to be

    A. an emphasis on self-sufficiency
    B. a refocusing of service delivery from diagnostic categories to individual needs
    C. a universal set of professional standards
    D. a set of fixed service delivery principles

3. The basic underlying deficit of autistic clients is a(n)

    A. inability to perform basic self-care functions such as eating and grooming
    B. lack of gross motor control
    C. inability to exist independently of caretakers
    D. severe receptive and expressive language impairment

4. Which of the following is most likely to be a secondary condition related to the primary effects of a disability?

    A. Learning disability
    B. Speech disorder
    C. Dystrophy
    D. Mental retardation

5. A person's self-help skills would most accurately be categorized as a(n) _____ of life factor.

    A. physical
    B. cognitive
    C. material
    D. social

6. Which of the following types of behavior treatment techniques is not widely used with clients who have a physical disability?

    A. Biofeedback
    B. Cognitive strategies
    C. Positive reinforcement
    D. Aversive control

7. Which of the following is a guideline that should be used in composing a client's behavioral outcomes?

   A. Specify the conditions under which the behavior will occur.
   B. Leave the date for final accomplishment open to allow for setbacks and adaptations.
   C. Avoid the use of contingency phrases
   D. Use the phrase "the client" or a suitable pronoun to avoid personalizing the objectives.

8. Which of the following is a diagnostic condition that is most likely to result in cognitive/developmental impairment?

   A. Fetal alcohol syndrome
   B. Spina bifida
   C. Hemiplegia
   D. Encephalocele

9. The main therapeutic goal for a hemiplegic client should be to

   A. teach the client to accomplish tasks with only one hand, by using substitutes for the other hand
   B. strengthen the leg of the weaker side
   C. outfit the client with the adequate number and type of prostheses that will be needed for basic self-care functions
   D. strengthen the arm of the weaker side

10. Research has shown that the prevalence of mental retardation corresponds with age, with sharp increases until about _____ and a marked decline after _____.

    A. 12;15
    B. 18; 21
    C. 25; 35
    D. 32; 45

11. A serious health hazard of severely mentally retarded clients is the ingestion of non-nutritive substances, known as

    A. mastication
    B. pica
    C. nostrum
    D. coprophagy

12. Among mentally retarded persons, which of the following activities is likely to require the greatest degree of intervention and rehabilitation?

    A. Language reception
    B. Socialization
    C. Hygiene
    D. Physical coordination

13. For teaching toileting skills to autistic or dual-diagnosis clients, the best approach is probably to use a combination of

    A. modeling and faded guidance
    B. overcorrection and response contingent stimulation
    C. faded guidance and extinction
    D. positive reinforcement and overcorrection

14. Which of the following is LEAST likely to be a reason why a person with neuromuscular impairment might exhibit symptoms of incontinence?

    A. Kidney infection
    B. Shyness or embarrassment at needing assistance to use the bathroom
    C. Bladder infection
    D. Sphincter weakness associated with the disease

15. Clients with high blood levels of anticonvulsants are likely to display any or all of the following side effects, except

    A. personality changes
    B. motor slowness
    C. auditory hallucinations
    D. reduced intellectual function

16. Which of the following movements is generally possible for a client with L2 spina bifida?

    A. Hip flexion
    B. Hip adduction
    C. Ankle plantarflexion
    D. Knee extension

17. A client receives reinforcement every fifth time he drinks from his cup without spilling. This is an example of _____ reinforcement.

    A. variable interval
    B. fixed interval
    C. variable ratio
    D. fixed ratio

18. Which of the following is a field of language teaching that attempts to account for language in terms of its uses in social contexts and discourse?

    A. Euphonies
    B. Pragmatics
    C. Mentalistics
    D. Sociolinguistics

19. A mentally-retarded client ruminates constantly throughout the day, despite verbal reprimands from habilitation staff. Probably the best approach to eliminating this behavior would be to

    A. begin providing positive reinforcement
    B. provide large quantities of food and allow the client to consume as much as she likes

C. ignore the behavior as much as possible
D. offer the client only two meals, supervised, each day

20. From a habilitation planning perspective, there are significant trends among persons whose primary diagnosis is either mental retardation, epilepsy, cerebral palsy, or dual diagnosis. Which of the following is not one of these?

    A. There are significant group differences in the mean level of assistance scores on learning
    B. There are few group differences in the level of economic self-sufficiency
    C. There are significant group differences in the ability to live independently
    D. There are few group differences in the level of self-care

20.____

21. For reducing the aggressive behaviors of autistic or dual-diagnosis clients, effective approaches include
    I. generalized positive reinforcement
    II. time-outs
    III. extinction
    IV. response contingent stimulation

    A. I and II
    B. II, III and IV
    C. III and IV
    D. I, II, III and IV

21.____

22. The federal law that requires an Individualized Education Plan (IEP) for school children who qualify for special education and related services is the

    A. Americans with Disabilities Act (ADA)
    B. Developmental Disabilities Assistance and Bill of Rights Act
    C. Individuals with Disabilities Education Act (IDEA)
    D. Rehabilitation Act

22.____

23. Of the following areas of life activity, adults diagnosed as mentally retarded are LEAST likely to have deficits in the area of

    A. language
    B. self-direction
    C. economic self-sufficiency
    D. learning

23.____

24. For a young client with spina bifida, clean intermittent catheterization (CIC) should be performed _____ a day.

    A. once
    B. twice
    C. 3 or 4 times
    D. 5 or 6 times

24.____

25. Each of the following is a disadvantage associated with the use of categorical or diagnostic definitions in relation to service delivery and program design, except
    A. difficulty determining a general set of disabilities that need to be addressed
    B. overly rigid adherence to exclusionary policies
    C. insufficient acknowledgement of individual differences within a category
    D. lack of sensitivity in evaluation instruments

KEY (CORRECT ANSWERS)

1.	B	11.	B
2.	B	12.	B
3.	D	13.	D
4.	B	14.	D
5.	D	15.	C
6.	B	16.	B
7.	A	17.	D
8.	A	18.	B
9.	A	19.	B
10.	A	20.	A

21. C
22. D
23. A
24. D
25. A

EXAMINATION SECTION
TEST 1

DIRECTIONS: Each question or incomplete statement is followed by several suggested answers or completions. Select the one that BEST answers the question or completes the statement. *PRINT THE LETTER OF THE CORRECT ANSWER IN THE SPACE AT THE RIGHT.*

1. Clinical observations and research on motor functioning of the mentally retarded indicate that
   A. there is a marked discrepancy in motor functioning between tasks requiring precise and those requiring complex movements
   B. there is a high degree of correspondence between general mental ability and motor performance
   C. there is no difference in the motor performance of moderately retarded and mildly retarded individuals
   D. degree of stimulation has no effect on motor performance

2. The incidence of the diagnosis of mental retardation in males as compared with that of females is
   A. considerably higher
   B. considerably lower
   C. slightly lower
   D. about the same

3. In terms of their behavior and the causes of their deficiency, mentally retarded children would be classified as a _____ group.
   A. very homogeneous
   B. moderately homogeneous
   C. very heterogeneous
   D. moderately heterogeneous

4. In terms of socioeconomic status, MOST trainable children come from families that in socioeconomic status.
   A. are rated low
   B. range from middle class to high
   C. are middle class
   D. range the spectrum

5. While phenylketonuria accounts for somewhat less than one percent of the mentally retarded, it is one of the few forms of mental retardation that can be
   A. identified as a causative agent in the first three months of pregnancy
   B. vitiated by early psychiatric treatment
   C. alleviated through strict adherence to a high phenyla-lanine diet
   D. prevented by specific medical intervention

6. A child who has been diagnosed as having cerebral aphasia shows _____ speech.
   A. lack of   B. perseverative   C. echolalic   D. repetitive

7. The PRIMARY distinguishing characteristic between the mentally retarded and the mentally deficient lies in the area of _____ competency.
   A. academic   B. social   C. occupational   D. physical

8. The educational program for the mentally retarded may BEST be described as

   A. the same as that for the socially handicapped, but with varying emphasis
   B. the same as that for the normal, but using specialist teachers
   C. a different developmental program from that for the normal, but basically with the same ultimate goal
   D. a different developmental program from that for the normal, but with different goals

9. Follow-up studies indicate that the mentally retarded tend to

   A. remain on their initial job because they are fearful of change
   B. change jobs frequently in their early post-school years
   C. move up the ladder of success as do normals but at a slower pace
   D. stabilize in one job or one area of work in their early post-school years

10. The PRIMARY objective of special education for the preponderance of the mentally retarded is

    A. contribution to the community
    B. participation in family life
    C. adjustment to the neighborhood environment
    D. adjustment in a sheltered work situation

11. Mental deficiency resulting from organic impairment or birth injury has been classified as

    A. endogenous   B. familial
    C. primary amentia   D. exogenous

12. Current definitions of the educable mentally retarded emphasize

    A. retardation as an irremediable and irreversible condition
    B. prediction of their future personal and social incompetence
    C. level of functioning at various stages of life as the important determinant of retardation
    D. potential for academic learning as the determinant of educability or trainability

13. Resources in the community for treating the emotional problems of mentally retarded children are

    A. more difficult to obtain than for non-retarded children
    B. under-utilized because of parental resistance to accepting retardation
    C. under-utilized because the retardation tends to mask emotional difficulties
    D. not effective with most types of retarded children

14. The retarded child who refuses to attend school and cries, throws up, and clings to the parent when it comes time to leave each morning is MOST probably showing symptoms of

    A. overdependence   B. school phobia
    C. psychopathic behavior D. improper nutrition

15. One of the MOST promising new developments in institutional care for the high level retardate is the

    A. addition of attendants to the inter-disciplinary staffs of installations
    B. organization of a well-rounded recreation program
    C. inclusion of psychotherapy in the institutional program
    D. establishment of a self-government program

16. The National Association for Retarded Children is a(n)

    A. youth group for the retarded, similar in design to the 4-H Clubs
    B. group of non-professionals associated with the American Association on Mental Deficiency
    C. association of parents' groups for the retarded
    D. association of teachers of the retarded, organized by the National Education Association

17. In MOST instances, parental inability to accept retardation in their child as a fact can be attributed primarily to their

    A. feelings of guilt
    B. fear of being viewed as subnormal themselves
    C. lack of knowledge of children's development
    D. being too close to the child to see him objectively

18. MOST authorities in the field agree that when children are admitted to state institutions for the mentally retarded, such commitment should be

    A. voluntary   B. made by the school
    C. made by a public agency   D. made by a court

19. Which one of the following descriptions MOST accurately characterizes the degree to which the mentally retarded will be able to function in social-vocational areas when they reach adulthood?

    A. Little more than self-care
    B. Partial self-support in a supervised environment, such as a sheltered workshop
    C. Employment, when given assistance from medical personnel in correcting physical or emotional deficiencies
    D. Employment in the community with the aid of appropriate school and community agencies when necessary

20. The process whereby an individual acquires his moral, social, and emotional attitudes from the people with whom he comes in frequent contact is called

    A. projection   B. introjection
    C. transfer of learning   D. transference

21. A resident of this state of working age, who has a permanent disability that is an employment handicap, is eligible for vocational rehabilitation if he

    A. is unemployable
    B. requires custodial care for an extended period of time
    C. is employable in a sheltered workshop only
    D. can become employable within a reasonable length of time

22. Of those listed below, the MOST likely jobs for the mentally retarded are:

    A. Messenger, hospital tray worker
    B. Foot press operator, practical nurse
    C. Shoeshine man, barber
    D. Plumber's helper, elevator operator

23. Of the following, which one is the MOST common etiological factor in clinical cases of mental retardation?

    A. Phenylketonuria
    B. Down's syndrome
    C. Organic brain damage
    D. Environmental deprivation

24. Which of the following types of recreational activity are MOST appropriate for the mentally retarded?

    A. Basketball, swimming
    B. Dancing, bowling
    C. Football, boxing
    D. Stickball, roller skating

25. Workers in the field of special education have recently shown renewed interest in the educational theories and methods of sensorial training developed for young children by

    A. Pestalozzi
    B. Rousseau
    C. Froebel
    D. Montessori

KEY (CORRECT ANSWERS)

1. B		11. D	
2. A		12. C	
3. C		13. A	
4. D		14. B	
5. D		15. D	
6. A		16. C	
7. B		17. A	
8. C		18. A	
9. B		19. D	
10. A		20. B	

21. D
22. A
23. C
24. B
25. D

TEST 2

DIRECTIONS: Each question or incomplete statement is followed by several suggested answers or completions. Select the one that BEST answers the question or completes the statement. *PRINT THE LETTER OF THE CORRECT ANSWER IN THE SPACE AT THE RIGHT.*

1. The instructional program for the trainable mentally retarded stresses

    A. association
    B. configuration
    C. perseveration
    D. habit formation

    1.____

2. Of the following, the MAJOR goal of the education of retarded children is to enable them to

    A. become skilled workers in selected jobs
    B. develop a better understanding of their problems and make a better adjustment to them
    C. become completely socially adequate in their communities
    D. develop qualities of leadership in limited areas

    2.____

3. Sheltered workshops for the mentally retarded are operated, in the main, by

    A. The Division of Vocational Rehabilitation
    B. The Department of Mental Hygiene
    C. associations of parents of retarded children
    D. The Department of Labor

    3.____

4. The incidence of mentally retarded individuals in the United States today is estimated to be

    A. 1 in 20   B. 1 in 40   C. 1 in 60   D. 1 in 80

    4.____

5. The MAJOR way in which the development of the retarded child resembles that of the normal child in the early years of life is in the attainment of

    A. locomotion skills
    B. manual dexterity
    C. language skills
    D. physical size

    5.____

6. Which one of the following agencies conducts the MOST extensive recreational program for the mentally retarded?

    A. Association for the Help of Retarded Children
    B. Association for Children with Retarded Mental Development
    C. American Association on Mental Deficiency
    D. Council for Exceptional Children

    6.____

7. The terminology used in characterizing retardates has changed over the years. Which one of the following CORRECTLY gives the order in which the terms have appeared?

    A. Mentally deficient, mentally handicapped, feebleminded
    B. Mentally deficient, feebleminded, mentally retarded
    C. Feebleminded, mentally deficient, mentally retarded
    D. Mentally retarded, feebleminded, mentally deficient

    7.____

8. Pavlov's influence on the training of mentally retarded children is BEST exemplified in the

   A. Institute for Neurological Diseases and Blindness
   B. National Institute of Mental Health
   C. National Foundation for Birth Defects
   D. Institute of Defectology

9. As the severely retarded child approaches adolescence and adulthood, there is a tendency for the IQ to

   A. decline
   B. remain static
   C. show slight but positive increases
   D. show significant increases

10. A colleague approaches the teacher of a mentally retarded class with a story about a 10-year-old boy whose head is *big* and *heavy*. The child needs assistance in dressing, toileting, and eating.
    She PROBABLY is describing a

    A. mongoloid   B. cretin
    C. microcephalic   D. hydrocephalic

11. When used with reference to mentally retarded children, the term *adaptive behavior* refers to the child's

    A. ability to shift readily from one learning situation to another
    B. prognosis for anti-social behavior
    C. effectiveness in coping with the social demands of the environment
    D. functioning level as determined by a projective testing technique

12. In presenting areas of interest for the adolescent retardate:
    I. Budgeting
    II. Study of Job Areas
    III. The Worker as a Citizen and Social Being
    IV. Choosing, Getting, and Holding a Job
    The MOST appropriate sequence is

    A. II, IV, I, III   B. IV, III, II, I
    C. I, II, III, IV   D. IV, I, III, II

13. Studies comparing the forgetting of completed and incompleted tasks tend to show that

    A. completed tasks tend to be forgotten more rapidly than incompleted ones
    B. incompleted tasks tend to be forgotten more rapidly than completed ones
    C. there is no difference in retention of the two types of tasks
    D. the inconclusive results that have been obtained make it impossible to generalize

14. Of the following, which is generally MOST conducive to the mastery of a skill?

    A. The practice of the skill in a daily routine
    B. Emphasis on speed rather than accuracy in early practice
    C. Overlearning
    D. Lack of emotion and pressure during practice

15. Degree of maturity, amount of previous experience, and motivation are all factors affecting the degree of _____ shown by a learner.

    A. intelligent activity
    B. transfer of skills
    C. readiness
    D. retention

16. Of the following, which one is of relatively minor effectiveness in determining the amount of transfer of learning from one subject to another? The

    A. degree of relationship between the two subjects involved
    B. methods used by the teacher to establish a relationship- between the subjects involved
    C. amount of study time put in by the learner on the material
    D. ability of the learner to make generalizations

17. Where there are no adequate public facilities for the instruction of a mentally handicapped child who can reasonably be expected to profit from such instruction, the parent

    A. may keep the child at home until a facility becomes available
    B. may educate the child privately, deducting the costs from state and federal taxes as legitimate medical expenses
    C. may register the child in a class conducted by a parents' organization in the state, with the state paying tuition charges
    D. can apply for state aid under an appropriate section of the Education Law

18. Learning and maturation differ from one another as forms of behavior development in that the latter

    A. depends on special training during a critical period
    B. is continuous, while the former is not
    C. must be externally prompted
    D. appears spontaneously

19. The long retention of skills such as swimming is generally explained by reference to the

    A. law of multiple response
    B. law of effect
    C. effect of overlearning
    D. process of redisintegration

20. Which one of the following psychologists identified the five stages (sensorimotor operations, preconceptual thought, intuitive thought, concrete operations, and formal operations) in intellectual development?

    A. Edward L. Thorndike
    B. Frances L. Ilg
    C. Jean Piaget
    D. Arnold Gesell

21. A practical application of the *stimulus-response* theory of learning is BEST exemplified in the classroom by the use of

    A. audio-visual aids
    B. experience charts
    C. developmental reading techniques
    D. teaching machines

22. Of the following, the use of the *conditioned-response* method of learning has been found MOST successful in dealing with

    A. enuresis
    B. epileptic seizures
    C. attitudes
    D. reading disabilities

23. The type of forgetting in which people tend to forget the names of persons they do not like is generally termed

    A. negative retention
    B. repression
    C. proactive inhibition
    D. retroactive inhibition

24. Experimental evidence suggests that the MOST effective learning and retention of material such as poetry takes place when the material is memorized

    A. as a whole unit
    B. word by word
    C. line by line
    D. stanza by stanza

25. The MOST recent theories of the causation of reading disabilities stress as a major factor

    A. perceptual dysfunctions and lags
    B. lack of cultural stimulation
    C. minimal brain damage
    D. lack of parental interest and aspiration

KEY (CORRECT ANSWERS)

1. D
2. B
3. C
4. B
5. D

6. A
7. C
8. D
9. A
10. D

11. C
12. A
13. A
14. C
15. C

16. C
17. D
18. D
19. C
20. C

21. D
22. A
23. B
24. A
25. A

EXAMINATION SECTION
TEST 1

DIRECTIONS: Each question or incomplete statement is followed by several suggested answers or completions. Select the one that BEST answers the question or completes the statement. *PRINT THE LETTER OF THE CORRECT ANSWER IN THE SPACE AT THE RIGHT.*

1. Which of the following statements is TRUE?　　　　　　　　　　　　　　　　1.____

    A. The goal of normalization is to allow one to do whatever one likes.
    B. Normalization involves making a person become normal.
    C. Normalization advocates that whenever possible, people's perceptions of developmentally disabled individuals must be enhanced or improved.
    D. Normalization advocates encouraging the developmentally disabled to be just like everyone else.

2. It is important to view the developmentally disabled as　　　　　　　　　　　2.____

    A. helpless
    B. unable to make decisions
    C. deviant
    D. none of the above

3. All of the following would be considered good practice EXCEPT　　　　　　　3.____

    A. providing residential services in the community, rather than in an isolated area
    B. placing residential homes next to rural prisons
    C. providing access in residences to accommodate those who are non-ambulatory
    D. avoiding excessive rules that tend to separate staff from residents

4. All of the following are true in normalization EXCEPT　　　　　　　　　　　4.____

    A. family involvement in normalization is usually not helpful to achieving the goal
    B. clients should be involved, when possible, in selecting programming in order to develop independence
    C. program options should emphasize autonomy, independence, integration, and productivity
    D. it is a good idea when possible to have day programming located apart from the living setting

5. Benefits of normalization include all of the following EXCEPT　　　　　　　　5.____

    A. development of self-confidence and self-esteem in the developmentally disabled
    B. social integration of the developmentally disabled
    C. positive changes in societal attitudes regarding the developmentally disabled
    D. societal acceptance of deviance

6. All of the following statements are true EXCEPT:　　　　　　　　　　　　　6.____

    A. Normalization means that normal conditions of life should be made available to developmentally disabled people
    B. Attitudes toward the mentally retarded have a great effect on the way they are treated, and, consequently, on their chances for living a productive, normal life

C. It is highly unlikely that efforts at normalization will succeed in most communities
D. What is normal or typical in one society may not be normal or typical in another

7. In normalization, the means used to teach a skill are as important as the skill itself. In teaching adults, which of the following would be MOST appropriate?

   A. Working individually with someone after dinner in order to teach him or her how to brush their teeth
   B. Teaching pouring skills with sand in a sandbox
   C. Teaching how to button clothes by using a doll for practice
   D. Teaching how to tie shoelaces by first working With a baby shoe

8. Which of the following statements is TRUE?

   A. Residents' chore duties in a community residence should only change three times a year.
   B. Entrance into a community residence should be solely determined by an individual's need for a place to live.
   C. Using a task analysis for a client would involve breaking down a complex task into smaller, more understandable parts.
   D. Clients should be allowed to eat when and what they choose.

9. Select the one statement below that is NOT true of supervised community residences. A supervised community residence

   A. can provide short-term residence for individuals who need only training and experience in activities of daily living after a period of institutionalization or as an alternative to institutionalization
   B. can provide an institutional setting for those people who need it
   C. can provide long-term residence for individuals who are unlikely to acquire the skills necessary for more independent living
   D. usually requires staff on site at all times

10. All of the following are goals of community residences EXCEPT

    A. providing a home environment for developmentally disabled persons
    B. providing a setting where clients can learn the skills necessary to live in the least restrictive environment
    C. providing a setting where the developmentally disabled can acquire the skills necessary to live as independently as possible
    D. the community residence allows for the maximum level of independence inconsistent with a person's disability and functional level

11. All of the following statements are true EXCEPT:

    A. A community residence does not need to adhere to the principle of normalization in its physical or social structure
    B. The term least restrictive environment refers to an environment which most resembles that of non-handicapped peers where the needs of developmentally disabled persons can be met

C. A person's length of stay in a community residence extends only until a person has attained the skills and motivation to function successfully in a less restrictive setting
D. The purposes of a community residence may vary so that people with different ranges of abilities and levels of functioning may be served

12. All of the following statements are true EXCEPT:

   A. Developmentally disabled persons residing in community residences must be afforded privacy, personal space, and freedom of access to the house as is consistent with their age and program needs
   B. Transportation should be available from the nearest institution so that people in community residences have access to the community
   C. The service needs of each person in a community residence should be individually planned by an interdisciplinary team
   D. An interdisciplinary team should include staff of the community residence, providers of program and support services, and, if appropriate, the developmentally disabled person's correspondent

13. All of the following statements are true EXCEPT:

   A. Supportive community residences are not required to provide staff on site 24 hours a day
   B. Residents in supervised community residences may need more assistance in activities of daily living than persons residing in supportive community residences
   C. An aim of a community residence is to maintain a family and home-like environment
   D. Those living in a community residence shall spend at least three hours per weekday and one evening per week in programs and activities at the residence

14. In working in treatment teams, it is MOST important for team members to

   A. communicate effectively with each other
   B. keep morale high
   C. attend meetings on time
   D. enjoy working with each other

15. All of the following statements are true EXCEPT:

   A. In teaching self-care skills, many tasks may need to be divided into sub-parts
   B. Tasks which are easiest to learn should generally be taught first
   C. Changes in routine are very helpful when teaching the mentally retarded a new skill
   D. The severely retarded do not learn as well from verbal instruction as they do from demonstration of a skill

16. All of the following statements are true EXCEPT:

   A. It is important to evaluate the client's readiness to attempt learning a particular task before starting to teach the task
   B. It is better to do a task for a client if the task may take much time and effort on his or her part
   C. People generally learn faster when their efforts lead to an enjoyable activity
   D. It is best when teaching a certain skill to begin with a small group when possible

17. All of the following statements are true EXCEPT:

    A. The expectations of a staff person of how well a client will be able to perform a certain task can influence daily living skills
    B. Environmental factors can influence daily living skills
    C. After seeing a skill demonstrated, a client should practice the skill
    D. A client will make a greater effort if he or she feels ill at ease with the instructor, and knows the instructor will become impatient if he or she continues to make mistakes

18. Of the following, the BEST way to teach a client an activity of daily living is to

    A. describe the steps to the client
    B. read the directions to the client
    C. break the activity into steps and have the client learn one step at a time
    D. have a client who can perform the task teach the client who cannot

19. All of the following are important steps in teaching a living skill EXCEPT

    A. defining the skill clearly
    B. determining the size of the skill
    C. breaking down each major step into substeps and sub-substeps as necessary
    D. rewarding the accomplishment of each step with candy

20. When teaching a daily living skill, it is important to keep in mind all of the following EXCEPT

    A. using concrete and specific language
    B. punishment can be a highly effective learning device
    C. matching the size of the skill to the client's ability level
    D. demonstrating what you want the resident to do

KEY (CORRECT ANSWERS)

1.	C	11.	A
2.	D	12.	B
3.	B	13.	D
4.	A	14.	A
5.	D	15.	C
6.	C	16.	B
7.	A	17.	D
8.	C	18.	C
9.	B	19.	D
10.	D	20.	B

TEST 2

DIRECTIONS: Each question or incomplete statement is followed by several suggested answers or completions. Select the one that BEST answers the question or completes the statement. *PRINT THE LETTER OF THE CORRECT ANSWER IN THE SPACE AT THE RIGHT.*

1. All of the following would be considered qualities of a developmental disability EXCEPT the disability

    A. may be attributable to mental retardation or autism
    B. has continued or can be expected to continue indefinitely
    C. can be easily overcome
    D. may be attributable to cerebral palsy or neurological impairment

    1.____

2. The condition of autism

    A. applies to those people who have little or no control over their motor skills
    B. is hereditary
    C. is characterized by severe disorders of communication and behavior
    D. begins most frequently in adulthood

    2.____

3. Secondary childhood autism differs from primary childhood autism in that

    A. primary childhood autism is more difficult to treat
    B. secondary childhood autism is secondary to disturbances such as brain damage
    C. secondary childhood autism is not as severe a disorder
    D. secondary childhood autism is less likely to interfere with behavior patterns

    3.____

4. Which of the following would be LEAST adversely affected by autism?

    A. Interpersonal relations
    B. Learning
    C. Developmental rate and sequences
    D. Motor skills

    4.____

5. Which of the following statements is NOT true?

    A. Cerebral palsy refers to a condition resulting from damage to the brain that may occur before, during or after birth and results in the loss of control over voluntary muscles in the body.
    B. Ataxic cerebral palsy is characterized by an inability to maintain normal balance.
    C. Someone with athetoid cerebral palsy would find it easier to maintain purposefulness of movements than someone with spastic cerebral palsy.
    D. Mixed cerebral palsy refers to the combination of two or more of the following categories of cerebral palsy such as the spastic, athetoid, ataxic, tremor, and rigid types.

    5.____

6. All of the following are true about epilepsy EXCEPT

    A. epilepsy does not usually involve a loss of consciousness
    B. an *aura* often appears to the individual before a *grand mal* seizure occurs

    6.____

C. people experiencing *petit mal* seizures are seldom aware that a seizure has occurred
D. status epilepticus, psychomotor, and Jacksonian are all forms of epilepsy

7. All of the following statements are true of mental retardation EXCEPT:

   A. The prevalence of mental retardation in the general total population is less than 3% of the population
   B. Approximately 89% of the mentally retarded population is mildly retarded
   C. School-age children who are mildly retarded can usually acquire practical skills and useful reading and arithmetic skills
   D. Adults who are mildly retarded can not usually achieve social and vocational skills adequate for minimum self-support

8. Which of the following statements is NOT true of mental retardation?

   A. Approximately 6% of the mentally retarded population is moderately retarded (I.Q. 36-51), 3.5% of the mentally retarded population is severely retarded (I.Q. 20-35), and 1.5% of this population is profoundly retarded (I.Q. 19 and below).
   B. A profoundly retarded person could never achieve limited self-care.
   C. Moderately retarded adults may achieve self-maintenance in unskilled work or semi-skilled work under sheltered conditions.
   D. Severely retarded children can profit from systematic skills training.

9. All of the following refer to neurological impairment EXCEPT

   A. childhood aphasia is a condition characterized by the failure to develop, or difficulty in using, language and speech
   B. epilepsy
   C. minimal brain dysfunction is associated with deviations of the central nervous system
   D. neurological impairment refers to a group of disorders of the central nervous system characterized by dysfunction in one or more, but not all, skills affecting communicative, perceptual, cognitive, memory, attentional, motor control, and appropriate social behaviors

10. Which of the following statements is TRUE?

    A. Autistic children are below average in intelligence level.
    B. All cerebral palsied persons are mentally retarded.
    C. Once an epileptic seizure has started, it cannot be stopped.
    D. Autism is due to faulty early interactional patterns between child and mother.

11. All of the following are false EXCEPT

    A. recent investigations have found that parents of autistic children have no specific common personality traits and no unusual environmental stresses
    B. cerebral palsied persons cannot understand directions
    C. it is not true that unless controlled seizures can cause further brain damage
    D. the majority of the mentally retarded are in institutions

12. In serving the needs of autistic persons, the one of the following which is usually LEAST important is the need   12.____

    A. for training in social skills
    B. for language stimulation
    C. to deal with potentially self-injurious, repetitive, and aggressive behaviors
    D. to teach skills that would improve intelligence

13. In serving the needs of persons with cerebral palsy, the one of the following which is usually LEAST important is the need   13.____

    A. to experience normal movement and sensations as much as possible
    B. to develop fundamental movement patterns which the person can regulate
    C. for experience and guidance in social settings
    D. to restrict their environment

14. All of the following statements are true EXCEPT: 14.____

    A. It is important that epileptic persons have balanced diets
    B. Pica, a craving for unnatural food, occurs with all mentally retarded persons
    C. It has been projected that 50% of those individuals who have cerebral palsy are also mentally retarded
    D. When working with the mentally retarded, it is important to encourage sensory-motor stimulation, physical stimulation, language stimulation, social skills training, and the performance of daily living skills

15. When working with neurologically impaired persons, all of the following are true EXCEPT: 15.____

    A. There is usually a need for perceptual training
    B. It is important to keep in mind that an individual may know something one day and not know it the next
    C. It may be necessary to remove distracting stimuli
    D. It is important to keep in mind that neurologically impaired persons usually have substantially lower I.Q.'s than the average person

16. The developmentally disabled do NOT have the right to   16.____

    A. register and vote in elections
    B. marry
    C. confidentiality of records
    D. hit someone who teases them

17. Which of the following statements is TRUE?   17.____

    A. It is important for staff members not to make all of the choices for their mentally retarded clients.
    B. Distraction is not a good technique to use when trying to channel potentially violent or destructive behavior to a socially acceptable outlet.
    C. Severely and profoundly retarded children do not appear to have a strong need for personal contact.
    D. It is primarily the mildly or moderately retarded child that exhibits the behavior usually associated with mental retardation.

18. All of the following are causes of mental retardation EXCEPT

    A. organic defects
    B. brain lesions
    C. increased sexual activity
    D. chromosomal abnormalities

19. A mentally retarded patient who is *acting out*

    A. may be trying to communicate that he or she is physically uncomfortable or needs something
    B. should be ignored
    C. should be severely punished
    D. feels comfortable in his or her surroundings

20. In working with the developmentally disabled, all of the following would be appropriate EXCEPT

    A. remembering that seemingly small things, both positive and negative, can be very important to the client
    B. allowing choices whenever possible
    C. maintaining a calm, level-headed attitude during an anxiety-producing situation will reassure clients and help them relax and feel safer
    D. after basic self-help skills have been mastered, it is not necessary to encourage further development

---

KEY (CORRECT ANSWERS)

1.	C	11.	A
2.	C	12.	D
3.	B	13.	D
4.	D	14.	B
5.	C	15.	D
6.	A	16.	D
7.	D	17.	A
8.	B	18.	C
9.	B	19.	A
10.	C	20.	D

EXAMINATION SECTION
TEST 1

DIRECTIONS: Each question or incomplete statement is followed by several suggested answers or completions. Select the one that BEST answers the question or completes the statement. *PRINT THE LETTER OF THE CORRECT ANSWER IN THE SPACE AT THE RIGHT.*

1. A patient tells you that the other patients are plotting to kill him. This is MOST likely an example of

    A. a manic-depressive reaction
    B. a paranoid reaction
    C. excellent perceptual skills on the part of the patient
    D. a compulsive reaction

2. Which of the following statements is TRUE?

    A. Diagnoses are, by their very nature, always accurate.
    B. Phobic reactions are the most common reasons people are admitted to mental hospitals.
    C. People with neuroses are far less likely to be hospitalized than people with psychoses.
    D. Severely depressed patients are less of a suicide risk than any other patient group, except paranoid schizophrenics.

3. The LARGEST single diagnostic group of psychotic patients are

    A. neurotic depressive   B. schizophrenic
    C. obsessive-compulsive   D. paranoid reactive

4. The personality type that would BEST be characterized by the description that *he or she has no conscience* would be the

    A. drug addict   B. exhibitionist
    C. sociopath   D. manic-depressive

5. Of the following, the marked inability to organize one's thoughts is found MOST commonly and severely in

    A. schizophrenics
    B. amnesiacs
    C. those suffering from anxiety neuroses
    D. sociopaths

6. Someone who constantly feels tense, anxious, and worried but is unable to identify exactly why is MOST likely to be suffering from

    A. anxiety neurosis   B. schizophrenia
    C. dissociative reaction   D. a conversion reaction

7. A patient always insists upon twirling around six times before entering a new room, or she fears she will die. This is an example of

    A. paranoid reaction   B. obsessive-compulsive reaction
    C. dissociative reaction   D. anxiety neurosis

8. Of the following, those who suffer from neuroses would USUALLY complain of

   A. rejections, dissociation, and frequent inability to remember what day it is
   B. delusions, rejections, and feeling tired
   C. tiredness, fears, and hallucinations
   D. fears, physical complaints, and anxieties

9. The category that is caused by a disorder of the brain for which physical pathology can be demonstrated is

   A. neurotic depressive reaction
   B. schizophrenia
   C. functional psychoses
   D. organic psychoses

10. Of the following, which is NOT true?

    A. Someone who is suddenly unable to hear for psychological reasons would be considered to be suffering from a conversion reaction.
    B. If someone is in fugue, they have combined amnesia with flight.
    C. *Multiple personalities* is a dissociative reaction that affects primarily the elderly.
    D. General symptoms of schizophrenia include an ability to deal with reality, the presence of delusions or hallucinations, and inappropriate affect.

11. Which one of the following is TRUE?

    A. Calling an elderly person *gramps* or *granny* makes them feel more secure.
    B. It is important for an elderly person to maintain his or her independence whenever possible.
    C. When elderly patients start acting like children, they should be treated like children.
    D. It is important to encourage the elderly to hurry because they tend to move so slowly.

12. It has been found that older patients learn BEST when one does all but which one of the following?

    A. Allowing plenty of time for them to practice and learn
    B. Creating a relaxing environment for them
    C. Dealing with one thing at a time
    D. Assuming little knowledge on their part

13. Which of the following contains the main factors that should be considered before administering medications to elderly patients?

    A. How popular the medication is with the patient and the team leader's recommendations
    B. Any organic brain damage, liver dysfunction, and body weight
    C. Liver dysfunction, the patient's medical history, and decreased body weight
    D. Decreased body weight, impaired circulation, liver dysfunction, and increased sensitivity to medications

14. When communicating with the hearing impaired, it is BEST to do all of the following EXCEPT

   A. make sure the person can see your lips
   B. speak slowly and clearly
   C. use gestures
   D. shout

15. The three most common visual disorders in the elderly are cataracts, diabetic retinopathy, and glaucoma.
    Of the following statements about these, the one that is NOT true is that

   A. the symptoms for cataracts are a need for brighter light and a need to hold things very near the eyes
   B. diabetic retinopathy, if untreated, can cause blindness, so any vision or eye problems in diabetics should be promptly reported
   C. glaucoma develops slowly, so it is much easier to detect than cataracts or diabetic retinopathy
   D. some of the symptoms of glaucoma are loss of vision out of the corner of the eye, headaches, nausea, eye pain, tearing, blurred vision, and halos around objects of light

16. Which of the following is NOT true?

   A. Most of the elderly hospitalized for psychiatric problems suffer from senile brain atrophy or brain changes that occur due to arteriosclerosis.
   B. It is important to allow the elderly who wish to, the right to always live in the past.
   C. The majority of the elderly are competent, alert, and functioning well in their communities.
   D. Many elderly patients feel that they are no longer valued members of our society.

17. Of the following, which is NOT a good reason for helping the elderly patient stay active? Activity

   A. promotes good health by stimulating appetite and regulating bowel function
   B. prevents the complications of inactivity such as pneumonia, bed sores, and joint immobility
   C. can create an interest in taking more medication
   D. can increase blood circulation

18. Staff members must come to an understanding of their own feelings about the elderly because

   A. the staff may then be more helpful
   B. any negative feelings one has may be difficult to hide
   C. feelings of fear or aversion can be easily transmitted
   D. all of the above

19. An elderly patient will probably eat better if

    A. food servings are large
    B. the foods are chewy
    C. he or she is allowed to finish his/her meals at a leisurely pace
    D. cooked food is served cold

20. The MOST common accident to the elderly involves

    A. falls B. burns C. bruises D. cuts

21. Which of the following is TRUE?

    A. Children should be considered and treated as miniature adults.
    B. Children are growing, developing human beings who will react to situations according to their level of development and the experiences to which they have been subjected.
    C. Children who are brought to a mental health center are usually calm and non-apprehensive on their first visit.
    D. The problems of adolescents are usually overestimated.

22. In working with adolescents, it would be BEST to

    A. neither bend over backwards to give in to demands, nor control them by rigid and punitive means
    B. dress the way most adolescents do
    C. staff those units with young people
    D. watch television with them regularly

23. Of the following, when working with children, it is MOST important to be

    A. consistent
    B. strict
    C. more concerned for their welfare than for the welfare of the other patients
    D. well-liked

24. Of the following, the element that is MOST lacking in relationships between adolescents and adults is

    A. respect B. fear C. trust D. sensitivity

25. Of the following, the BEST reason for grouping children together would be

    A. they should be protected from the influences of all adult patients
    B. children tend to feel more comfortable with other children
    C. children are less likely to *act out* when they are with other children
    D. they would be unable to bother adult patients

26. All of the following statements are true EXCEPT:

    A. Accidents, reactions to drugs, fevers, and disease may each contribute to mental or emotional problems
    B. How effectively an individual reacts to and manages stress contributes to his or her mental health
    C. There is significant research that indicates that mental illness is caused primarily by genetic transmittal
    D. A person's upbringing, his or her relationships with family or friends, past experiences, and present living conditions may all contribute to the status of his or her mental health

27. All of the following are basic psychological needs which must be met for a person to have self-esteem EXCEPT

    A. acceptance and understanding
    B. trust, respect, and security
    C. a rewarding romantic relationship
    D. pleasant interactions with other people

28. All of the following statements are true EXCEPT:

    A. Most people become mentally ill because they are unable to cope with or adapt to the stresses and problems of life
    B. People with emotional problems can rarely be helped enough to live independently
    C. Most of the diseases and symptoms of the body which plague people have a large emotional component as their cause
    D. Environmental and familial factors are more important than genetic factors in mental illness

29. The following are all optimal aspects of family functioning EXCEPT

    A. communication is open and direct
    B. expression of emotion is more often positive than negative
    C. minor problems are ignored, knowing they will go away on their own
    D. there is a high degree of congruence or harmony between the family's values and the actual realities of the society

30. All of the following statements are true EXCEPT:

    A. People who are wealthy rarely become mentally ill
    B. Physical disease may influence emotional balance
    C. People who are mentally ill are often very sensitive to what is happening in their environment
    D. Most people doubt their own sanity at one time or another

31. All of the following statements are true EXCEPT:

    A. Hereditary factors are not the primary cause of mental illness
    B. A person may react to an extremely traumatic experience by becoming mentally ill
    C. Early recognition and treatment does not affect the course of mental illness
    D. Mental illness can develop suddenly

32. All of the following statements are true EXCEPT:

    A. Emotionally disturbed people are usually very sensitive to how other people feel towards them
    B. People do not inherit mental disorders, but may inherit a predisposition to certain types of mental problems
    C. There are many factors which can cause mental illness
    D. Mood swings are signs of mental illness

33. Which of the following statements is LEAST accurate?

    A. The difference between being mentally healthy and mentally ill often lies in the intensity and frequency of inappropriate behavior.
    B. The way a person views a situation determines his or her response to the situation.
    C. The mentally ill are permanently disabled.
    D. Different personal experiences cause a difference in what a person perceives as stressful, and how much stress a person can tolerate.

34. All of the following statements are true EXCEPT:

    A. Most experts in the field of mental health believe that the experiences which occur during the first twenty, or the first six, years of life are the most significant
    B. An unfortunate characteristic of children is that they tend to blame themselves for failures of their parents, and thus may develop feelings of inadequacy which may affect them all of their lives
    C. If neglect is severe enough, an infant or young child may withdraw from reality into a fantasy world which feels less threatening
    D. Human beings develop in the exact same pattern and almost at the same rate

35. Schizophrenia is

    A. genetically caused
    B. most often caused by the habitual use of drugs
    C. the result of a complex relationship between biological, psychological, and sociological factors
    D. most commonly caused by the inhalation of toxic gases

KEY (CORRECT ANSWERS)

1.	B	16.	B
2.	C	17.	C
3.	B	18.	D
4.	C	19.	C
5.	A	20.	A
6.	A	21.	B
7.	B	22.	A
8.	D	23.	A
9.	D	24.	C
10.	C	25.	B
11.	B	26.	C
12.	D	27.	C
13.	D	28.	B
14.	D	29.	C
15.	C	30.	A

31. C
32. D
33. C
34. D
35. C

TEST 2

DIRECTIONS: Each question or incomplete statement is followed by several suggested answers or completions. Select the one that BEST answers the question or completes the statement. *PRINT THE LETTER OF THE CORRECT ANSWER IN THE SPACE AT THE RIGHT.*

1. Tardive dyskenesia is a(n) 1.___

   A. antidepressant
   B. birth-related serious injury
   C. serious side effect of phenothiazine derivatives
   D. antiparkinsons drug

2. People taking psychotropic drugs are MOST likely to be sensitive to 2.___

   A. long exposures to sunlight
   B. darkness
   C. noise
   D. other patients

3. An antipsychotic drug that is a phenothiazine derivative would MOST likely be used for 3.___

   A. helping a patient lose weight
   B. calming a patient
   C. helping a patient sleep
   D. reducing the frequency of delusions in a patient

4. Of the following, an antidepressant such as Elavil would MOST likely be used for 4.___

   A. the immediate prevention of suicidal action in a newly admitted patient
   B. helping a patient lose weight
   C. elevating a patient's mood
   D. diuretic purposes

5. Which of the following statements is NOT true? 5.___

   A. Antianxiety tranquilizers such as sparine, librium, and vistaril are useful primarily with psychoneurotic and psychosomatic disorders.
   B. Minor or antianxiety tranquilizers tend to be less habit-forming than major or antipsychotic tranquilizers.
   C. Akinesia, pseudoparkinsonism, and tardive dyskenesia are serious side effects of antipsychotic drugs, or phenothiazine derivatives.
   D. Generally, those using tranquilizers like sparine or librium are in less danger of deadly drug overdoses than those using barbituates.

6. All of the following statements are false EXCEPT: 6.___

   A. Antipsychotic drugs promote increased sexual interest
   B. Patients no longer need to take their medication when they feel better
   C. Phenothiazines are psychotropic drugs
   D. One of the main difficulties with antipsychotic drugs is that they tend to be habit-forming

7. Yellowing of the skin or eyes, sensitivity to light and pseudoparkinsonism may occur in patients receiving

    A. mellaril or thorazine
    B. librium or tranxene
    C. valium or vistaril
    D. antiparkinson drugs

8. Which of the following is NOT true of extrapyramidal symptoms (EPS)? They

    A. may appear after many weeks of use of phenothiazines
    B. can safely be controlled without medical assistance
    C. may appear after the patient has been taking the drug for only a few days
    D. may include pseudoparkinsonism

9. The time required to reach an effective blood level for an antidepressant medication would MOST likely be three

    A. days
    B. hours
    C. weeks
    D. months

10. An example of a psychotropic drug would be

    A. seconal
    B. aspirin
    C. librium
    D. perichloz

11. In evaluating a patient you are meeting for the first time, it would be best NOT to

    A. be as objective as possible
    B. question one's own motives and reactions when processing data during and after the meeting
    C. be extremely goal-oriented
    D. not allow any praise or criticism directed at you by the patient to influence your assessment

12. All of the following statements are true EXCEPT:

    A. People communicate non-verbally via their behavior and their body posture
    B. Non-verbal clues may be a better indication of a patient's true feelings than what the patient actually says
    C. A patient who is highly anxious is easier to evaluate than a patient who is relatively calm
    D. People should be judged objectively

13. When asking a patient a question, one should do all of the following EXCEPT

    A. phrase questions in order to receive a yes or no response
    B. ask only relevant questions
    C. listen carefully to the response before asking the next question
    D. phrase questions clearly

14. The MAIN purpose for extensive record keeping is to

    A. provide an accurate description of the patient's diagnosis
    B. provide a subjective report of the patient's behavior
    C. provide an objective report of the patient's behavior
    D. give mental health personnel something to do

15. When talking to a patient for the first time, one must realize that

    A. hostile behavior indicates an extremely severe disorder in the patient
    B. a patient's physical appearance will indicate how successful you will be in communicating with the patient
    C. the patient is extremely nervous
    D. you are both strangers to each other

16. Of the following, which statement is NOT true?

    A. The rapid assessment of a patient is not necessarily accomplished by asking a series of routine questions.
    B. There is value, in assessing a patient, in creating a conversational bridge which has *here and now* relevance.
    C. One can assess a patient's state by his or her reaction to a warm greeting given to him or her.
    D. There is some value in routinely asking certain questions, when needed, in order to check a patient's orientation and memory.

17. All of the following could be signs that someone is moving towards mental illness EXCEPT

    A. exhibiting a degree of prolonged, constant anxiety, apprehension, or fear which is out of proportion with reality
    B. severe appetite disturbances
    C. occasional depression
    D. abrupt changes in a person's behavior

18. The first few minutes of interaction with a patient can reveal all but

    A. a patient's contact with reality
    B. whether you are comfortable with a patient
    C. a patient's mood
    D. a patient's chances for recovery

19. Which of the following statements is TRUE?

    A. The tentative diagnosis made when a patient is first admitted is the most accurate diagnosis.
    B. One should always try and keep in mind the state the patient was in when first admitted.
    C. A diagnosis is actually an ongoing process.
    D. When assessing patients' behavior, it is best to be suspicious of what may look like progress.

20. All of the following are examples of defense mechanisms EXCEPT

    A. projection
    B. complimenting someone
    C. displacement
    D. regression

21. A treatment plan is likely to be MOST effective if the

    A. patient's suggestions are always incorporated
    B. patient is voluntarily and wholeheartedly participating in the treatment plan designed for him or her

C. patient has daily contact with his or her family
D. patient respects the team leader

22. All of the following are true EXCEPT:

    A. Patients do not become well simply by people doing something for them
    B. A patient's well-being is enhanced when one or more team members can forge a *therapeutic alliance* with that patient
    C. The most important purpose of the treatment team is to administer the proper medications to patients
    D. It is important that a patient be seen as an individual, and not just as a *case* or a *number*

23. Of the following, a member of the treatment team can BEST assist a patient by

    A. commanding respect from other team members
    B. carefully observing the behavior of patients
    C. avoiding spending too much time with patients
    D. becoming friends with a patient

24. Of the following, which is LEAST important when considering a treatment plan?

    A. Involving the patient
    B. Setting reasonable goals
    C. Being as specific as possible in setting completion dates for goals, and sticking to them
    D. Detailing the methods to be followed, and the work assignments

25. All of the following are true EXCEPT:

    A. A treatment team should help patients understand that they can improve their condition if they will cooperate with the treatment plan
    B. Patients should be encouraged to participate in the programs designed for them
    C. Patients should be encouraged to revise their treatment plans
    D. One's approach should be tailored for each individual, whenever possible

26. All of the following could be considered appropriate goals for patients to work towards, EXCEPT to

    A. expand one's capacity to find or create acceptable options
    B. learn to be less dependent
    C. give up feeling persecuted
    D. learn how to get what one needs, at any cost

27. In working in treatment teams, it is MOST important for team members to

    A. communicate effectively with each other
    B. enjoy working with each other
    C. keep morale high
    D. attend meetings on time

28. One of the purposes of the treatment team is to

    A. decrease the amount of work
    B. coordinate and integrate services to patients
    C. provide training
    D. provide patients with basic counseling skills they can use

29. When working with someone exhibiting a manic-depressive psychosis, depressed type, it is BEST to

    A. concern yourself primarily with his or her eating habits
    B. focus primarily on their sleeping habits
    C. take every statement he or she may make about suicide seriously
    D. allow them to watch a great deal of television

30. In working with a paranoid patient, all of the following are true EXCEPT:
    It

    A. is important to listen with respect
    B. is helpful to establish a trusting relationship
    C. is good to try and talk the patient out of his or her fears
    D. would not be a good practice to agree with their statements, if they are not true

31. It is important, when dealing with verbally abusive patients, to keep in mind all of the following EXCEPT:

    A. Patients usually become abusive because of frustrating circumstances beyond their control
    B. In most cases, the patients do not mean anything personal by their abusive remarks; they are displacing anger
    C. It is important for staff members to remain calm and controlled when patients have emotional outbursts
    D. It is a good idea to allow an angry patient to draw you into an argument, as this will eventually help calm him or her down

32. When dealing with a patient who insists upon doing a number of rituals before brushing his teeth, it would be BEST to

    A. attempt to tease him out of his behavior
    B. not be critical of the ritualistic behavior
    C. perform the same rituals so that he feels more secure
    D. insist that he eliminate one step of the ritual each week

33. A patient tells you that he is balancing an automobile on the top of his head, and asks you what you think of that.
    An APPROPRIATE response for you to make would be:

    A. to ask him to take you for a ride
    B. *Stop saying ridiculous things*
    C. *I know you believe you are balancing a car on your head but I don't see it, therefore I have to assume that you're not*
    D. *Is it an invisible car*

34. A new patient, who is very paranoid, refuses to take off his clothes before getting into bed.
    Which would be MOST helpful?

    A. Getting another staff member to assist in removing his clothes
    B. Leaving the room until he comes to his senses
    C. Trying to find out why the patient does not want to undress
    D. Allowing the patient to stay up all night

35. In handling depressed patients, it is BEST to

    A. encourage them to participate in activities
    B. remind them often that things will be better tomorrow
    C. remember that depressed patients have few feelings of guilt
    D. let them know that you know just how they are feeling

36. A patient tells you that she is very depressed over the recent death of her brother.
    Which of the following would be the MOST appropriate response?

    A. *Everybody gets depressed when they lose someone they love.*
    B. *It could have been worse; at least he was ill only a short time.*
    C. *I know just how you feel.*
    D. *This must be very difficult for you.*

37. A patient who recently suffered a stroke refuses to let you help her bathe.
    This is probably because

    A. it is hard for her to accept that she can no longer do things for herself that she could do before the stroke
    B. she does not like you
    C. she is extremely independent and should be encouraged to be less so
    D. you need to review your methods for bathing patients

38. All of the following would be appropriate in working with a patient who is hallucinating EXCEPT

    A. carefully watch what you are non-verbally communicating
    B. ask concrete, reality-oriented questions
    C. provide a calm, structured environment
    D. agree with the patient, if asked, that you are experiencing the same state he or she is

39. In dealing with overactive patients, it is BEST to

    A. not give most of your attention to these patients, leaving the quieter patients to look after themselves
    B. keep in mind that overactive patients are always more interesting than other patients
    C. remember that overactive patients need more care than other patients
    D. forcibly restrain them whenever possible

40. A patient with mild organic brain damage is very withdrawn and negativistic. The BEST approach, of the following, would be

    A. *I need a partner to play cards with me*
    B. *Your family is very disappointed in you when you act like this*
    C. *Your doctor said you should participate in all activities here, so you'd better do that*
    D. *Would you like to go to your room so you can be alone?*

KEY (CORRECT ANSWERS)

1.	C	11.	C	21.	B	31.	D
2.	A	12.	C	22.	C	32.	B
3.	D	13.	A	23.	B	33.	C
4.	C	14.	C	24.	C	34.	C
5.	B	15.	D	25.	C	35.	A
6.	C	16.	C	26.	D	36.	D
7.	A	17.	C	27.	A	37.	A
8.	B	18.	D	28.	B	38.	D
9.	C	19.	C	29.	C	39.	A
10.	C	20.	B	30.	C	40.	A

EXAMINATION SECTION
TEST 1

DIRECTIONS: Each question or incomplete statement is followed by several suggested answers or completions. Select the one that BEST answers the question or completes the Statement. *PRINT THE LETTER OF THE CORRECT ANSWER IN THE SPACE AT THE RIGHT.*

Questions 1-5.

DIRECTIONS: Answer questions 1 through 5 on the basis of the following passage.

Mental disorders are found in a fairly large number of the inmates in correctional institutions. There are no exact figures as to the inmates who are mentally disturbed -- partly because it is hard to draw a precise line between "mental disturbance" and "normality" -- but 'experts find that somewhere between 15% and 25% of inmates are suffering from disorders that are obvious enough to show up in routine psychiatric examinations. Society has not yet really come to grips with the problem of what to do with mentally disturbed offenders. There is not enough money available to set up treatment programs for all the people identified as mentally disturbed; and there would probably not be enough qualified psychiatric personnel available to run such programs even if they could be set up. Most mentally disturbed offenders are therefore left to serve out their time in correctional institutions, and the burden of dealing with them falls on correction officers. This means that a correction offcer must be sensitive enough to human behavior to know when he is dealing with a person who is not mentally normal, and that the officer must be imaginative enough to be able to sense how an abnormal individual might react under certain circumstances.

1. According to the above passage, mentally disturbed inmakes in correctional institutions   1._____

    A. are usually transferred to mental hospitals when their condition is noticed
    B. cannot be told from other inmates, because tests cannot distinguish between insane people and normal people
    C. may constitute as mich as 25% of the total inmate population
    D. should be regarded as no different from all the other inmates

2. The passage says that today the job of handling mentally disturbed inmates is MAINLY up to   2._____

    A. psychiatric personnel   B. other inmates
    C. correction officers   D. administrative officials

3. Of the following, which is a reason given in the passage for society's failure to provide adequate treatment programs for mentally disturbed inmates?   3._____

    A. Law-abiding citizens should not have to pay for fancy treatment programs for criminals.
    B. A person who breaks the law should not expect society to give him special help.
    C. It is impossible to tell whether an inmate is mentally disturbed.
    D. There are not enough trained people to provide the kind of treatment needed.

4. The expression *abnormal individual,* as used in the last sentence of the passage, refers to an individual who is

    A. of average intelligence   B. of superior intelligence
    C. completely normal   D. mentally disturbed

5. The reader of the passage would MOST likely agree that

    A. correction officers should not expect mentally disturbed persons to behave the same way a normal person would behave
    B. correction officers should not report infractions of the rules committed by mentally disturbed persons
    C. mentally disturbed persons who break the law should be treated exactly the same way as anyone else
    D. mentally disturbed persons who have broken the law should not be imprisoned

Questions 6-12.

DIRECTIONS: Questions 6 through 12 are based on the roster of patients, the instructions, the table, and the sample question given below.

Twelve patients of a mental institution are divided into three permanent groups in their workshop. They must be present and accounted for in these groups at the beginning of each workday. During the day, the patients check out of their groups for various activities. They check back in again when those activities have been completed. Assume that the day is divided into three activity periods.

ROSTER OF PATIENTS

GROUP X	Ted	Frank	George	Harry
GROUP Y	Jack	Ken	Larry	Mel
GROUP Z	Phil	Bob	Sam	Vic

The following table shows the movements of these patients from their groups during the day. Assume that all were present and accounted for at the beginning of Period I.

		GROUP X	GROUP Y	GROUP Z
Period I	Check-outs	Ted, Frank	Ken, Larry	Phil
Period II	Check-ins	Frank	Ken, Larry	Phil
	Check-outs	George	Jack, Mel	Bob, Sam, Vic
Period III	Check-ins	George	Mel, Jack	Sam, Bob, Vic
	Check-outs	Frank, Harry	Ken	Vic

SAMPLE QUESTION: At the end of Period II, the patients remaining in Group X were

    A. Ted, Frank, Harry   C. Ted, George
    B. Frank, Harry   D. Frank, Harry, George

During Period I, Ted and Frank were checked out from Group X. During Period II, Frank was checked back in and George was checked out. Therefore, the members of the group remaining out are Ted and George. The two other members of the group, Frank and Harry, should be present. The CORRECT answer is B.

6. At the end of Period I, the TOTAL number of patients remaining in their own permanent groups was

   A. 8   B. 7   C. 6   D. 5

7. At the end of Period I, the patients remaining in Group Z were

   A. George and Harry
   B. Jack and Mel
   C. Bob, Sam, and Vic
   D. Phil

8. At the end of Period II, the patients remaining in Group Y were

   A. Ken and Larry
   B. Jack, Ken, and Mel
   C. Jack and Ken
   D. Ken, Mel, and Larry

9. At the end of Period II, the TOTAL number of patients remaining in their own permanent groups was

   A. 8   B. 7   C. 6   D. 5

10. At the end of Period II, the patients who were NOT present in Group Z were

    A. Phil, Bob, and Sam
    B. Sam, Bob, and Vic
    C. Sam, Vic, and Phil
    D. Vic, Phil, and Bob

11. At the end of Period II, the patients remaining in Group Y were

    A. Ted, Frank, and George
    B. Jack, Mel, and Ken
    C. Jack, Larry, and Mel
    D. Frank and Harry

12. At the end of Period III, the TOTAL number of patients NOT present in their own permanent groups was

    A. 4   B. 5   C. 6   D. 7

13. The one of the following conditions which bears no causative relationship to feeblemindedness is

    A. heredity
    B. cerebral defect
    C. early postnatal trauma
    D. dementia

14. Physical conditions which are caused by emotional conflicts are generally referred to as being

    A. psycho-social
    B. hypochondriacal
    C. psychosomatic
    D. psychotic

15. Of the following conditions, the one in which anxiety is NOT generally found is

    A. psychopathic personality
    B. mild hysteria
    C. psychoneurosis
    D. compulsive-obsessive personality

16. Kleptomania may BEST be described as a

    A. neurotic drive to accumulate personal property through compulsive acts in order to dispose of it to others with whom one wishes friendship
    B. type of neurosis which manifests itself in an uncontrollable impulse to steal without economic motivation
    C. psychopathic trait which is probably hereditary in nature
    D. manifestation of punishment-inviting behavior based upon guilt feelings for some other crime or wrong-doing, fantasied or real, committed as a child

17. The one of the following tests which is NOT ordinarily used as a protective technique is the

    A. Wechsler Bellevue Scale
    B. Rorschach Test
    C. Thematic Apperception Test
    D. Jung Free Association Test

18. The outstanding personality test in use at the present time is the Rorschach Test. Of the following considerations, the GREATEST value of this test to the psychiatrist and social worker is that it

    A. provides practical recommendations with reference to further educational and vocational training possibilities for the person tested
    B. reveals in quick, concise form the hereditary factors affecting the individual personality
    C. helps in substantiating a diagnosis of juvenile delinquency
    D. helps in a diagnostic formulation and in determining differential treatment

19. Of the following, the one through which ethical values are MOST generally acquired is

    A. heredity
    B. early training in school
    C. admonition and strict corrective measures by parents and other supervising adults
    D. integration into the self of parental values and attitudes

20. Delinquent behavior is MOST generally a result of

    A. living and growing up in an environment that is both socially and financially deprived
    B. a lack of educational opportunity for development of individual skills
    C. multiple factors -- psychological, bio-social, emotional and environmental
    D. low frustration tolerance of many parents toward problems of married life

21. Alcoholism in the United States is USUALLY caused by

    A. the sense of frustration in one's work
    B. inadequacy of recreational facilities
    C. neurotic conflicts expressed in drinking excessively
    D. shyness and timidity

22. The MOST distinctive characteristic of the chronic alcoholic is that he drinks alcohol   22.____

    A. socially   B. compulsively
    C. periodically   D. secretly

23. The chronic alcoholic is the person who cannot face reality without alcohol, and yet   23.____
    whose adequate adjustment to reality is impossible so long as he uses alcohol.
    On the basis of this statement, it is MOST reasonable to conclude that individuals
    overindulge in alcohol because alcohol

    A. deadens the sense of conflict, giving the individual an illusion of social competence
       and a feeling of well-being and success
    B. provides the individual with an outlet to display his feelings of good-fellowship and
       cheerfulness which are characteristic of his extroverted personality
    C. affords an escape technique from habitual irrational fears, but does not affect ratio-
       nal fears
    D. offers an escape from imagery and feelings of superiority which cause tension and
       anxiety

24. The one of the following drugs to which a person is LEAST likely to become addicted is   24.____

    A. opium   B. morphine   C. marijuana   D. heroin

25. Teenagers who become addicted to the use of drugs are MOST generally   25.____

    A. mentally defective   B. paranoid
    C. normally adventurous   D. emotionally disturbed

26. In the light of the current high rate of addiction to drugs among youths throughout the   26.____
    country, the one of the following statements which is generally considered to be LEAST
    correct is that

    A. a relatively large number of children and youths who experiment with drugs
       become addicts
    B. youths who use narcotics do so because of some emotional and personality distur-
       bance
    C. youthful addicts are found largely among those who suffer to an abnormal extent
       deprivations in their personal development and growth
    D. the great majority of youthful addicts have had unfortunate home experiences and
       practically no contact with established community agencies

27. The one of the following terms which BEST describes the psychological desire to repeat   27.____
    the use of a drug intermittently or continously because of emotional needs is

    A. habituation   B. euphoria   C. tolerance   D. addiction

28. The desire for special clothing in a mental institution usually is concerned with   28.____

    A. shoes   B. sox   C. trousers   D. underwear

29. A study entitled "A preliminary evaluation of the relationship between group psychother-   29.____
    apy and the adjustment of adolescent inmates (16-21 years) in a short-term penal institu-
    tion" was conducted by the Diagnostic Staff at Rikers Island in New York. A conclusion
    which was drawn as a result of the study was that

A. a repetition of the study was necessary with smaller therapy and non-therapy groups
B. group psychotherapy subjects displayed a better institutional adjustment than those not receiving group therapy
C. no follow-up study was necessary because of the negative results from the original study
D. a smaller proportion of experimental group subjects improved after receiving group psychotherapy when compared to those who did not receive group therapy

30. The one of the following statements which is MOST accurate concerning group psychotherapy is that group psychotherapy

    A. is in a way an outgrowth of the concept of patient self-government
    B. is of little value with deviant personality types
    C. should make the group members resent help from their fellow patients
    D. reflects a punitive rather than a rehabilitative aim

31. In group counseling and psychotherapy it is USUALLY true that persons are more defensive and argumentative than in individualized counseling and therapy sessions. The reason for this tendency is that

    A. individuals in a group setting feel it more necessary to protect their personality
    B. people in group settings are motivated by the characteristically free atmosphere
    C. people would rather argue in a group setting than in an individualized setting
    D. the group session is more poorly organized and therefore uncontrolled

32. There is a group of mentally ill patients who have a <u>functional psychosis.</u> The word "functional" in this case indicates that

    A. it is an organic psychosis
    B. the psychosis is caused by alcoholism or drug addiction
    C. there are no demonstrable changes in the brain
    D. there are clinical findings of senile arteriosclerosis

33. "Sociopaths" is a fairly new word used to describe

    A. confirmed narcotics addicts
    B. latent male homosexuals
    C. neurotic adolescents
    D. psychopathic personalities

34. The incarceration of the geriatric presents many problems in mental administration. The word "geriatric" means MOST NEARLY

    A. dipsomanic (alcoholic)
    B. moronic (mentally deficient)
    C. pertaining to split personality types
    D. pertaining to individuals of advanced years

35. Jobs for ex-patients can MOST often be found in

    A. big corporations
    B. domestic service
    C. government agencies
    D. small private enterprises

KEY (CORRECT ANSWERS)

1. C
2. C
3. D
4. D
5. A

6. B
7. C
8. A
9. D
10. B

11. C
12. B
13. D
14. C
15. A

16. B
17. A
18. D
19. D
20. C

21. C
22. B
23. A
24. C
25. D

26. A
27. A
28. A
29. B
30. A

31. A
32. C
33. D
34. D
35. D

INTERVIEWING

EXAMINATION SECTION
TEST 1

DIRECTIONS: Each question or incomplete statement is followed by several suggested answers or completions. Select the one that BEST answers the question or completes the statement. *PRINT THE LETTER OF THE CORRECT ANSWER IN THE SPACE AT THE RIGHT.*

1. Of the following, the MAIN advantage to the supervisor of using the indirect (or nondirective) interview, in which he asks only guiding questions and encourages the employee to do most of the talking, is that he can

    A. obtain a mass of information about the employee in a very short period of time
    B. easily get at facts which the employee wishes to conceal
    C. get answers which are not slanted or biased in order to win his favor
    D. effectively deal with an employee's serious emotional problems

2. An interviewer under your supervision routinely closes his interview with a reassuring remark such as, "I'm sure you soon will be well," or "Everything will soon be all right." This practice is USUALLY considered

    A. *advisable*, chiefly because the interviewer may make the patient feel better
    B. *inadvisable*, chiefly because it may cause a patient who is seriously ill to doubt the worker's understanding of the situation
    C. *advisable*, chiefly because the patient becomes more receptive if further interviews are needed
    D. *inadvisable*, chiefly because the interviewer should usually not show that he is emotionally involved

3. An interviewer has just ushered out a client he has interviewed. As the interviewer is preparing to leave, the client mentions a fact that seems to contradict the information he has given.
   Of the following, it would be BEST for the interviewer at this time to

    A. make no response but write the fact down in his report and plan to come back another day
    B. point out to the client that he has contradicted himself and ask for an explanation
    C. ask the client to elaborate on the comment and attempt to find out further information about the fact
    D. disregard the comment since the client was probably exhausted and not thinking clearly

4. A client who is being interviewed insists on certain facts. The interviewer knows that these statements are incorrect. In regard to the rest of the client's statements, the interviewer is MOST justified to

    A. disregard any information the client gives which cannot be verified
    B. try to discover other misstatements by confronting the client with the discrepancy
    C. consider everything else which the client has said as the truth unless proved otherwise
    D. ask the client to prove his statements

5. Immediately after the interviewer identifies himself to a client, she says in a hysterical voice that he is not to be trusted.
Of the following, the BEST course of action for the interviewer to follow would be to

   A. tell the woman sternly that if she does not stay calm, he will leave
   B. assure the woman that there is no cause to worry
   C. ignore the woman until she becomes quiet
   D. ask the woman to explain her problem

6. Assume that you are an interviewer and that one of your interviewees has asked you for advice on dealing with a personal problem.
Of the following, the BEST action for you to take is to

   A. tell him about a similar problem which you know worked out well
   B. advise him not to worry
   C. explain that the problem is quite a usual one and that the situation will be brighter soon
   D. give no opinion and change the subject when practicable

7. All of the following are, *generally*, good approaches for an interviewer to use in order to improve his interviews EXCEPT

   A. developing a routine approach so that interviews can be standardized
   B. comparing his procedure with that of others engaged in similar work
   C. reviewing each interview critically, picking out one or two weak points to concentrate on improving
   D. comparing his own more successful and less successful interviews

8. Assume that a supervisor suggests at a staff meeting that tape recording machines be provided for interviewers. Following are four arguments *against* the use of tape recorders that are raised by other members of the staff that might be valid:
   I. Recorded interviews provide too much unnecessary information
   II. Recorded interviews provide no record of manner or gestures.
   III. Tape recorders are too cumbersome and difficult for the average supervisor to manage.
   IV. Tape recorders may inhibit the interviewee.

   Which one of the following choices MOST accurately classifies the above into those which are generally *valid* and those which are *not*?

   A. I and II are generally valid, but III and IV are not.
   B. IV is generally valid, but I, II and III are not.
   C. I, II and IV are generally valid, but III is not.
   D. I, II, III and IV are generally valid.

9. During an interview the PRIMARY advantage of the technique of using questions as opposed to allowing the interviewee to talk freely is that questioning

   A. gives the interviewer greater control
   B. provides a more complete picture
   C. makes the interviewee more relaxed
   D. decreases the opportunity for exaggeration

3 (#1)

10. Assume that, in conducting an interview, an interviewer takes into consideration the age, sex, education, and background of the subject.
This practice is GENERALLY considered

   A. *undesirable,* mainly because an interviewer may be prejudiced by such factors
   B. *desirable,* mainly because these are factors which might influence a person's response to certain questions
   C. *undesirable,* mainly because these factors rarely have any bearing on the matter being investigated
   D. *desirable,* mainly because certain categories of people answer certain questions in the same way

10.____

11. If a client should begin to tell his life story during an interview, the BEST course of action for an interviewer to take is to

   A. interrupt immediately and insist that they return to business
   B. listen attentively until the client finishes and then ask if they can return to the subject
   C. pretend to have other business and come back later to see the client
   D. interrupt politely at an appropriate point and direct the client's attention to the subject

11.____

12. An interviewer who is trying to discover the circumstances surrounding a client's accident would be MOST successful during an interview if he avoided questions which

   A. lead the client to discuss the matter in detail
   B. can easily be answered by either "yes" or "no"
   C. ask for specific information
   D. may be embarrassing or annoying to the client

12.____

13. A client being interviewed may develop an emotional reaction (positive or negative) toward the interviewer. The BEST attitude for the interviewer to take toward such feelings is that they are

   A. *inevitable;* they should be accepted but kept under control
   B. *unusual;* they should be treated impersonally
   C. *obstructive;* they should be resisted at all costs
   D. *abnormal;* they should be eliminated as soon as possible

13.____

14. Encouraging the client being interviewed to talk freely at first is a technique that is supported by all of the following reasons EXCEPT that it

   A. tends to counteract any preconceived ideas that the interviewer may have entertained about the client
   B. gives the interviewer a chance to learn the best method of approach to obtain additional information
   C. inhibits the client from looking to the interviewer for support and advice
   D. allows the client to reveal the answers to many questions before they are asked

14.____

15. Of the following, *generally,* the MOST effective way for an interviewer to assure full cooperation from the client he is interviewing is to

   A. sympathize with the client's problems and assure him of concern
   B. tell a few jokes before beginning to ask questions

15.____

C. convince the patient that the answers to the questions will help him as well as the interviewer
D. arrange the interview when the client feels best

16. Since many elderly people are bewildered and helpless when interviewed, special consideration should be given to them.
Of the following, the BEST way for an interviewer to *initially* approach elderly clients who express anxiety and fear is to

   A. assure them that they have nothing to worry about
   B. listen patiently and show interest in them
   C. point out the specific course of action that is best for them
   D. explain to them that many people have overcome much greater difficulties

17. Assume that, in planning an initial interview, an interviewer determines in advance what information is needed in order to fulfill the purpose of the interview.
Of the following, this procedure usually does NOT

   A. reduce the number of additional interviews required
   B. expedite the processing of the case
   C. improve public opinion of the interviewer's agency
   D. assure the cooperation of the person interviewed

18. Sometimes an interviewer deliberately introduces his own personal interests and opinions into an interview with a client.
In general, this practice should be considered

   A. *desirable,* primarily because the relationship between client and interviewer becomes social rather than businesslike
   B. *undesirable,* primarily because the client might complain to his supervisor
   C. *desirable;* primarily because the focus of attention is directed toward the client
   D. *undesirable;* primarily because an argument between client and interviewer could result

19. The one of the following types of interviewees who presents the LEAST difficult problem to handle is the person who

   A. answers with a great many qualifications
   B. talks at length about unrelated subjects so that the interviewer cannot ask questions
   C. has difficulty understanding the interviewer's vocabulary
   D. breaks into the middle of sentences and completes them with a meaning of his own

20. A man being interviewed is entitled to Medicaid, but he refuses to sign up for it because he says he cannot accept any form of welfare.
Of the following, the *best* course of action for an interviewer to take FIRST is to

   A. try to discover the reason for his feeling this way
   B. tell him that he should be glad financial help is available
   C. explain that others cannot help him if he will not help himself
   D. suggest that he speak to someone who is already on Medicaid

21. Of the following, the outcome of an interview by an interviewer depends MOST heavily on the

    A. personality of the interviewee
    B. personality of the interviewer
    C. subject matter of the questions asked
    D. interaction between interviewer and interviewee

22. Some clients being interviewed by an interviewer are primarily interested in making a favorable impression. The interviewer should be aware of the fact that such clients are MORE likely than *other* clients to

    A. try to anticipate the answers the interviewer is looking for
    B. answer all questions openly and frankly
    C. try to assume the role of interviewer
    D. be anxious to get the interview over as quickly as possible

23. The type of interview which a hospital care interviewer usually conducts is *substantially different* from most interviewing situations in all of the following aspects EXCEPT the

    A. setting
    B. kinds of clients
    C. techniques employed
    D. kinds of problems

24. During an interview, an interviewer uses a "leading question." This type of question is so-called because it, *generally.*,

    A. starts a series of questions about one topic
    B. suggests the answer which the interviewer wants
    C. forms the basis for a following "trick" question
    D. sets, at the beginning, the tone of the interview

25. An interviewer may face various difficulties when he tries to obtain information from a client.
    Of the following, the difficulty which is EASIEST for the interviewer to *overcome* occurs when a client

    A. is unwilling to reveal the information
    B. misunderstands what information is needed
    C. does not have the information available to him
    D. is unable to coherently give the information requested

KEY (CORRECT ANSWERS)

1.	C	11.	D
2.	B	12.	B
3.	C	13.	A
4.	C	14.	C
5.	D	15.	C
6.	D	16.	B
7.	A	17.	D
8.	C	18.	D
9.	A	19.	C
10.	B	20.	A

21.	D
22.	A
23.	C
24.	B
25.	B

TEST 2

DIRECTIONS: Each question or incomplete statement is followed by several suggested answers or completions. Select the one that BEST answers the question or completes the statement. *PRINT THE LETTER OF THE CORRECT ANSWER IN THE SPACE AT THE RIGHT.*

1. Of the following, the MOST appropriate manner for an interviewer to assume during an interview with a client is   1._____

    A. authoritarian   B. paternal   C. casual   D. businesslike

2. The systematic study of interviewing theory, principles and techniques by an interviewer will, *usually*   2._____

    A. aid him to act in a depersonalized manner
    B. turn his interviewes into stereotyped affairs
    C. make the people he interviews feel manipulated
    D. give him a basis for critically examining his own practice

3. Compiling in advance a list of general questions to ask a client during an interview is a technique *usually* considered   3._____

    A. *desirable,* chiefly because reference to the list will help keep the interview focused on the important issues
    B. *undesirable,* chiefly because use of such a list will discourage the client from speaking freely
    C. *desirable,* chiefly because the list will serve as a record of what questions were asked
    D. *undesirable,* chiefly because use of such a list will make the interview too mechanical and impersonal

4. The one of the following which is usually of GREATEST importance in winning the cooperation of a person being interviewed while achieving the purpose of the interview is the interviewer's ability to   4._____

    A. gain the confidence of the person being interviewed
    B. stick to the subject of the interview
    C. handle a person who is obviously lying
    D. prevent the person being interviewed from withholding information

5. While interviewing clients, an interviewer should use the technique of interruption, beginning to speak when a client has temporarily paused at the end of a phrase or sentence, in order to   5._____

    A. limit the client's ability to voice his objections or complaints
    B. shorten, terminate or redirect a client's response
    C. assert authority when he feels that the client is too conceited
    D. demonstrate to the client that pauses in speech should be avoided

6. An interviewer might gain background information about a client by being aware of the person's speech during an interview.
Which one of the following patterns of speech would offer the LEAST accurate information about a client? The   6._____

A. number of slang expressions and the level of vocabulary
B. presence and degree of an accent
C. rate of speech and the audibility level
D. presence of a physical speech defect

7. Suppose that you are interviewing a distressed client who claims that he was just laid off from his job and has no money to pay his rent.
Your FIRST action should be to

   A. ask if he has sought other employment or has other sources of income
   B. express your sympathy but explain that he must pay the rent on time
   C. inquire about the reasons he was laid off from work
   D. try to transfer him to a smaller apartment which he can afford

8. Suppose you have some background information on an applicant whom you are interviewing. During the interview it appears that the applicant is giving you *false* information. The BEST thing for you to do at that point is to

   A. pretend that you are not aware of the written facts and let him continue
   B. tell him what you already know and discuss the discrepancies with him
   C. terminate the interview and make a note that the applicant is untrustworthy
   D. tell him that, because he is making false statements, he will not be eligible for an apartment

9. A Spanish-speaking applicant may want to bring his bilingual child with him to an interview to act as an interpreter. Which of the following would be LEAST likely to affect the value of an interview in which an applicant's child has acted as interpreter?

   A. It may make it undesirable to ask certain questions.
   B. A child may do an inadequate job of interpretation.
   C. A child's answers may indicate his feelings toward his parents.
   D. The applicant may not want to reveal all information in front of his child.

10. Assume you are assigned to interview applicants.
Of the following, which is the BEST attitude for you to take in dealing with applicants?

    A. Assume they will enjoy being interviewed because they believe that you have the power of decision
    B. Expect that they have a history of anti-social behavior in the family, and probe deeply into the social development of family members
    C. Expect that they will try to control the interview, thus you should keep them on the defensive
    D. Assume that they will be polite and cooperative and attempt to secure the information you need in a business-like manner

11. If you are interviewing an applicant who is a minority group member in reference to his eligibility, it would be BEST for you to use language that is

    A. *informal,* using ethnic expressions known to the applicant
    B. *technical,* using the expressions commonly used in the agency
    C. *simple,* using words and phrases which laymen understand
    D. *formal,* to remind the applicant that he is dealing with a government agency

12. When interviewing an applicant to determine his eligibility, it is MOST important to   12._____
    A. have a prior mental picture of the typical eligible applicant
    B. conduct the interview strictly according to a previously prepared script
    C. keep in mind the goal of the interview, which is to determine eligibility
    D. get an accurate and detailed account of the applicant's life history

13. The practice of trying to imagine yourself in the applicant's place during an interview is   13._____
    A. *good;* mainly because you will be able to evaluate his responses better
    B. *good;* mainly because it will enable you to treat him as a friend rather than as an applicant
    C. *poor;* mainly because it is important for the applicant to see you as an impartial person
    D. *poor;* mainly because it is too time-consuming to do this with each applicant

14. When dealing with clients from different ethnic backgrounds, you should be aware of certain tendencies toward prejudice.   14._____
    Which of the following statements is LEAST likely to be valid?
    A. Whites prejudiced against blacks are more likely to be prejudiced against Puerto Ricans than whites not prejudiced against blacks.
    B. The less a white is in competition with blacks, the less likely he is to be prejudiced against them.
    C. Persons who have moved from one social group to another are likely to retain the attitudes and prejudices of their original social group.
    D. When there are few blacks or Puerto Ricans in a project, whites are less likely to be prejudiced against them than when there are many.

15. Of the following, the one who is MOST likely to be a good interviewer of people seeking assistance, is one who   15._____
    A. tries to get applicants to apply to another agency instead
    B. believes that it is necessary to get as much pertinent information as possible in order to determine the applicant's real needs
    C. believes that people who seek assistance are likely to have persons with a history of irresponsible behavior in their households
    D. is convinced that there is no need for a request for assistance

KEYS (CORRECT ANSWERS)

1. D
2. D
3. A
4. A
5. B

6. C
7. A
8. B
9. C
10. D

11. C
12. C
13. A
14. C
15. B

COMMUNICATION
EXAMINATION SECTION
TEST 1

DIRECTIONS: Each question or incomplete statement is followed by several suggested answers or completions. Select the one that BEST answers the question or completes the statement. *PRINT THE LETTER OF THE CORRECT ANSWER IN THE SPACE AT THE RIGHT.*

1. In some agencies the counsel to the agency head is given the right to bypass the chain of command and issue orders directly to the staff concerning matters that involve certain specific processes and practices.
   This situation *most nearly* illustrates the PRINCIPLE of

   A. the acceptance theory of authority B. multiple - linear authority
   C. splintered authority D. functional authority

2. It is commonly understood that communication is an important part of the administrative process.
   Which of the following is NOT a valid principle of the communication process in administration?

   A. The channels of communication should be spontaneous
   B. The lines of communication should be as direct and as short as possible
   C. Communications should be authenticated
   D. The persons serving in communications centers should be competent

3. Of the following, the *one* factor which is generally considered LEAST essential to successful committee operations is

   A. stating a clear definition of the authority and scope of the committee
   B. selecting the committee chairman carefully
   C. limiting the size of the committee to four persons
   D. limiting the subject matter to that which can be handled in group discussion

4. Of the following, the failure by line managers to accept and appreciate the benefits and limitations of a new program or system *very frequently* can be traced to the

   A. budgetary problems involved
   B. resultant need to reduce staff
   C. lack of controls it engenders
   D. failure of top management to support its implementation

5. If a manager were thinking about using a committee of subordinates to solve an operating problem, which of the following would generally NOT be an *advantage* of such use of the committee approach?

   A. Improved coordination B. Low cost
   C. Increased motivation D. Integrated judgment

6. Every supervisor has many occasions to lead a conference or participate in a conference of some sort.
Of the following statements that pertain to conferences and conference leadership, which is generally considered to be MOST valid?

   A. Since World War II, the trend has been toward fewer shared decisions and more conferences.
   B. The most important part of a conference leader's job is to direct discussion.
   C. In providing opportunities for group interaction, management should avoid consideration of its past management philosophy.
   D. A good administrator cannot lead a good conference if he is a poor public speaker.

7. Of the following, it is usually LEAST desirable for a conference leader to

   A. call the name of a person after asking a question
   B. summarize proceedings periodically
   C. make a practice of repeating questions
   D. ask a question without indicating who is to reply

8. Assume that, in a certain organization, a situation has developed in which there is little difference in status or authority between individuals.
Which of the following would be the *most likely* result with regard to communication in this organization?

   A. Both the accuracy and flow of communication will be improved.
   B. Both the accuracy and flow of communication will substantially decrease.
   C. Employees will seek more formal lines of communication.
   D. Neither the flow nor the accuracy of communication will be improved over the former hierarchical structure.

9. The main function of many agency administrative officers is "information management." Information that is received by an administrative officer may be classified as active or passive, depending upon whether or not it requires the recipient to take some action.
Of the following, the item received which is *clearly* the MOST active information is

   A. an appointment of a new staff member
   B. a payment voucher for a new desk
   C. a press release concerning a past event
   D. the minutes of a staff meeting

10. Of the following, the one LEAST considered to be a communication barrier is

    A. group feedback   B. charged words
    C. selective perception   D. symbolic meanings

11. Management studies support the hypothesis that, in spite of the tendency of employees to censor the information communicated to their supervisor, subordinates are *more likely* to communicate problem-oriented information UPWARD when they have a

    A. long period of service in the organization
    B. high degree of trust in the supervisor
    C. high educational level
    D. low status on the organizational ladder

12. Electronic data processing equipment can produce more information faster than can be generated by any other means. In view of this, the MOST important problem faced by management at present is to

    A. keep computers fully occupied
    B. find enough computer personnel
    C. assimilate and properly evaluate the information
    D. obtain funds to establish appropriate information systems

    12.____

13. A well-designed management information system *essentially* provides each executive and manager the information he needs for

    A. determining computer time requirements
    B. planning and measuring results
    C. drawing a new organization chart
    D. developing a new office layout

    13.____

14. It is generally agreed that management policies should be periodically reappraised and restated in accordance with current conditions.
    Of the following, the approach which would be MOST effective in determining whether a policy should be revised is to

    A. conduct interviews with staff members at all levels in order to ascertain the relationship between the policy and actual practice
    B. make proposed revisions in the policy and apply it to current problems
    C. make up hypothetical situations using both the old policy and a revised version in order to make comparisons
    D. call a meeting of top level staff in order to discuss ways of revising the policy

    14.____

15. Your superior has asked you to notify division employees of an important change in one of the operating procedures described in the division manual. Every employee presently has a copy of this manual.
    Which of the following is normally the MOST practical way to get the employees to understand such a change?

    A. Notify each employee individually of the change and answer any questions he might have
    B. Send a written notice to key personnel, directing them to inform the people under them
    C. Call a general meeting, distribute a corrected page for the manual, and discuss the change
    D. Send a memo to employees describing the change in general terms and asking them to make the necessary corrections in their copies of the manual

    15.____

16. Assume that the work in your department involves the use of many technical terms.
    In such a situation, when you are answering inquiries from the general public, it would *usually* be BEST to

    A. use simple language and avoid the technical terms
    B. employ the technical terms whenever possible
    C. bandy technical terms freely, but explain each term in parentheses
    D. apologize if you are forced to use a technical term

    16.____

17. Suppose that you receive a telephone call from someone identifying himself as an employee in another city department who asks to be given information which your own department regards as confidential.
Which of the following is the BEST way of handling such a request?

    A. Give the information requested, since your caller has official standing
    B. Grant the request, provided the caller gives you a signed receipt
    C. Refuse the request, because you have no way of knowing whether the caller is really who he claims to be
    D. Explain that the information is confidential and inform the caller of the channels he must go through to have the information released to him

18. Studies show that office employees place high importance on the social and human aspects of the organization. What office employees like best about their jobs is the kind of people with whom they work. So strive hard to group people who are most likely to get along well together.
Based on this information, it is *most reasonable* to assume that office workers are MOST pleased to work in a group which

    A. is congenial
    B. has high productivity
    C. allows individual creativity
    D. is unlike other groups

19. A certain supervisor does not compliment members of his staff when they come up with good ideas. He feels that coming up with good ideas is part of the job and does not merit special attention.
This supervisor's practice is

    A. *poor,* because recognition for good ideas is a good motivator
    B. *poor,* because the staff will suspect that the supervisor has no good ideas of his own
    C. *good,* because it is reasonable to assume that employees will tell their supervisor of ways to improve office practice
    D. *good,* because the other members of the staff are not made to seem inferior by comparison

20. Some employees of a department have sent an anonymous letter containing many complaints to the department head. Of the following, what is this *most likely* to show about the department?

    A. It is probably a good place to work.
    B. Communications are probably poor.
    C. The complaints are probably unjustified.
    D. These employees are probably untrustworthy.

21. Which of the following actions would usually be MOST appropriate for a supervisor to take *after* receiving an instruction sheet from his superior explaining a new procedure which is to be followed?

    A. Put the instruction sheet aside temporarily until he determines what is wrong with the old procedure
    B. Call his superior and ask whether the procedure is one he must implement immediately

C. Write a memorandum to the superior asking for more details
D. Try the new procedure and advise the superior of any problems or possible improvements

22. Of the following, which one is considered the PRIMARY advantage of using a committee to resolve a problem in an organization?

    A. No one person will be held accountable for the decision since a group of people was involved
    B. People with different backgrounds give attention to the problem
    C. The decision will take considerable time so there is unlikely to be a decision that will later be regretted
    D. One person cannot dominate the decision-making process

23. Employees in a certain office come to their supervisor with all their complaints about the office and the work. Almost every employee has had at least one minor complaint at some time.
The situation with respect to complaints in this office may BEST be described as *probably*

    A. *good;* employees who complain care about their jobs and work hard
    B. *good;* grievances brought out into the open can be corrected
    C. *bad;* only serious complaints should be discussed
    D. *bad;* it indicates the staff does not have confidence in the administration

24. The administrator who allows his staff to suggest ways to do their work will *usually* find that

    A. this practice contributes to high productivity
    B. the administrator's ideas produce greater output
    C. clerical employees suggest inefficient work methods
    D. subordinate employees resent performing a management function

25. The MAIN purpose for a supervisor's questioning the employees at a conference he is holding is to

    A. stress those areas of information covered but not understood by the participants
    B. encourage participants to think through the problem under discussion
    C. catch those subordinates who are not paying attention
    D. permit the more knowledgeable participants to display their grasp of the problems being discussed

KEYS (CORRECT ANSWERS)

1.	D	11.	B
2.	A	12.	C
3.	C	13.	B
4.	D	14.	A
5.	B	15.	C
6.	B	16.	A
7.	C	17.	D
8.	D	18.	A
9.	A	19.	A
10.	A	20.	B

21. D
22. B
23. B
24. A
25. B

TEST 2

DIRECTIONS: Each question or incomplete statement is followed by several suggested answers or completions. Select the one that BEST answers the question or completes the statement. *PRINT THE LETTER OF THE CORRECT ANSWER IN THE SPACE AT THE RIGHT.*

1. For a superior to use *consultative supervision* with his subordinates effectively, it is ESSENTIAL that he   1.____

    A. accept the fact that his formal authority will be weakened by the procedure
    B. admit that he does not know more than all his men together and that his ideas are not always best
    C. utilize a committee system so that the procedure is orderly
    D. make sure that all subordinates are consulted so that no one feels left out

2. The "grapevine" is an informal means of communication in an organization. The attitude of a supervisor with respect to the grapevine should be to   2.____

    A. ignore it since it deals mainly with rumors and sensational information
    B. regard it as a serious danger which should be eliminated
    C. accept it as a real line of communication which should be listened to
    D. utilize it for most purposes instead of the official line of communication

3. The supervisor of an office that must deal with the public should realize that planning in this type of work situation   3.____

    A. is *useless* because he does not know how many people will request service or what service they will request
    B. *must be done at a higher level* but that he should be ready to implement the results of such planning
    C. is *useful* primarily for those activities that are not concerned with public contact
    D. is *useful* for all the activities of the office, including those that relate to public contact

4. Assume that it is your job to receive incoming telephone calls. Those calls which you cannot handle yourself have to be transferred to the appropriate office.   4.____
If you receive an outside call for an extension line which is busy, the one of the following which you should do FIRST is to

    A. interrupt the person speaking on the extension and tell him a call is waiting
    B. tell the caller the line is busy and let him know every thirty seconds whether or not it is free
    C. leave the caller on "hold" until the extension is free
    D. tell the caller the line is busy and ask him if he wishes to wait

5. Your superior has subscribed to several publications directly related to your division's work, and he has asked you to see to it that the publications are circulated among the supervisory personnel in the division. There are eight supervisors involved. The BEST method of insuring that all eight see these publications is to   5.____

    A. place the publication in the division's general reference library as soon as it arrives
    B. inform each supervisor whenever a publication arrives and remind all of them that they are responsible for reading it

C. prepare a standard slip that can be stapled to each publication, listing the eight supervisors and saying, "Please read, initial your name, and pass along"
D. send a memo to the eight supervisors saying that they may wish to purchase individual subscriptions in their own names if they are interested in seeing each issue

6. Your superior has telephoned a number of key officials in your agency to ask whether they can meet at a certain time next month. He has found that they can all make it, and he has asked you to confirm the meeting.
Which of the following is the BEST way to confirm such a meeting?

   A. Note the meeting on your superior's calendar
   B. Post a notice of the meeting on the agency bulletin board
   C. Call the officials on the day of the meeting to remind them of the meeting
   D. Write a memo to each official involved, repeating the time and place of the meeting

7. Assume that a new city regulation requires that certain kinds of private organizations file information forms with your department. You have been asked to write the short explanatory message that will be printed on the front cover of the pamphlet containing the forms and instructions.
Which of the following would be the MOST appropriate way of beginning this message?

   A. Get the readers' attention by emphasizing immediately that there are legal penalties for organizations that fail to file before a certain date
   B. Briefly state the nature of the enclosed forms and the types of organizations that must file
   C. Say that your department is very sorry to have to put organizations to such an inconvenience
   D. Quote the entire regulation adopted by the city, even if it is quite long and is expressed in complicated legal language

8. Suppose that you have been told to make up the vacation schedule for the 18 employees in a particular unit. In order for the unit to operate effectively, only a few employees can be on vacation at the same time.
Which of the following is the MOST advisable approach in making up the schedule?

   A. Draw up a schedule assigning vacations in alphabetical order
   B. Find out when the supervisors want to take their vacations, and randomly assign whatever periods are left to the non-supervisory personnel
   C. Assign the most desirable times to employees of longest standing and the least desirable times to the newest employees
   D. Have all employees state their own preference, and then work out any conflicts in consultation with the people involved

9. Assume that you have been asked to prepare job descriptions for various positions in your department.
Which of the following are the basic points that should be covered in a *job description*?

   A. General duties and responsibilities of the position, with examples of day-to-day tasks
   B. Comments on the performances of present employees

C. Estimates of the number of openings that may be available in each category during the coming year
D. Instructions for carrying out the specific tasks assigned to your department

10. Of the following, the biggest DISADVANTAGE in allowing a free flow of communications in an agency is that such a free flow

    A. *decreases* creativity
    B. *increases* the use of the "grapevine"
    C. *lengthens* the chain of command
    D. *reduces* the executive's power to direct the flow of information

10.____

11. A downward flow of authority in an organization is one example of _____ communication.

    A. horizontal   B. informal   C. circular   D. vertical

11.____

12. Of the following, the one that would *most likely* block effective communication is

    A. concentration only on the issues at hand
    B. lack of interest or commitment
    C. use of written reports
    D. use of charts and graphs

12.____

13. An ADVANTAGE of the *lecture* as a teaching tool is that it

    A. enables a person to present his ideas to a large number of people
    B. allows the audience to retain a maximum of the information given
    C. holds the attention of the audience for the longest time
    D. enables the audience member to easily recall the main points

13.____

14. An ADVANTAGE of the *small-group* discussion as a teaching tool is that

    A. it always focuses attention on one person as the leader
    B. it places collective responsibility on the group as a whole
    C. its members gain experience by summarizing the ideas of others
    D. each member of the group acts as a member of a team

14.____

15. The one of the following that is an ADVANTAGE of a *large-group* discussion, when compared to a small-group discussion, is that the large-group discussion

    A. moves along more quickly than a small-group discussion
    B. allows its participants to feel more at ease, and speak out more freely
    C. gives the whole group a chance to exchange ideas on a certain subject at the same occasion
    D. allows its members to feel a greater sense of personal responsibility

15.____

KEYS (CORRECT ANSWERS)

1. D
2. C
3. D
4. D
5. C

6. D
7. B
8. D
9. A
10. D

11. D
12. B
13. A
14. D
15. C

READING COMPREHENSION
UNDERSTANDING AND INTERPRETING WRITTEN MATERIAL
EXAMINATION SECTION
TEST 1

Questions 1-8.

DIRECTIONS: Each question or incomplete statement is followed by several suggested answers or completions. Select the one that BEST answers the question or completes the statement. *PRINT THE LETTER OF THE CORRECT ANSWER IN THE SPACE AT THE RIGHT.*

Questions 1 and 2.

DIRECTIONS: Your answers to Questions 1 and 2 must be based ONLY on the information given in the following paragraph.

Hospitals maintained wholly by public taxation may treat only those compensation cases which are emergencies and may not treat such emergency cases longer than the emergency exists; provided, however, that these restrictions shall not be applicable where there is not available a hospital other than a hospital maintained wholly by taxation.

1. According to the above paragraph, compensation cases

    A. are regarded as emergency cases by hospitals maintained wholly by public taxation
    B. are seldom treated by hospitals maintained wholly by public taxation
    C. are treated mainly by privately endowed hospitals
    D. may be treated by hospitals maintained wholly by public taxation if they are emergencies

1.____

2. According to the above paragraph, it is MOST reasonable to conclude that where a privately endowed hospital is available,

    A. a hospital supported wholly by public taxation may treat emergency compensation cases only so long as the emergency exists
    B. a hospital supported wholly by public taxation may treat any compensation cases
    C. a hospital supported wholly by public taxation must refer emergency compensation cases to such a hospital
    D. the restrictions regarding the treatment of compensation cases by a tax-supported hospital are not wholly applicable

2.____

Questions 3-7.

DIRECTIONS: Answer Questions 3 through 7 ONLY according to the information given in the following passage.

THE MANUFACTURE OF LAUNDRY SOAP

The manufacture of soap is not a complicated process. Soap is a fat or an oil, plus an alkali, water and salt. The alkali used in making commercial laundry soap is caustic soda. The salt used is the same as common table salt. A fat is generally an animal product that is not a liquid at room temperature. If heated, it becomes a liquid. An oil is generally liquid at room temperature. If the temperature is lowered, the oil becomes a solid just like ordinary fat.

At the soap plant, a huge tank five stories high, called a *kettle,* is first filled part way with fats and then the alkali and water are added. These ingredients are then heated and boiled together. Salt is then poured into the top of the boiling solution; and as the salt slowly sinks down through the mixture, it takes with it the glycerine which comes from the melted fats. The product which finally comes from the kettle is a clear soap which has a moisture content of about 34%. This clear soap is then chilled so that more moisture is driven out. As a result, the manufacturer finally ends up with a commercial laundry soap consisting of 88% clear soap and only 12% moisture.

3. An ingredient used in making laundry soap is

   A. table sugar
   B. potash
   C. glycerine
   D. caustic soda

4. According to the above passage, a difference between fats and oils is that fats

   A. cost more than oils
   B. are solid at room temperature
   C. have less water than oils
   D. are a liquid animal product

5. According to the above passage, the MAIN reason for using salt in the manufacture of soap is to

   A. make the ingredients boil together
   B. keep the fats in the kettle melted
   C. remove the glycerine
   D. prevent the loss of water from the soap

6. According to the passage, the purpose of chilling the clear soap is to

   A. stop the glycerine from melting
   B. separate the alkali from the fats
   C. make the oil become solid
   D. get rid of more moisture

7. According to the passage, the percentage of moisture in commercial laundry soap is

   A. 12%   B. 34%   C. 66%   D. 88%

8. The x-ray has gone into business. Developed primarily to aid in diagnosing human ills, the machine now works in packing plants, in foundries, in service stations, and in a dozen ways to contribute to precision and accuracy in industry.
The above statement means *most nearly* that the x-ray

   A. was first developed to aid business
   B. is of more help to business than it is to medicine
   C. is being used to improve the functioning of business
   D. is more accurate for packing plants than it is for foundries

8.____

Questions 9-25.

DIRECTIONS: Each question consists of a statement. You are to indicate whether the statement is TRUE (T) or FALSE (F). *PRINT THE LETTER OF THE CORRECT ANSWER IN THE SPACE AT THE RIGHT.*

Questions 9-12.

DIRECTIONS: Read the paragraph below about *shock* and then answer Questions 9 through 12 according to the information given in the paragraph.

SHOCK

While not found in all injuries, shock is present in all serious injuries caused by accidents. During shock, the normal activities of the body slow down. This partly explains why one of the signs of shock is a pale, cold skin, since insufficient blood goes to the body parts during shock.

9. If the injury caused by an accident is serious, shock is sure to be present. 9.____

10. In shock, the heart beats faster than normal. 10.____

11. The face of a person suffering from shock is usually red and flushed. 11.____

12. Not enough blood goes to different parts of the body during shock. 12.____

Questions 13-18.

DIRECTIONS: Questions 13 through 18, inclusive, are to be answered SOLELY on the basis of the information contained in the following statement and NOT upon any other information you may have.

Blood transfusions are given to patients at the hospital upon recommendation of the physicians attending such cases. The physician fills out a *Request for Blood Transfusion* form in duplicate and sends both copies to the Medical Director's office, where a list is maintained of persons called *donors* who desire to sell their blood for transfusions. A suitable donor is selected, and the transfusion is given. Donors are, in many instances, medical students and employees of the hospital. Donors receive twenty-five dollars for each transfusion.

13. According to the above paragraph, a blood donor is paid twenty-five dollars for each transfusion. 13.____

14. According to the above paragraph, only medical students and employees of the hospital are selected as blood donors.

15. According to the above paragraph, the *Request for Blood Transfusion* form is filled out by the patient and sent to the Medical Director's office.

16. According to the above paragraph, a list of blood donors is maintained in the Medical Director's office.

17. According to the above paragraph, cases for which the attending physicians recommend blood transfusions are usually emergency cases.

18. According to the above paragraph, one copy of the *Request for Blood Transfusion* form is kept by the patient and one copy is sent to the Medical Director's office.

Questions 19-25.

DIRECTIONS: Questions 19 through 25, inclusive, are to be answered SOLELY on the basis of the information contained in the following passage and NOT upon any other information you may have.

Before being admitted to a hospital ward, a patient is first interviewed by the Admitting Clerk, who records the patient's name, age, sex, race, birthplace, and mother's maiden name. This clerk takes all of the money and valuables that the patient has on his person. A list of the valuables is written on the back of the envelope in which the valuables are afterwards placed. Cash is counted and placed in a separate envelope, and the amount of money and the name of the patient are written on the outside of the envelope. Both envelopes are sealed, fastened together, and placed in a compartment of a safe.

An orderly then escorts the patient to a dressing room where the patient's clothes are removed and placed in a bundle. A tag bearing the patient's name is fastened to the bundle. A list of the contents of the bundle is written on property slips, which are made out in triplicate. The information contained on the outside of the envelopes containing the cash and valuables belonging to the patient is also copied on the property slips.

According to the above passage,

19. patients are escorted to the dressing room by the Admitting Clerk.

20. the patient's cash and valuables are placed together in one envelope.

21. the number of identical property slips that are made out when a patient is being admitted to a hospital ward is three.

22. the full names of both parents of a patient are recorded by the Admitting Clerk before a patient is admitted to a hospital ward.

23. the amount of money that a patient has on his person when admitted to the hospital is entered on the patient's property slips.

24. an orderly takes all the money and valuables that a patient has on his person.

25. the patient's name is placed on the tag that is attached to the bundle containing the patient's clothing.

KEY (CORRECT ANSWERS)

1. D
2. A
3. D
4. B
5. C

6. D
7. A
8. C
9. T
10. F

11. F
12. T
13. T
14. F
15. F

16. T
17. T
18. F
19. F
20. F

21. T
22. F
23. T
24. F
25. T

TEST 2

DIRECTIONS: Each question or incomplete statement is followed by several suggested answers or completions. Select the one that BEST answers the question or completes the statement. *PRINT THE LETTER OF THE CORRECT ANSWER IN THE SPACE AT THE RIGHT.*

Questions 1-4.

DIRECTIONS: Questions 1 through 4 are to be answered in accordance with the following paragraphs.

One fundamental difference between the United States health care system and the health care systems of some European countries is the way that hospital charges for long-term illnesses affect their citizens.

In European countries such as England, Sweden, and Germany, citizens can face, without fear, hospital charges due to prolonged illness, no matter how substantial they may be. Citizens of these nations are required to pay nothing when they are hospitalized, for they have prepaid their treatment as taxpayers when they were well and were earning incomes.

On the other hand, the United States citizen, in spite of the growth of payments by third parties which include private insurance carriers as well as public resources, has still to shoulder 40 percent of hospital care costs, while his private insurance contributes only 25 percent and public resources the remaining 35 percent.

Despite expansion of private health insurance and social legislation in the United States, out-of-pocket payments for hospital care by individuals have steadily increased. Such payments, currently totalling $23 billion, are nearly twice as high as ten years ago.

Reform is inevitable and, when it comes, will have to reconcile sharply conflicting interests. Hospital staffs are demanding higher and higher wages. Hospitals are under pressure by citizens, who as patients demand more and better services but who as taxpayers or as subscribers to hospital insurance plans, are reluctant to pay the higher cost of improved care. An acceptable reconciliation of these interests has so far eluded legislators and health administrators in the United States.

1. According to the above passage, the one of the following which is an ADVANTAGE that citizens of England, Sweden, and Germany have over United States citizens is that, when faced with long-term illness,

    A. the amount of out-of-pocket payments made by these European citizens is small when compared to out-of-pocket payments made by United States citizens
    B. European citizens have no fear of hospital costs no matter how great they may be
    C. more efficient and reliable hospitals are available to the European citizen than is available to the United States citizens
    D. a greater range of specialized hospital care is available to the European citizens than is available to the United States citizens

2. According to the above passage, reform of the United States system of health care must reconcile all of the following EXCEPT

    A. attempts by health administrators to provide improved hospital care
    B. taxpayers' reluctance to pay for the cost of more and better hospital services
    C. demands by hospital personnel for higher wages
    D. insurance subscribers' reluctance to pay the higher costs of improved hospital care

2.____

3. According to the above passage, the out-of-pocket payments for hospital care that individuals made ten years ago was APPROXIMATELY _____ billion.

    A. $32   B. $23   C. $12   D. $3

3.____

4. According to the above passage, the GREATEST share of the costs of hospital care in the United States is paid by

    A. United States citizens   B. private insurance carriers
    C. public resources   D. third parties

4.____

Questions 5-8.

DIRECTIONS: Questions 5 through 8 are to be answered SOLELY on the basis of the information contained in the following passage.

    Effective cost controls have been difficult to establish in most hospitals in the United States. Ways must be found to operate hospitals with reasonable efficiency without sacrificing quality and in a manner that will reduce the amount of personal income now being spent on health care and the enormous drain on national resources. We must adopt a new public objective of providing higher quality health care at significantly lower cost. One step that can be taken to achieve this goal is to carefully control capital expenditures for hospital construction and expansion. Perhaps the way to start is to declare a moratorium on all hospital construction and to determine the factors that should be considered in deciding whether a hospital should be built. Such factors might include population growth, distance to the nearest hospital, availability of medical personnel, and hospital bed shortage.

    A second step to achieve the new objective is to increase the ratio of out-of-hospital patient to in-hospital patient care. This can be done by using separate health care facilities other than hospitals to attract patients who have increasingly been going to hospital clinics and overcrowding them. Patients should instead identify with a separate health care facility to keep them out of hospitals.

    A third step is to require better hospital operating rules and controls. This step might include the review of a doctor's performance by other doctors, outside professional evaluations of medical practice, and required refresher courses and re-examinations for doctors. Other measures might include obtaining mandatory second opinions on the need for surgery in order to avoid unnecessary surgery, and outside review of work rules and procedures to eliminate unnecessary testing of patients.

    A fourth step is to halt the construction and public subsidizing of new medical schools and to fill whatever needs exist in professional coverage by emphasizing the medical training of physicians with specialities that are in short supply and by providing a better geographic distribution of physicians and surgeons.

5. According to the above passage, providing higher quality health care at lower cost can be achieved by the

   A. greater use of out-of-hospital facilities
   B. application of more effective cost controls on doctors' fees
   C. expansion of improved in-hospital patient care services at hospital clinics
   D. development of more effective training programs in hospital administration

6. According to the above passage, the one of the following which should be taken into account in determining if a hospital should be constructed is the

   A. number of out-of-hospital health care facilities
   B. availability of public funds to subsidize construction
   C. number of hospitals under construction
   D. availability of medical personnel

7. According to the above passage, it is IMPORTANT to operate hospitals efficiently because

   A. they are currently in serious financial difficulties
   B. of the need to reduce the amount of personal income going to health care
   C. the quality of health care services has deteriorated
   D. of the need to increase productivity goals to take care of the growing population in the United States

8. According to the above passage, which one of the following approaches is MOST LIKELY to result in better operating rules and controls in hospitals?

   A. Allocating doctors to health care facilities on the basis of patient population
   B. Equalizing the workloads of doctors
   C. Establishing a physician review board to evaluate the performance of other physicians
   D. Eliminating unnecessary outside review of patient testing

Questions 9-14.

DIRECTIONS: Questions 9 through 14 are to be answered SOLELY on the basis of the information contained in the following passage.

The United States today is the only major industrial nation in the world without a system of national health insurance or a national health service. Instead, we have placed our prime reliance on private enterprise and private health insurance to meet the need. Yet, in a recent year, of the 180 million Americans under 65 years of age, 34 million had no hospital insurance, 38 million had no surgical insurance, 63 million had no out-patient x-ray and laboratory insurance, 94 million had no insurance for prescription drugs, and 103 million had no insurance for physician office visits or home visits. Some 35 million Americans under the age of 65 had no health insurance whatsoever. Some 64 million additional Americans under age 65 had health insurance coverage that was less than that provided to the aged under Medicare.

Despite more than three decades of enormous growth, the private health insurance industry today pays benefits equal to only one-third of the total cost of private health care, leaving the rest to be borne by the patient—essentially the same ratio which held true a decade ago. Moreover, nearly all private health insurance is limited; it provides partial benefits, not comprehensive benefits; acute care, not preventive care; it siphons off the young and healthy, and ignores the poor and medically indigent. The typical private carrier usually pays only the cost of hospital care, forcing physicians and patients alike to resort to wasteful and inefficient use of hospital facilities, thereby giving further impetus to the already soaring costs of hospital care. Valuable hospital beds are used for routine tests and examinations. Unnecessary hospitalization, unnecessary surgery, and unnecessarily extended hospital stays are encouraged. These problems are exacerbated by the fact that administrative costs of commercial carriers are substantially higher than they are for Blue Shield, Blue Cross, or Medicare.

9. According to the above passage, the PROPORTION of total private health care costs paid by private health insurance companies today as compared to ten years ago has

   A. *increased* by approximately one-third
   B. *remained* practically the same
   C. *increased* by approximately two-thirds
   D. *decreased* by approximately one-third

10. According to the above passage, the one of the following which has contributed MOST to wasteful use of hospital facilities is the

    A. increased emphasis on preventive health care
    B. practice of private carriers of providing comprehensive health care benefits
    C. increased hospitalization of the elderly and the poor
    D. practice of a number of private carriers of paying only for hospital care costs

11. Based on the information in the above passage, which one of the following patients would be LEAST likely to receive benefits from a typical private health insurance plan?
    A

    A. young patient who must undergo an emergency appendectomy
    B. middle-aged patient who needs a costly series of x-ray and laboratory tests for diagnosis of gastrointestinal complaints
    C. young patient who must visit his physician weekly for treatment of a chronic skin disease
    D. middle-aged patient who requires extensive cancer surgery

12. Which one of the following is the MOST accurate inference that can be drawn from the above passage?

    A. Private health insurance has failed to fully meet the health care needs of Americans.
    B. Most Americans under age 65 have health insurance coverage better than that provided to the elderly under Medicare.
    C. Countries with a national health service are likely to provide poorer health care for their citizens than do countries that rely primarily on private health insurance.
    D. Hospital facilities in the United States are inadequate to meet the nation's health care needs.

13. Of the total number of Americans under age 65, what percentage belonged in the combined category of persons with NO health insurance or health insurance less than that provided to the aged under Medicare?

    A. 19% B. 36% C. 55% D. 65%

14. According to the above passage, the one of the following types of health insurance which covered the SMALLEST number of Americans under age 65 was

    A. hospital insurance
    B. surgical insurance
    C. insurance for prescription drugs
    D. insurance for physician office or home visits

Questions 15-17.

DIRECTIONS: Questions 15 through 17 are to be answered SOLELY on the basis of the information contained in the following passage.

Statistical studies have demonstrated that disease and mortality rates are higher among the poor than among the more affluent members of our society. Periodic surveys conducted by the United States Public Health Service continue to document a higher prevalence of infectious and chronic diseases within low income families. While the basic life style and living conditions of the poor are to a considerable extent responsible for this less favorable health status, there are indications that the kind of health care received by the poor also plays a significant role. The poor are less likely to be aware of the concepts and practices of scientific medicine and less likely to seek health care when they need it. Moreover, they are discouraged from seeking adequate health care by the depersonalization, disorganization, and inadequate emphasis on preventive care which characterize the health care most often provided for them.

To achieve the objective of better health care for the poor, the following approaches have been suggested: encouraging the poor to seek preventive care as well as care for acute illness and to establish a lasting one-to-one relationship with a single physician who can treat the poor patient as a whole individual; sufficient financial subsidy to put the poor on an equal footing with *paying patients,* thereby giving them the opportunity to choose from among available health services providers; inducements to health services providers to establish public clinics in poverty areas; and legislation to provide for health education, earlier detection of disease, and coordinated health care.

15. According to the above passage, the one of the following which is a function of the United States Public Health Service is

    A. gathering data on the incidence of infectious diseases
    B. operating public health clinics in poverty areas lacking private physicians
    C. recommending legislation for the improvement of health care in the United States
    D. encouraging the poor to participate in programs aimed at the prevention of illness

16. According to the above passage, the one of the following which is MOST characteristic of the health care currently provided for the poor is that it

    A. aims at establishing clinics in poverty areas
    B. enables the poor to select the health care they want through the use of financial subsidies
    C. places insufficient stress on preventive health care
    D. over-emphasizes the establishment of a one-to-one relationship between physician and patient

16.____

17. The above passage IMPLIES that the poor lack the financial resources to

    A. obtain adequate health insurance coverage
    B. select from among existing health services
    C. participate in health education programs
    D. lobby for legislation aimed at improving their health care

17.____

Questions 18-20.

DIRECTIONS: Questions 18 through 20 are to be answered SOLELY on the basis of the information contained in the following passage.

    The concept of *affiliation,* developed more than ten years ago, grew out of a series of studies which found evidence of faulty care, surgery of *questionable* value and other undesirable conditions in the city's municipal hospitals. The affiliation agreements signed shortly thereafter were designed to correct these deficiencies by assuring high quality medical care. In general, the agreements provided the staff and expertise of a voluntary hospital—sometimes connected with a medical school—to operate various services or, in some cases, all of the professional divisions of a specific municipal hospital. The municipal hospitals have paid for these services, which last year cost the city $200 million, the largest single expenditure of the Health and Hospitals Corporation. In addition, the municipal hospitals have provided to the voluntary hospitals such facilities as free space for laboratories and research. While some experts agree that affiliation has resulted in improvements in some hospital care, they contend that many conditions that affiliation was meant to correct still exist. In addition, accountability procedures between the Corporation and voluntary hospitals are said to be so inadequate that audits of affiliation contracts of the past five years revealed that there may be more than $200 million in charges for services by the voluntary hospitals which have not been fully substantiated. Consequently, the Corporation has proposed that future agreements provide accountability in terms of funds, services supplied, and use of facilities by the voluntary hospitals.

18. According to the above passage, *affiliation* may BEST be defined as an agreement whereby

    A. voluntary hospitals pay for the use of municipal hospital facilities
    B. voluntary and municipal hospitals work to eliminate duplication of services
    C. municipal hospitals pay voluntary hospitals for services performed
    D. voluntary and municipal hospitals transfer patients to take advantage of specialized services

18.____

19. According to the above passage, the MAIN purpose for setting up the *affiliation* agreement was to

    A. supplement the revenues of municipal hospitals
    B. improve the quality of medical care in municipal hospitals
    C. reduce operating costs in municipal hospitals
    D. increase the amount of space available to municipal hospitals

20. According to the above passage, inadequate accountability procedures have resulted in

    A. unsubstantiated charges for services by the voluntary hospitals
    B. emphasis on research rather than on patient care in municipal hospitals
    C. unsubstantiated charges for services by the municipal hospitals
    D. economic losses to voluntary hospitals

Questions 21-25.

DIRECTIONS: Questions 21 through 25 are to be answered SOLELY on the basis of the information contained in the following passage.

The payment for medical services covered under the Outpatient Medical Insurance Plan (OMI) may be made, by OMI, directly to a physician or to the OMI patient. If the physician and the patient agree that the physician is to receive payment directly from OMI, the payment will be officially assigned to the physician; this is the assignment method. If payment is not assigned, the patient receives payment directly from OMI based on an itemized bill he submits, regardless of whether or not he has already paid his physician.

When a physician accepts assignment of the payment for medical services, he agrees that total charges will not be more than the allowed charge determined by the OMI carrier administering the program. In such cases, the OMI patient pays any unmet part of the $85 annual deductible, plus 10 percent of the remaining charges to the physician. In unassigned claims, the patient is responsible for the total amount charged by the physician. The patient will then be reimbursed by the program 90 percent of the allowed charges in excess of the annual deductible.

The rates of acceptance of assignments provide a measure of how many OMI patients are spared *administrative participation* in the program. Because physicians are free to accept or reject assignments, the rate in which assignments are made provide a general indication of the medical community's satisfaction with the OMI program, especially with the level of amounts paid by the program for specific services and the promptness of payment.

21. According to the above passage, in order for a physician to receive payment directly from OMI for medical services to an OMI patient, the physician would have to accept the assignment of payment, to have the consent of the patient, AND to

    A. submit to OMI a paid itemized bill
    B. collect from the patient 90% of the total bill
    C. collect from the patient the total amount of the charges for his services, a portion of which he will later reimburse the patient
    D. agree that his charges for services to the patient will not exceed the amount allowed by the program

22. According to the above passage, if a physician accepts assignment of payment, the patient pays

   A. the total amount charged by the physician and is reimbursed by the program for 90 percent of the allowed charges in excess of the applicable deductible
   B. any unmet part of the $85 annual deductible, plus 90 percent of the remaining charges
   C. the total amount charged by the physician and is reimbursed by the program for 10 percent of the allowed charges in excess of the $85 annual deductible
   D. any unmet part of the $85 annual deductible, plus 10 percent of the remaining charges

23. A physician has accepted the assignment of payment for charges to an OMI patient. The physician's charges, all of which are allowed under OMI, amount to $115. This is the first time the patient has been eligible for OMI benefits and the first time the patient has received services from this physician.
   According to the above passage, the patient must pay the physician

   A. $27   B. $76.50   C. $88   D. $103.50

24. In an unassigned claim, a physician's charges, all of which are allowed under OMI, amount to $165. The patient paid the physician the full amount of the bill.
   If this is the FIRST time the patient has been eligible for OMI benefits, he will receive from OMI a reimbursement of

   A. $72   B. $80   C. $85   D. $93

25. According to the above passage, if the rate of acceptance of assignments by physicians is high, it is LEAST appropriate to conclude that the medical community is generally satisfied with the

   A. supplementary medical insurance program
   B. levels of amounts paid to physicians by the program
   C. number of OMI patients being spared administrative participation in the program
   D. promptness of the program in making payment for services

KEY (CORRECT ANSWERS)

1.	B	11.	C	21.	D
2.	A	12.	A	22.	D
3.	C	13.	C	23.	C
4.	D	14.	D	24.	A
5.	A	15.	A	25.	C
6.	D	16.	C		
7.	B	17.	B		
8.	C	18.	C		
9.	B	19.	B		
10.	D	20.	A		

READING COMPREHENSION
UNDERSTANDING AND INTERPRETING WRITTEN MATERIAL
EXAMINATION SECTION

DIRECTIONS: Each question or incomplete statement is followed by several suggested answers or completions. Select the one that BEST answers the question or completes the statement. *PRINT THE LETTER OF THE CORRECT ANSWER IN THE SPACE AT THE RIGHT.*

Questions 1-5.

DIRECTIONS: Questions 1 through 5 are to be answered SOLELY on the basis of the following paragraph.

   In counting the poor, the Social Security Administration has developed two poverty thresholds that designate families as either *poor* or *near poor*. The Administration assumed that the poor would spend the same proportion of income on food as the rest of the population but that, obviously, since their income was smaller, their range of selection would be narrower. In the Low Cost Food Plan, the amount allocated to food from the average expenditure was cut to the minimum that the Agriculture Department said could still provide American families with an adequate diet. This Low Cost Food Plan was used to characterize the *near poor* category, and an even lower Economy Food Plan was used to characterize the *poor* category. The Economy Food Plan was based on $7.00 a person for food each day, assuming that all food would be prepared at home. The Agriculture Department estimates that only about 10 percent of persons spending $7.00 or less for food each day actually were able to get a nutritionally adequate diet.

1. Of the following, the MOST suitable for the above paragraph would be
    A. THE SUPERIORITY OF THE ECONOMY PLAN OVER THE LOW COST PLAN
    B. THE NEED FOR A NUTRITIONALLY ADEQUATE DIET
    C. FOOD EXPENDITURES OF THE POOR AND THE NEAR POOR
    D. DIET IN THE UNITED STATES

2. According to the above paragraph, the Social Security Administration assumed, in setting its poverty levels, that the poor
    A. spend a smaller proportion of income for food than the average non-poor
    B. would not eat in restaurants
    C. as a group includes only those with a nutritionally inadequate diet
    D. spend more money on food than the near poor

3. According to the above paragraph, it would be CORRECT to state that the Low Cost Food Plan
    A. is above the minimum set by the Agriculture Department for a nutritionally adequate diet
    B. gives most people a nutritionally inadequate diet

1.___

2.___

3.___

C. is lower than the Economy Food Plan
D. represents the amount spent by the *near poor*

4. As estimated by the Department of Agriculture, the percentage of people spending $7.00 or less a day for food who did NOT get a nutritionally adequate diet was
   A. 100%   B. 90%   C. 10%   D. 0%

5. As used in the above paragraph, the underlined words allocated to mean MOST NEARLY
   A. offered for   B. assigned to
   C. wasted on   D. spent on

Questions 6-11.

DIRECTIONS: Questions 6 through 11 are to be answered SOLELY on the basis of the information given in the paragraphs below.

Three years ago, the city introduced a program of reduced transit rates for the elderly. It was hoped that this program would increase the travel of the elderly and help them maintain a greater measure of independence. About 600,000 of the 800,000 eligible residents are currently enrolled in the program. To be eligible, a person must be 65 years of age or older and not employed full-time. Riding for reduced fare is permitted between 10:00 A.M. and 4:00 P.M. and between 7:00 P.M. and Midnight on weekdays, and 24 hours a day on Saturdays, Sundays, and holidays.

In a city university study, based on a sampling of 728 enrollees interviewed, it was learned that 51 percent are able to travel more and 30.8 percent had been able to save enough money to make a noticeable difference in their budgets as a result of the reduced-fare program.

It has been recommended that reduced-fare programs be extended to encourage the use of transit lines in off hours by other groups such as the poor, the very young, housewives, and the physically handicapped. To implement this recommendation, it would be necessary for the Federal government to increase transit subsidies.

6. Which one of the following would be the BEST title for the above passage?
   A. A PROGRAM OF REDUCED TRANSIT RATES FOR THE ELDERLY
   B. RECOMMENDATIONS FOR EXTENDING PROGRAMS FOR THE ELDERLY
   C. CITY UNIVERSITY STUDY ON THE RELATIONSHIP OF AGE AND TRAVEL
   D. ELIGIBILITY REQUIREMENTS FOR THE REDUCED RATE PROGRAM

7. Approximately what percentage of the eligible residents is currently enrolled in the reduced-fare program?
   A. 25%   B. 50%   C. 65%   D. 75%

8. Which one of the following persons is NOT eligible for   8.___
   the reduced-fare program?
   A
     A. woman, age 67, employed part-time as a stenographer
     B. handicapped man, age 62
     C. blind man, age 66, employed part-time as a trans-
        cribing typist
     D. housewife, age 70

9. At which one of the following times would the reduced-   9.___
   fare NOT be permitted for an eligible elderly person?
     A. Sunday, 6:00 P.M.   B. Christmas Day, 2:00 A.M.
     C. Tuesday, 9:00 A.M.   D. Thursday, 8:00 P.M.

10. Of the 728 enrollees interviewed in the city university   10.___
    study of the reduced-fare program, it was found that
      A. the majority traveled more and saved money at the
         same time
      B. more than half traveled less and, therefore, saved
         money
      C. about half traveled more and about one-third saved
         money
      D. the majority saved money but traveled the same rate
         as before

11. According to the above passage, what would be necessary   11.___
    to extend the reduced-fare program to other groups of
    people?
      A. Increasing the eligible age to 68
      B. Reducing the hours when half-fare is permitted
      C. Increasing the fare for other riders
      D. Increasing the transit subsidies by the Federal
         government

Questions 12-14.

DIRECTIONS: Questions 12 through 14 are to be answered SOLELY on
            the basis of the following passage.

   Local public welfare agencies, in general, recognize that more
time is required for Aid to Dependent Children cases and General
Assistance cases than for Old Age Assistance cases, and that the
intensive work required in Child Welfare Service cases necessitates
special planning with regard to limiting caseloads for workers to
prevent their carrying too large a number of cases. A General
Assistance case often includes several persons, while Old Age Assistance cases are on an individual basis. Although the average cost of
a case per month has continued to increase for all assistance programs,
these programs have retained their relative cost positions. The
average monthly cost of a case has been lowest for Aid to the Aged,
followed, in ascending order, by Aid to the Blind, Aid to Dependent
Children, and General Assistance, with the cost per case of the last
mentioned program averaging more than four times that for Aid to the
Aged. On the other hand, the proportion of Aid to the Aged cases is
rising while the percentage of General Assistance cases is declining.

12. Some types of cases require more time or more intensive work than others.
The one of the following statements which MOST accurately illustrates this point, according to the above paragraph, is:
    A. Aid to the Blind cases often include several persons and, therefore, are very time-consuming, while Old Age Assistance cases require intensive casework
    B. Aid to Dependent Children cases often involve complicated situations and, therefore, require intensive casework, while Aid to the Blind cases are extremely time-consuming
    C. Old Age Assistance cases are relatively less time-consuming, while Child Welfare Service cases entail detailed casework
    D. Old Age Assistance cases are time-consuming, while General Assistance cases are comparatively simple

12.___

13. If a public welfare official were to set up several case-loads, with each caseload containing the same total number of cases but with a varying number in each of the different types of assistance, the caseload which would MOST likely require the GREATEST expenditure of time would be the one with a majority of
    A. Aid to the Blind cases and Aid to Dependent Children cases
    B. General Assistance cases and Aid to Dependent Children cases
    C. Old Age Assistance cases and Aid to the Blind cases
    D. Old Age Assistance cases and General Assistance cases

13.___

14. According to the above paragraph, the one of the following statements which is the MOST accurate with regard to the cost of welfare services is that
    A. the average monthly cost for each Aid to Dependent Children case was higher than for each Aid to the Blind case but lower than for each Aid to the Aged case
    B. the cost per case for General Assistance has risen four times as fast as the cost per case for Aid to the Aged
    C. there has been a decrease in the proportion of General Assistance cases, but the cost per case in this category has increased
    D. more than four times as much money was spent in total for all the cases in the General Assistance program than for those in the Aid to the Aged program

14.___

Questions 15-17.

DIRECTIONS: Questions 15 through 17 are to be answered SOLELY on the basis of the following passage.

Aid to dependent children shall be given to a parent or other relative as herein specified for the benefit of a child or children under sixteen years of age or of a minor or minors between sixteen and eighteen years of age if in the judgment of the administrative agency: (1) the granting of an allowance will be in the interest of such child or minor, and (2) the parent or other relative is a fit person to bring up such child or minor so that his physical, mental, and moral well-being will be safeguarded, and (3) aid is necessary to enable such parent or other relative to do so, and (4) such child or minor is a resident of the state on the date of application for aid, and (5) such minor between sixteen and eighteen years of age is regularly attending school in accordance with the regulations of the department. An allowance may be granted for the aid of such child or minor who has been deprived of parental support or care by reason of the death, continued absence from the home, or physical or mental incapacity of a parent, and who is living with his father, mother, grandfather, grandmother, brother, sister, stepfather, stepmother, stepbrother, stepsister, uncle, or aunt. In making such allowances, consideration shall be given to the ability of the relative making application and of any other relatives to support and care for or to contribute to the support and care of such child or minor. In making all such allowances, it shall be made certain that the religious faith of the child or minor shall be preserved and protected.

15. The above passage is concerned PRIMARILY with
    A. the financial ability of persons applying for public assistance
    B. compliance on the part of applicants with the *settlement* provisions of the law
    C. the fitness of parents or other relatives to bring up physically, mentally, or morally delinquent children between the ages of sixteen and eighteen
    D. eligibility for aid to dependent children

16. On the basis of the above passage, the MOST accurate of the following statements is:
    A. Mary Doe, mother of John, age 18, is entitled to aid for her son if he is attending school regularly
    B. Evelyn Stowe, mother of Eleanor, age 13, is not entitled to aid for Eleanor if she uses her home for immoral purposes
    C. Ann Roe, cousin of Helen, age 14, is entitled to aid for Helen if the latter is living with her
    D. Peter Moe, uncle of Henry, age 15, is not entitled to aid for Henry if the latter is living with him

17. The above passage is PROBABLY an excerpt of the
    A. Administrative Code   B. Social Welfare Law
    C. Federal Security Act   D. City Charter

Questions 18-20.

DIRECTIONS: Questions 18 through 20 are to be answered SOLELY on the basis of the information contained in the following passage.

On the state level, in an effort to obtain better administration and delivery of services in the Medicaid program, the Governor has appointed a committee to advise the State Commissioner of Social Welfare on medical care services. Included on this committee are representatives of the medical, dental, pharmaceutical, nursing, and social work professions, as well as persons representing the fields of mental health, home health agencies, nursing homes, schools of health science, public health and welfare administrations, and the general public. Several of the committee members are physicians in private practice who represent and uphold the interests of the private physicians who care for Medicaid patients.

The committee not only makes recommendations on the standards, quality, and costs of medical services, personnel, and facilities, but also helps identify unmet needs, and assists in long-range planning, evaluation, and utilization of services. It advises, as requested, on administrative and fiscal matters, and also interprets the programs and goals to professional groups.

On the city level, representatives of the county medical societies of the city meet periodically with Medicaid administrators to discuss problems and consider proposals. It is hoped that the county medical societies will assume the responsibility of informing citizens as to where they can receive medical care under Medicaid.

18. Based on information in the above passage, it can be inferred that the group on the advisory committee likely to be LEAST objective in their recommendations would be the representatives of the
    A. public health and welfare administrations
    B. general public
    C. private physicians
    D. schools of health science

19. The above passage suggests that a problem with the Medicaid program is that
    A. the Mayor has not appointed a committee to work with the City Commissioner of Social Services
    B. many people do not know where they can go to obtain medical care under the program
    C. the county medical societies do not meet often enough with the Medicaid program administrators
    D. citizens do not take the initiative to seek out sources of available medical care under the program

20. According to the above passage, the Governor's objective in appointing the advisory committee was to 20.___
    A. obtain more cooperation from the county medical societies
    B. get the members of the committee to provide medical care services to Medicaid recipients
    C. help improve the Medicaid program in all its aspects, including administration and provision of services
    D. persuade a greater number of private physicians and other health care professionals to accept Medicaid patients

Questions 21-25.

DIRECTIONS: Questions 21 through 25 are to be answered SOLELY on the basis of the information contained in the following passage.

Any person who is living in the city and is otherwise eligible may be granted public assistance whether or not he has state residence. However, since the city does not contribute to the cost of assistance granted to persons who are without state residence, the cases of all recipients must be formally identified as to whether or not each member of the household has state residence.

To acquire state residence, a person must have resided in the state continuously for one year. Such residence is not lost unless the person is out of the state continuously for a period of one year or longer. Continuous residence does not include any period during which the individual is a patient in a hospital, an inmate of a public institution or of an incorporated private institution, a resident on a military reservation or a minor residing in a boarding home while under the care of an authorized agency. Receipt of public assistance does not prevent a person from acquiring state residence. State residence, once acquired, is not lost because of absence from the state while a person is serving in the United States Armed Forces or the Merchant Marine; nor does a member of the family of such a person lose state residence while living with or near that person in these circumstances.

Each person, regardless of age, acquires or loses state residence as an individual. There is no derivative state residence except for an infant at the time of birth. He is deemed to have state residence if he is in the custody of both parents and either one of them has state residence, or if the parent having custody of his has state residence.

21. According to the above passage, an infant is deemed to have state residence at the time of his birth if 21.___
    A. he is born in the state but neither of his parents is a resident
    B. he is in the custody of only one parent, who is not a resident but his other parent is a resident
    C. his brother and sister are residents
    D. he is in the custody of both his parents but only one of them is a resident

22. The Jones family consists of five members. Jack and Mary   22.___
    Jones have lived in New York State continuously for the
    past eighteen months after having lived in Ohio since they
    were born. Of their three children, one was born ten
    months ago and has been in the custody of his parents
    since birth. Their second child lived in Ohio until six
    months ago and then moved in with his parents. Their
    third child had never lived in New York until he moved
    with his parents to New York eighteen months ago. How-
    ever, he entered the Armed Forces one month later and has
    not lived in New York since that time.
    Based on the above passage, how many members of the Jones
    family are New York State residents?
        A. 2   B. 3   C. 4   D. 5

23. Assuming that each of the following individuals has lived   23.___
    continuously in the state for the past year, and has never
    previously lived in the state, which one of them is a
    state resident?
        A. Jack Salinas, who has been an inmate in a state
           correctional facility for six months of the year
        B. Fran Johnson, who has lived on an Army base for the
           entire year
        C. Arlene Snyder, who married a non-resident during the
           past year
        D. Gary Phillips, who was a patient in a Veterans
           Administration hospital for the entire year

24. The above passage implies that the reason for determining   24.___
    whether or not a recipient of public assistance is a
    state resident is that
        A. the cost of assistance for non-residents is not a
           city responsibility
        B. non-residents living in the city are not eligible for
           public assistance
        C. recipients of public assistance are barred from
           acquiring state residence
        D. the city is responsible for the full cost of assis-
           tance to recipients who are residents

25. Assume that the Rollins household in the city consists   25.___
    of six members at the present time - Anne Rollins, her
    three children, her aunt, and her uncle. Anne Rollins
    and one of her children moved to the city seven months
    ago. Neither of them had previously lived in the state.
    Her other two children have lived in the city continuous-
    ly for the past two years, as has her aunt. Anne Rollins'
    uncle had lived in the city continuously for many years
    until two years ago. He then entered the Armed Forces
    and has returned to the city within the past month.
    Based on the above passage, how many members of the
    Rollins' household are state residents?
        A. 2   B. 3   C. 4   D. 6

KEY (CORRECT ANSWERS)

1. C		11. D
2. B		12. C
3. D		13. B
4. B		14. C
5. B		15. D
6. A		16. B
7. D		17. B
8. B		18. C
9. C		19. B
10. C		20. C

21. D
22. B
23. C
24. A
25. C

TEST 2

DIRECTIONS: Each question or incomplete statement is followed by several suggested answers or completions. Select the one that BEST answers the question or completes the statement. *PRINT THE LETTER OF THE CORRECT ANSWER IN THE SPACE AT THE RIGHT.*

Questions 1-4.

DIRECTIONS: Questions 1 through 4 are to be answered SOLELY on the basis of the following passage.

The loss of control over the use of a drug -- called addiction where there is both physical and psychological dependence, and habituation where there is psychological dependence without physical dependence -- is, regardless of the particular drug involved, a disease. Both chronic alcoholism and narcotics addiction are usually recognized as diseases.

It is inappropriate to invoke the criminal process against persons who have lost control over the use of dangerous drugs solely because these persons are drug users. Once a person has lost control over his use of drugs, the existence of offenses such as drug use or simple possession will not deter his use. Having lost control, he cannot choose to conform his conduct to the requirements of the law by refraining from use. He is non-deterrable.

Admittedly, there may be times before a person loses control over his use of drugs when he did have a choice of whether to use or not to use, or to stop using. Because of this, punishing him for use or simple possession would not offend the principle that to be punishable conduct must be a result of free choice.

1. Of the following, the MOST suitable title for the above passage is
    A. DRUG ADDICTION
    B. DRUG ABUSE AND PUNISHMENT
    C. HABITUATION AND THE CRIMINAL PROCESS
    D. PREVENTING DRUG-RELATED CRIME

1.__

2. According to the above passage, addiction and habituation are
    A. identical in meaning because both are diseases related to drug use
    B. identical in meaning because both involve dependence on drugs
    C. similar to the extent that both involve physical dependence on a drug
    D. similar to the extent that both involve psychological dependence on a drug

2.__

3. According to the above passage, punishing drug abusers would be justifiable ONLY if their behavior were
   A. elective
   B. non-deterrable
   C. chronic
   D. dangerous

4. According to the above passage, punishing a person for simple possession of drugs is
   A. appropriate under certain circumstances
   B. inappropriate because the person could not have acted otherwise
   C. necessary for the protection of society
   D. unfair because it penalizes past conduct

Questions 5-8.

DIRECTIONS: Questions 5 through 8 are to be answered SOLELY on the basis of the following passage.

The usual explanation for drunken behavior is that alcohol, which is a physiological depressant, impairs reasoning and inhibition powers before it depresses the ability to act and to express emotion.

The purely physiological effects of alcohol are very much like those of fatigue. Individual personality and social and cultural influences apparently greatly determine how these effects are reflected in changed behavior as alcohol is consumed. Therefore, one can assert that alcohol alone does not cause drunken behavior; rather, drunken behavior expresses personal character, cultural traditions, and social circumstances, as they influence a person's reactions to the physiological effects of alcohol on his body.

For some people, and in some circumstances, these personal, cultural, and social factors may readily express themselves as criminal behavior. The most obvious case, of course, is public drunkenness.

The exact relationship between various crimes and various stages of intoxication is not completely known. G.M. Scott believes that the moderate stages of intoxication are the ones usually associated with crime since the latter states of intoxication make performance of crime impossible. Dr. Banay found that many drunks are drawn into crime not only by the need of money to replace wages that drinking prevents them from earning, but also by their increased irritability and pugnacity... He discovered that most of the sex offenses for which offenders are committed to state prisons show a relation between alcohol and the crime and that the average sex case is a clear-cut illustration of the hypothesis that alcohol covers up an underlying condition and that some dormant tendency is either brought to the surface or aggravated by alcohol.

In addition to drunken behavior resulting in criminal acts, it is also connected to several other important social problems. Reference can be made particularly to dependency, unemployment, desertion, divorce, vagrancy, and suicide. For all of these social ills, alcohol acts as the physiological depressing agent which influences one's deviation from normative behavior.

5. Discussions of intoxication customarily state that alcohol
   A. initially affects the analytic faculty
   B. initially affects the ability to express feelings
   C. reduces the desire for money
   D. stimulates perception of the true nature of one's condition

6. Which one of the following hypotheses would Dr. Banay MOST likely support?
   A. The casual drinker is LESS likely to commit a crime than the chronic drinker.
   B. An aggressive drunk is LIKELY to have aggressive tendencies when not under the influence of alcohol.
   C. The UNDERLYING cause of most sex offenses is excessive drinking.
   D. There is NO connection between cultural background and drunken behavior.

7. The title BEST suited for the above passage is
   A. HOW ALCOHOL INFLUENCES POTENTIAL SEXUAL OFFENDERS
   B. STAGES OF INTOXICATION
   C. THE ROLE OF ALCOHOLIC CONSUMPTION IN HUMAN BEHAVIOR
   D. THE RELATIONSHIP BETWEEN ALCOHOL AND EMOTION

8. The writer implies that
   A. a desire to destroy oneself is a frequent side effect of drinking intoxicating liquors
   B. a person who is drunk may find it easier to kill himself
   C. there is a pattern of drinking behavior in the background of most suicides
   D. there is no relationship between the problems of drinking and suicide

Questions 9-11.

DIRECTIONS: Questions 9 through 11 are to be answered SOLELY on the basis of the following paragraph.

A <u>substantial</u> source of opposition to legalizing heroin is those people who are convinced that this idea is simply another form of social and economic injustice. Instead of getting at the fundamental causes of addiction, they say, the result will be to turn hundreds of young addicts into the living dead.

9. According to the above paragraph, opposition to legalizing heroin is based, in part, on the belief that
   A. some addicts will become walking dead people
   B. the problem is entirely one of educating individuals
   C. the pushers will simply turn to other criminal activities
   D. the root causes of addiction are still mysterious

10. Which of the following treatment approaches would the author of the above paragraph be MOST likely to oppose?
    A. Ambulatory detoxification
    B. Methadone maintenance
    C. Drug-free therapeutic community
    D. Youth intervention program

11. As used in the above paragraph, the underlined word substantial means MOST NEARLY
    A. known   B. large   C. strange   D. unanimous

Questions 12-16.

DIRECTIONS: Questions 12 through 16 are to be answered SOLELY on the basis of the following paragraph.

In the past dozen years or so, there has emerged an argument which obviously has a certain persuasiveness among young people: that drugs are being used, not as an expression of antisocial behavior or for escape, but to define a different, anti-establishment culture. Drugs can, of course, be used that way; it's very possible to have a youth culture that uses drugs as a norm. But it's also possible to have a youth culture that is opposed to using drugs as a norm. For example, in China, around 1910, a very effective campaign against opium was led largely by students who felt that the use of drugs was the reason China had suffered so much at the hands of the Western powers.

12. According to the above paragraph, the Chinese students opposed the use of opium because
    A. it contradicted Chinese religious values
    B. it interfered with their studies
    C. they believed it weakened their country
    D. the Western powers encouraged addiction

13. The writer of the above paragraph seems to believe that there is no necessary connection between
    A. escapism and culture   B. norms and values
    C. students and politics   D. youth and drugs

14. According to the above paragraph, it is possible to have a youth culture that considers the use of drugs
    A. completely acceptable   B. legally defensible
    C. morally uplifting   D. physically beneficial

15. The underlined word emerged means MOST NEARLY
    A. come into view   B. gone through
    C. required to be   D. responded quickly

16. As used in the above paragraph, the underlined word norm means MOST NEARLY
    A. argument or explanation   B. error or mistake
    C. pleasure or reward   D. rule or average

Questions 17-20.

DIRECTIONS: Questions 17 through 20 are to be answered SOLELY on the basis of the following paragraph.

Alcoholics are to be found in both sexes, in every major religio and racial group, and at all socio-economic levels. What they share in common are psychiatric problems which they seek to ease or dull through alcohol. Ideally, every heavy drinker should be subjected to intensive psychiatric therapy. Unfortunately, even psychiatric treatment is not always successful, and in any case the nation has allocated neither the funds nor the personnel nor the facilities that would be required for such a massive therapeutic effort.

17. According to the above paragraph, national priorities in connection with psychiatric treatment for alcoholism do NOT provide for 17.___
    A. fair and impartial treatment
    B. large-scale programs
    C. proper religious values
    D. strict laws against alcoholism

18. According to the above paragraph, alcoholics are MOST likely to be 18.___
    A. emotionally disturbed   B. ultimately curable
    C. unable to function   D. under medical care

19. As used in the above paragraph, the underlined word intensive means MOST NEARLY 19.___
    A. concentrated   B. modern
    C. prompt   D. specialized

20. As used in the above paragraph, the underlined word allocated means MOST NEARLY 20.___
    A. assigned   B. conserved   C. desired   D. recognized

Questions 21-25.

DIRECTIONS: Questions 21 through 25 are to be answered SOLELY on the basis of the following paragraph.

The practice of occasionally adulterating marijuana complicates analysis of the effects of marijuana use in non-controlled settings. Behavioral changes which are attributed to marijuana may actually derive from the adulterants or from the interaction of tetrahydro-cannabinols and adulterants. Similarly, in today's society, marijuar is often used simultaneously or sequentially with other psychoactive drugs. When drug interactions occur, the simultaneous presence of two or more drugs in the body can exert effects which are more than that which would result from the simple addition of the effects of each drug used separately. Thus, the total behavioral response may be greater than the sum of its parts. For example, if a given dose of marijuana induced two units of perceptual distortion, and a certa dose of LSD given alone induced two units of perceptual distortion, the simultaneous administration of these doses of marijuana and LSD may induce not four but five units of perceptual distortion.

21. According to the above paragraph, the concurrent presence of two drugs in the body can
    A. compound the effects of both drugs
    B. reduce perceptual distortion
    C. simulate psychotic symptoms
    D. be highly toxic

21.___

22. Based on the above paragraph, it is MOST reasonable to assume that tetrahydrocannabinols are
    A. habit-forming substances
    B. components of marijuana
    C. similar to quinine or milk-sugar
    D. used as adulterants

22.___

23. Based on the above paragraph, it is MOST reasonable to state that marijuana is
    A. most affected by adulterants when used as a psycho-active drug
    B. erroneously considered to be less harmful than other drugs
    C. frequently used in connection with other mind-affecting drugs
    D. occasionally used as an adjunct to LSD in order to reduce bad reactions

23.___

24. As used in the above paragraph, the underlined word attributed means MOST NEARLY
    A. originally unsuspected   B. identical in action
    C. known as a reason   D. ascribed by way of cause

24.___

25. As used in the above paragraph, the underlined word induced means MOST NEARLY
    A. caused   B. projected   C. required   D. displayed

25.___

KEY (CORRECT ANSWERS)

1. B	6. B	11. B	16. D	21. A
2. D	7. C	12. C	17. B	22. B
3. A	8. B	13. D	18. A	23. C
4. A	9. A	14. A	19. A	24. D
5. A	10. B	15. A	20. A	25. A

EXAMINATION SECTION
TEST 1

DIRECTIONS: Each question or incomplete statement is followed by several suggested answers or completions. Select the one that BEST answers the question or completes the statement. *PRINT THE LETTER OF THE CORRECT ANSWER IN THE SPACE AT THE RIGHT.*

Questions 1-9

Questions 1 through 9 measure your ability to (1) determine whether statements from witnesses say essentially the same thing and (2) determine the evidence needed to make it reasonably certain that a particular conclusion is true.

1. Which of the following pairs of statements say essentially the same thing in two different ways?
   I. All Hoxie steelworkers are at least six feet tall. No steelworker is less than six feet tall.
   II. Some neutered pit bulls are not dangerous dogs. Some dangerous dogs are neutered pit bulls.

   A. I only
   B. I and II
   C. II only
   D. Neither I nor II

   1._____

2. Which of the following pairs of statements say essentially the same thing in two different ways?
   I. If we are in training today, it is definitely Wednesday. Every Wednesday there is training.
   II. You may go out tonight only after you clean your room. If you clean your room, you may go out tonight.

   A. I only
   B. I and II
   C. II only
   D. Neither I nor II

   2._____

3. Which of the following pairs of statements say essentially the same thing in two different ways?
   I. The case will be dismissed if either the defendant pleads guilty and agrees to perform community service, or the defendant pleads guilty and makes a full apology to the victim.
   The case will be dismissed if the defendant pleads guilty and either agrees to perform community service or makes a full apology to the victim.
   II. Long books are fun to read.
   Books that aren't fun to read aren't long.

   A. I only
   B. I and II
   C. II only
   D. Neither I nor II

   3._____

4. Which of the following pairs of statements say essentially the same thing in two different ways?

   I. If you live in a mansion, you have a big heating bill. If you do not have a big heating bill, you do not live in a mansion.
   II. Some clerks can both type and read shorthand. Some clerks can neither type nor read shorthand.

   A. I only
   B. I and II
   C. II only
   D. Neither I nor II

5. Summary of Evidence Collected to Date:
   I. Three students - Bob, Mary and Stan - each received a grade of A, C and F on the civil service exam.
   II. Stan did not receive an F on the exam.

   Prematurely Drawn Conclusion: Stan received an A.
   Which of the following pieces of evidence, if any, would make it *reasonably certain* that the conclusion drawn is true?

   A. Bob received an F
   B. Mary received a C
   C. Bob did not receive an A
   D. None of these

6. Summary of Evidence Collected to Date:
   I. At Walco, all the employees who work the morning shift work the evening shift as well.
   II. Some Walco employees who work the evening shift also work the afternoon shift.

   Prematurely Drawn Conclusion: If Ron, a Walco employee, works the morning shift, he does not work the afternoon shift.
   Which of the following pieces of evidence, if any, would make it *reasonably certain* that the conclusion drawn is true?

   A. Ron works only two shifts
   B. Ron works the evening shift
   C. All Walco employees work at least one shift
   D. None of these

7. Summary of Evidence Collected to Date:

   All the family counselors at the agency have an MTF certification and an advanced degree.

   Prematurely Drawn Conclusion: Any employee of the agency who has an advanced degree is a family counselor.

   Which of the following pieces of evidence, if any, would make it *reasonably certain* that the conclusion drawn is true?

A. Nobody at the agency who has an advanced degree is employed as anything other than a family counselor
B. Everyone who has an MTF certification is a family counselor
C. Each person at the agency who has an MTF certification also has an advanced degree
D. None of these

8. <u>Summary of Evidence Collected to Date:</u>   8._____
Margery, a worker at the elder agency, is working on recreational programs.
<u>Prematurely Drawn Conclusion:</u> Margery is not working on cases of elder abuse.
Which of the following pieces of evidence, if any, would make it *reasonably certain* that the conclusion drawn is true?

A. Elder abuse and recreational programs are unrelated fields
B. Nobody at the elder agency who works on cases of elder abuse works on recreation programs
C. Nobody at the elder agency who works on recreational programs works on cases of elder abuse
D. None of these

9. <u>Summary of Evidence Collected to Date:</u>   9._____
   I. St. Leo's Cathedral is not as tall as the FarCorp building.
   II. The FarCorp building and the Hyatt Uptown are the same height.
<u>Prematurely Drawn Conclusion:</u> The FarCorp building is not in Springfield.
Which of the following pieces of evidence, if any, would make it *reasonably certain* that the conclusion drawn is true?

A. No buildings in Springfield are as tall as the Hyatt Uptown
B. The Hyatt Uptown is not in Springfield
C. St. Leo's Cathedral is the oldest building in Springfield
D. None of these

Questions 10-14

Questions 10 through 14 refer to Map #1 and measure your ability to orient yourself within a given section of town, neighborhood or particular area. Each of the questions describes a starting point and a destination. Assume that you are driving a car in the area shown on the map accompanying the questions. Use the map as a basis for the shortest way to get from one point to another without breaking the law.

On the map, a street marked by arrows, or by arrows and the words "One Way," indicates one-way travel, and should be assumed to be one-way for the entire length, even when there are breaks or jogs in the street.

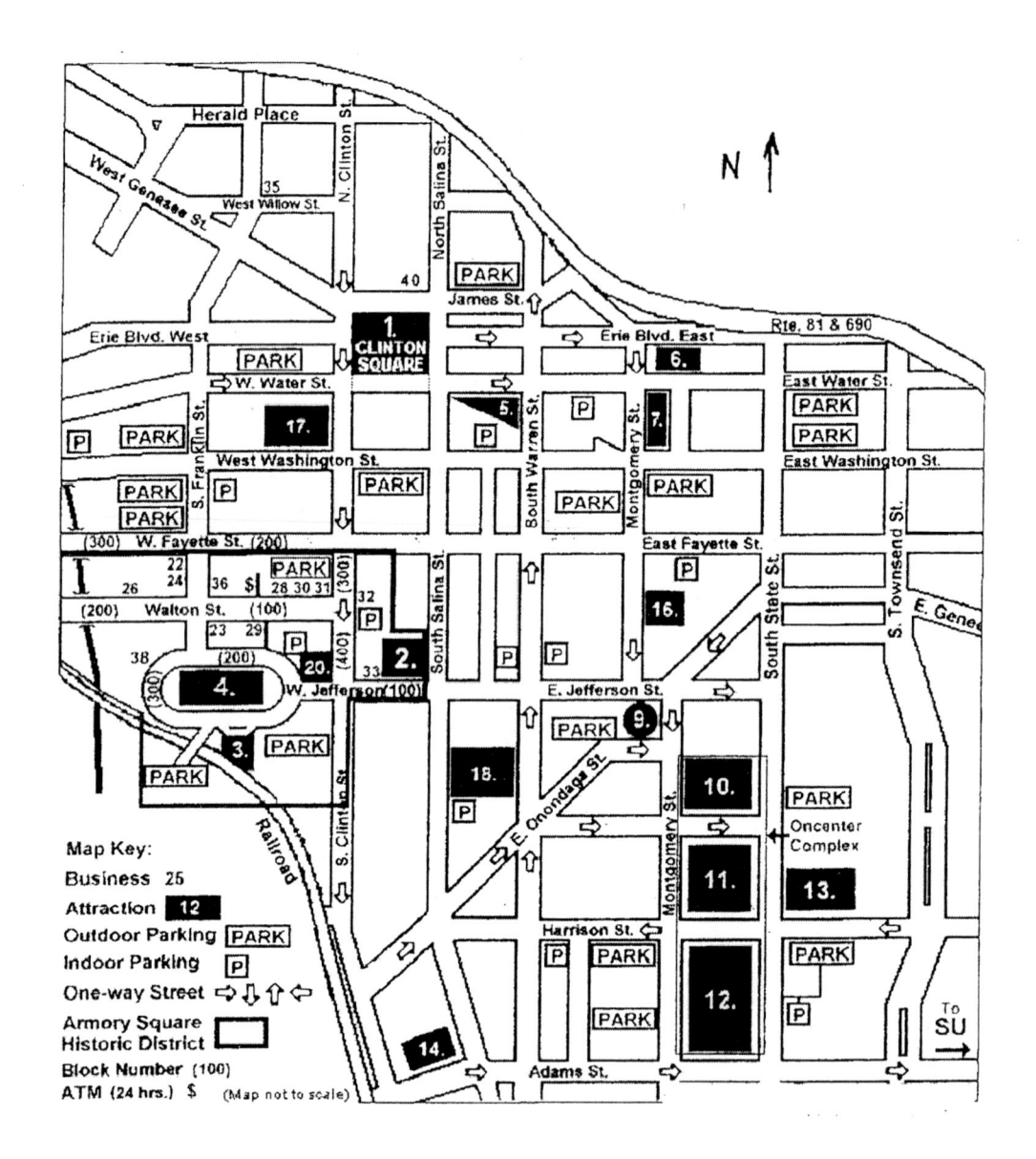

Map#1

1. Clinton Square
2. Landmark Theatre
3. OnTrack Commuter Rail Service
4. Museum of Science and Technology
5. Hanover Square
6. Erie Canal Museum
7. City Hall
9. Columbus Circle
10. Mulroy Civic Center Theaters
11. War Memorial
12. Convention Center
13. Everson Museum of Art
14. Convention and Visitors Bureau
16. Onondaga Historical Association
17. Federal Plaza
18. Galleries of Syracuse

10. The shortest legal way from Columbus Circle to Federal Plaza is

    A. west on Jefferson St., north on Salina St., west on Water St.
    B. east on Jefferson St., north on State St., west on Water St.
    C. north on Montgomery St., west on Washington St.
    D. south on Montgomery St., west on Harrison St., north on Salina St., west on Washington St.

11. The shortest legal way from Clinton Square to the Museum of Science and Technology is

    A. south on Clinton St., west on Fayette St., south on Franklin St.
    B. west on Erie Blvd., south on Franklin St.
    C. south on Clinton St., west on Water St., south on Franklin St.
    D. south on Clinton St., west on Jefferson St.

12. The shortest legal way from Hanover Square to Landmark Theatre is

    A. west on Water St., south on Salina St.
    B. east on Water St., south on Montgomery St., west on Fayette St., south on Salina St.
    C. east on Water St., south on Montgomery St., west on Fayette St., south on Clinton St., east on Jefferson St.
    D. south on Warren St., west on Jefferson St.

13. The shortest legal way from the Convention Center to the Erie Canal Museum is

    A. north on State St., west on Washington St., north on Montgomery St.
    B. north on Montgomery St., jog west on Jefferson St., north on Montgomery St.
    C. north on State St., west on Fayette St., north on Warren St., east on Water St.
    D. north on State St., west on Water St.

14. The shortest legal way from City Hall to Clinton Square is

    A. west on Washington St., north on Salina St.
    B. south on Montgomery St., west on Fayette St., north on Salina St.
    C. north on Montgomery St., west on Erie Blvd.
    D. west on Water St.

Questions 15-19

Questions 15 through 19 refer to Figure #1, on the following page, and measure your ability to understand written descriptions of events. Each question presents a description of an accident or event and asks you which of the five drawings in Figure #1 BEST represents it.

In the drawings, the following symbols are used:

Moving vehicle: ⌂   Non-moving vehicle: ⬢

Pedestrian or bicycle: ●

The path and direction of travel of a vehicle or pedestrian is indicated by a solid line.

The path and direction of travel of each vehicle or pedestrian directly involved in a collision from the point of impact is indicated by a dotted line.

In the space at the right, print the letter of the drawing that best fits the descriptions written below:

15. A driver heading north on Elm sideswipes a parked car, veers into the oncoming lane and travels through the intersection of Elm and Main. He then sideswipes an oncoming car, veers back into the northbound lane and flees.   15.__

16. A driver heading south on Elm sideswipes a car parked in the southbound lane, then loses control and veers through the intersection of Elm and Main. The driver then collides with the rear of another parked car, which is knocked forward after the impact.   16.__

17. A driver heading north on Elm strikes the rear of a parked car, which is knocked through the intersection of Elm and Main and strikes a parked car in the southbound lane head-on.   17.__

18. A driver heading north on Elm strikes the rear of a car that is stopped at a traffic light. The car at the light is knocked through the intersection of Elm and Main and strikes a parked car in the rear.   18.__

19. A driver heading south on Elm loses control and crosses into the other lane of traffic, where he sideswipes a car parked in the northbound lane, then veers back into the southbound lane, travels through the intersection of Elm and Main and collides with the rear end of a parked car.   19.__

FIGURE #1

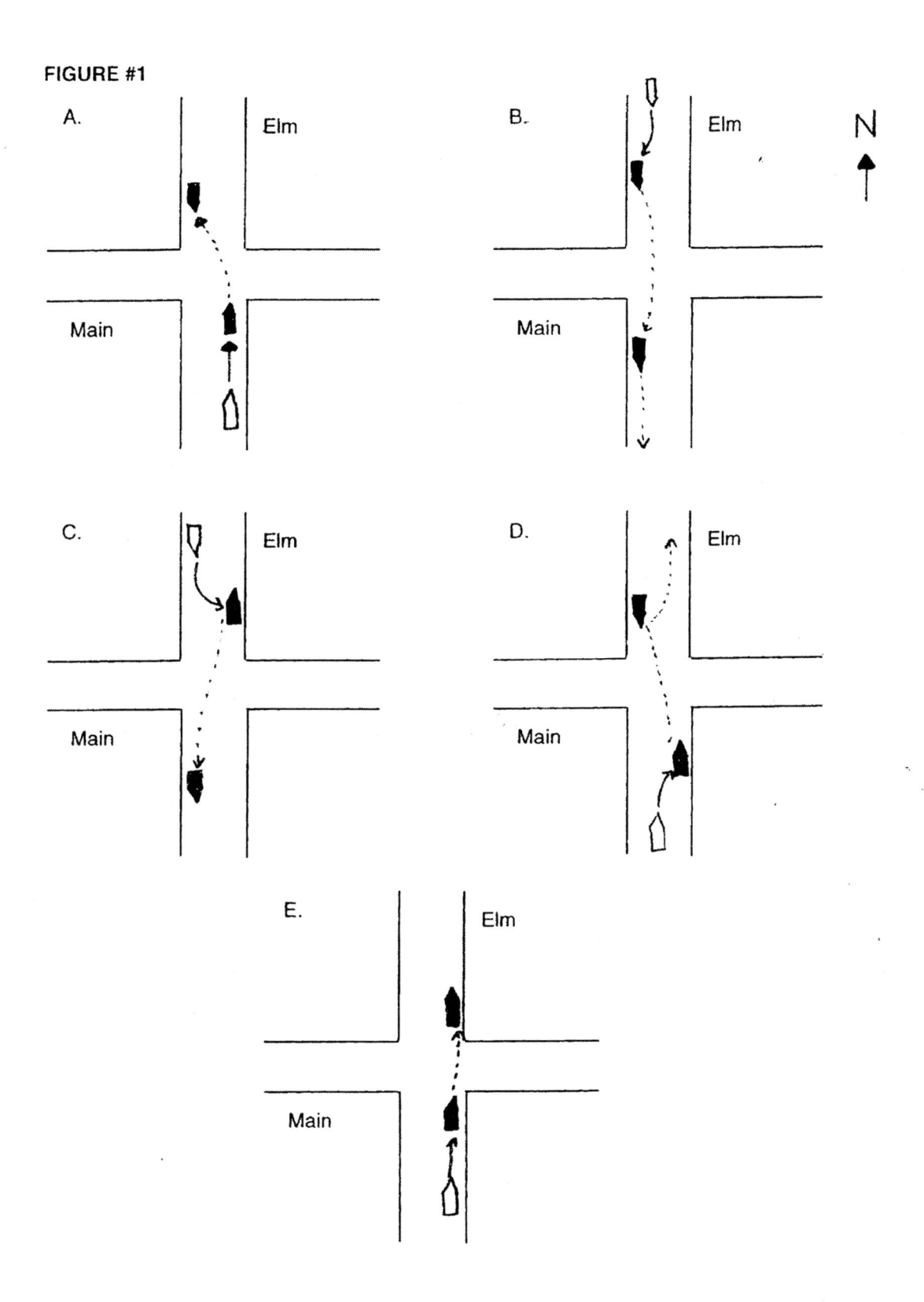

A.

Elm

Main

B.

Elm

Main

N

C.

Elm

Main

D.

Elm

Main

E.

Elm

Main

Questions 20-22

In questions 20 through 22, choose the word or phrase CLOSEST in meaning to the word or phrase printed in capital letters.

20. REDRESS 20.___

    A. suspend
    B. repeat
    C. compensate
    D. subdue

21. PRECEDENT 21.___

    A. cohort
    B. example
    C. obstruction
    D. elder

22. ADJUDICATION 22.___

    A. case
    B. judgment
    C. claim
    D. defendant

Questions 23-25

Questions 23 through 25 measure your ability to do fieldwork-related arithmetic. Each question presents a separate arithmetic problem for you to solve.

23. The Department of Sanitation purchased seven vehicles in the last year. Four of the vehicles were street sweepers that cost $95,000 each. Three were garbage compactors that cost $160,000 each. The average price of a vehicle purchased by the Department in the last year was about 23.___

    A. $98,000
    B. $108,000
    C. $122,000
    D. $145,000

24. Agent Frederick, whose car gets about 24 miles to the gallon, drives to Buffalo, 260 miles away. The average price of gasoline is $2.30 a gallon. How much did Agent Frederick spend on gas for the trip to Buffalo? 24.___

    A. $11   B. $25   C. $55   D. $113

25. Over the last four days, Precinct 11 has had 20 misdemeanor arrests each day. If the precinct records 15 misdemeanor arrests on the fifth day, what will its average daily number of misdemeanor arrests be? 25.___

    A. 16   B. 17   C. 18   D. 19

KEY (CORRECT ANSWERS)

1. D
2. C
3. A
4. A
5. B

6. A
7. A
8. C
9. A
10. B

11. A
12. B
13. C
14. A
15. D

16. B
17. A
18. E
19. C
20. C

21. B
22. B
23. C
24. B
25. D

TEST 2

DIRECTIONS: Each question or incomplete statement is followed by several suggested answers or completions. Select the one that BEST answers the question or completes the statement. *PRINT THE LETTER OF THE CORRECT ANSWER IN THE SPACE AT THE RIGHT.*

Questions 1-9

Questions 1 through 9 measure your ability to (1) determine whether statements from witnesses say essentially the same thing and (2) determine the evidence needed to make it reasonably certain that a particular conclusion is true.
To do well on this part of the test, you do NOT have to have a working knowledge of police procedures and techniques. Nor do you have to have any more familiarity with criminals and criminal behavior than that acquired from reading newspapers, listening to radio or watching TV. To do well in this part, you must read and reason carefully.

1. Which of the following pairs of statements say essentially the same thing in two different ways?
    I. All of the teachers at the school are wise, but some have proven to be bad-tempered.
    II. Teachers at the school are either wise or bad-tempered.
    III. If John can both type and do long division, he is qualified for this job. If John applies for this job, he can both type and do long division.

    A. I only
    B. I and II
    C. II only
    D. Neither I nor II

2. Which of the following pairs of statements say essentially the same thing in two different ways?
    I. If Carl rides the A train, the C train is down.
    II. Carl doesn't ride the A train unless the C train is down.
    III. If the three sides of a triangle are equal, the triangle is equilateral. A triangle is equilateral if the three sides are equal.

    A. I only
    B. I and II
    C. II only
    D. Neither I nor II

3. Which of the following pairs of statements say essentially the same thing in two different ways?
    I. If this dog has a red collar, it must be Slim.
    II. If this dog does not have a red collar, it can't be Slim.
    III. Dr. Slouka is not in his office during lunchtime. If it's not lunchtime, Dr. Slouka is in his office.

    A. I only
    B. I and II
    C. II only
    D. Neither I nor II

4. Which of the following pairs of statements say essentially the same thing in two different ways?
   I. At least one caseworker at Social Services has a degree in psychology.
      Not all the caseworkers at Social Services have a degree in psychology.
   II. If an officer doesn't pass the physical fitness test, he cannot be promoted.
      If an officer is not promoted, he hasn't passed the physical fitness test.

   A. I only
   B. I and II
   C. II only
   D. Neither I nor II

5. Summary of Evidence Collected to Date:
   I. All the Class II inspectors use multiplication when they inspect escalators.
   II. On some days, Fred, a Class II inspector, doesn't use multiplication at all.
   III. Fred's friend, Garth, uses multiplication every day.
   Prematurely Drawn Conclusion: Garth inspects escalators every day.
   Which of the following pieces of evidence, if any, would make it *reasonably certain* that the conclusion drawn is true?

   A. Garth is a Class II inspector
   B. Fred never inspects escalators
   C. Fred usually doesn't inspect escalators
   D. None of these

6. Summary of Evidence Collected to Date:
   I. Every one of the shelter's male pit bulls has been neutered.
   II. Some male pit bulls have also been muzzled.
   Prematurely Drawn Conclusion: Rex has been neutered.
   Which of the following pieces of evidence, if any, would make it *reasonably certain* that the conclusion drawn is true?

   A. Rex, a pit bull at the shelter, has been muzzled
   B. All of the pit bulls at the shelter are males
   C. Rex is one of the shelter's male pit bulls
   D. None of these

7. Summary of Evidence Collected to Date:
   I. Some of the social workers at the clinic have been welfare recipients.
   II. Some of the social workers at the clinic are college graduates.
   Prematurely Drawn Conclusion: Some of the social workers at the clinic who are college graduates have never received welfare benefits.
   Which of the following pieces of evidence, if any, would make it *reasonably certain* that the conclusion drawn is true?

   A. There are more college graduates at the clinic than those who have received welfare benefits
   B. There is an odd number of social workers at the clinic
   C. The number of college graduates and former welfare recipients at the clinic is the same
   D. None of these

8. Summary of Evidence Collected to Date:
Everyone who works at the library has read *War and Peace*. Most people who have read *War and Peace* have also read *Anna Karenina*.
Prematurely Drawn Conclusion: Marco has read *War and Peace*.
Which of the following pieces of evidence, if any, would make it *reasonably certain* that the conclusion drawn is true?

   A. Marco works at the library
   B. Marco has probably read *Anna Karenina*
   C. Everyone who has read *Anna Karenina* has read *War and Peace*
   D. None of these

9. Summary of Evidence Collected to Date:
Officer Skiles is working on the Martin investigation.
Prematurely Drawn Conclusion: Skiles is also working on the Bartlett case.
Which of the following pieces of evidence, if any, would make it *reasonably certain* that the conclusion drawn is true?

   A. Everyone who is working on the Martin investigation is also working on the Bartlett investigation
   B. Everyone who is working on the Bartlett investigation is also working on the Martin investigation
   C. The Martin investigation and Bartlett investigation are being conducted at the same time
   D. None of these

Questions 10-14

Questions 10 through 14 refer to Map #2 and measure your ability to orient yourself within a given section of town, neighborhood or particular area. Each of the questions describes a starting point and a destination. Assume that you are driving a car in the area shown on the map accompanying the questions. Use the map as a basis for the shortest way to get from one point to another without breaking the law.

On the map, a street marked by arrows, or by arrows and the words "One Way," indicates one-way travel, and should be assumed to be one-way for the entire length, even when there are breaks or jogs in the street. EXCEPTION: A street that does not have the same name over the full length.

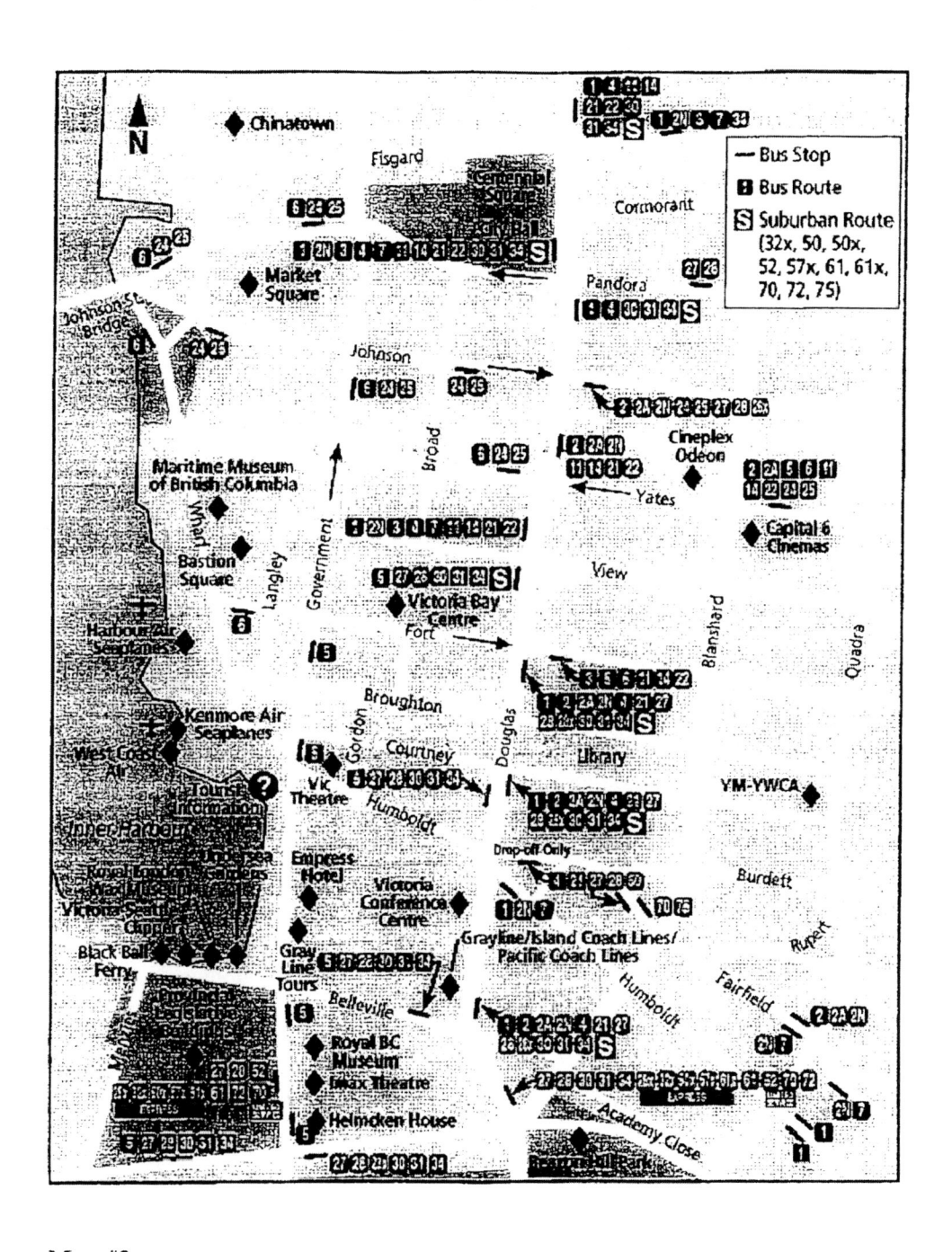

Map #2

10. The shortest legal way from the Royal London Wax Museum to the Chinatown block is

    A. east on Belleville, north on Douglas, west on Broughton, north on Government
    B. east on Belleville, north on Government
    C. east on Belleville, north on Government, west on Yates, north on Wharf
    D. east on Belleville, north on Douglas, west on Fisgard

11. The shortest legal way from the Maritime Museum of British Columbia to the Victoria Conference Centre is

    A. north on Wharf, east on Yates, south on Douglas
    B. south and west on Wharf, north on Government, east on Broughton, south on Douglas
    C. south on Wharf, east on Fort, south on Douglas
    D. south and west on Wharf, south on Government, east on Belleville, north on Douglas

12. The shortest legal way from Market Square to City Hall is

    A. north on Government, east on Fisgard, south on Douglas
    B. east on Pandora, north on Douglas
    C. east on Johnson, north on Blanshard, west on Pandora, north on Douglas
    D. east on Johnson, north on Douglas

13. The shortest legal way from the Victoria Bay Centre to Bastion Square is

    A. east on Fort, south on Douglas, west on Broughton, north on Wharf
    B. west on Fort, north on Government, west on Yates, south on Wharf
    C. west on Fort, north on Wharf
    D. east on Fort, north on Douglas, west on Johnson, south on Wharf

14. The shortest legal way from The Empress Hotel to the YM-YWCA is

    A. north on Government, east on Broughton
    B. north on Government, east on Courtney
    C. north on Government, southeast on Humboldt, north on Quadra
    D. north on Government, west on Courtney

Questions 15-19

Questions 15 through 19 refer to Figure #2, on the following page, and measure your ability to understand written descriptions of events. Each question presents a description of an accident or event and asks you which of the five drawings in Figure #2 BEST represents it.

In the drawings, the following symbols are used:

Moving vehicle: 〇   Non-moving vehicle: ▲

Pedestrian or bicycle: ●

The path and direction of travel of a vehicle or pedestrian is indicated by a solid line.

The path and direction of travel of each vehicle or pedestrian directly involved in a collision from the point of impact is indicated by a dotted line.

In the space at the right, print the letter of the drawing that best fits the descriptions written below:

15. A driver traveling north on Taylor strikes a parked car in the rear and knocks it forward, where it collides with a pedestrian in the crosswalk.   15.____

16. A driver headed south on Taylor strikes another car that is traveling east through the intersection of Taylor and Hayes. After the impact, the eastbound car veers to the right and strikes a pedestrian in the crosswalk on Jones.   16.____

17. A driver headed south on Taylor runs a red light and strikes another car that is headed east on Hayes. The eastbound car is knocked into a pedestrian that is using the crosswalk on Taylor   17.____

18. A driver traveling south on Taylor makes a sudden left turn onto Hayes. In the intersection, he strikes the front of an oncoming car and veers onto Hayes, where he strikes a pedestrian in the crosswalk.   18.____

19. A driver headed west on Hayes strikes a car that is traveling east through the intersection of Taylor and Hayes. After the impact, the eastbound car veers to the right and strikes a pedestrian in the crosswalk on Jones.   19.____

FIGURE #2

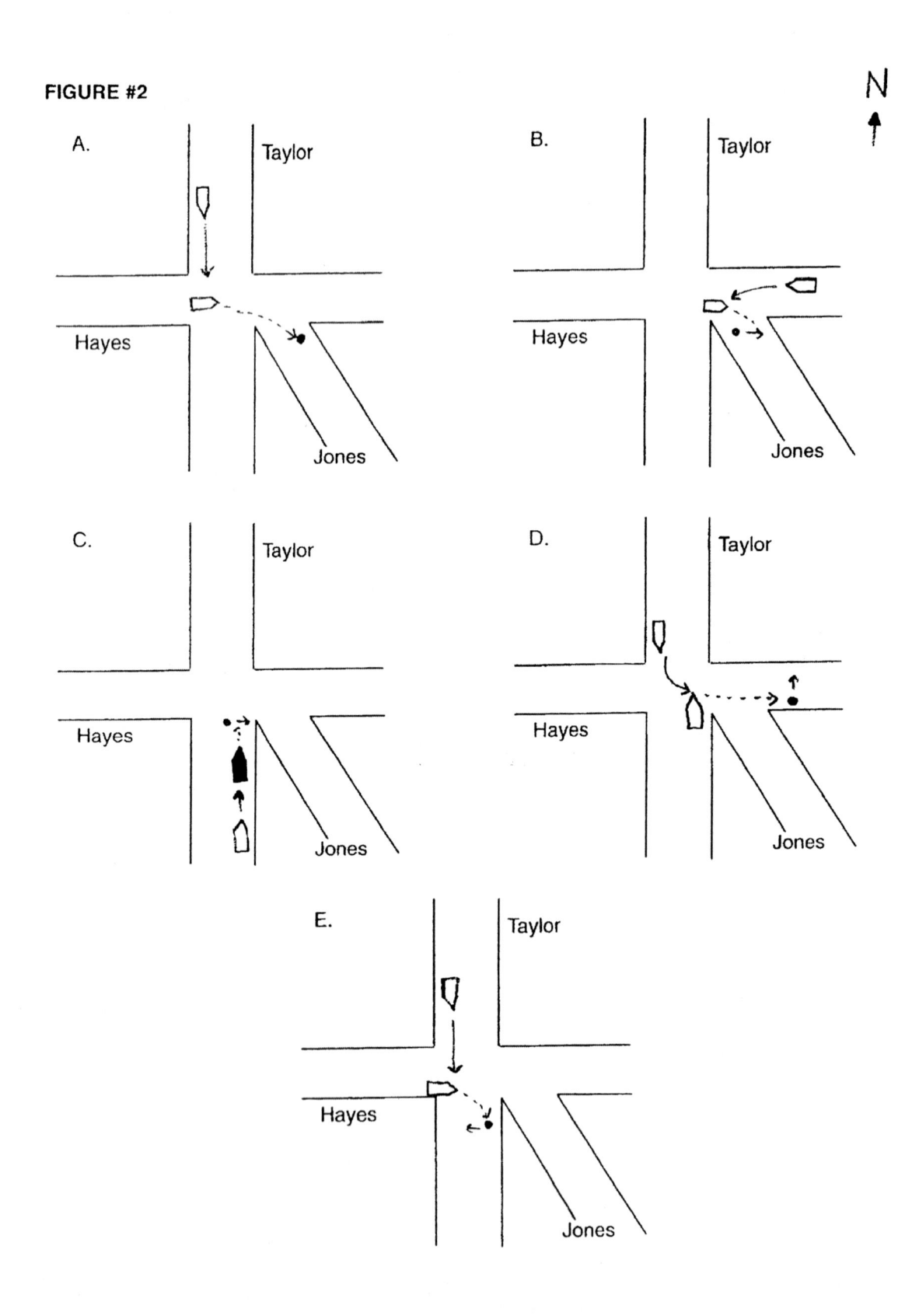

Questions 20-22

In questions 20 through 22, choose the word or phrase CLOSEST in meaning to the word or phrase printed in capital letters.

20. SEQUESTER

    A. follow
    B. separate
    C. endorse
    D. punish

21. EXECUTE

    A. carry out
    B. advance
    C. impede
    D. occur

22. SUPPRESS

    A. uphold
    B. convict
    C. forbid
    D. compensate

Questions 23-25

Questions 23 through 25 measure your ability to do fieldwork-related arithmetic. Each question presents a separate arithmetic problem for you to solve..

23. In the election for the presidency of Local Union 1134, Stan Fitz received 542 votes, Elizabeth Stuckey received 430 votes and Gene Sterner received 130 votes. Ninety percent of those eligible to vote did so. What was the number of eligible voters?

    A. 900
    B. 992
    C. 1102
    D. 1224

24. The Department of Records wants to sort its files alphabetically into boxes that hold an average of 50 files each. The Department has 1,140 records, an amount that is expected to double in the next ten years. To have enough boxes ten years from now, the Department should buy at least _____ boxes.

    A. 23   B. 38   C. 45   D. 47

25. The office's petty cash fund contains a total of $433 on Wednesday. At the beginning of the day, Arnold reimburses $270 that he had previously borrowed from the fund. Then Janet withdraws $158 for office supplies; Hank spends $87 on lunch for a committee meeting; and at the end of the day, Ernestine buys a new office calendar for $12. How much remains in the petty cash fund at the end of the day on Wednesday?

    A. $94   B. $257   C. $446   D. $527

KEY (CORRECT ANSWERS)

1.	D	11.	C
2.	B	12.	D
3.	A	13.	A
4.	D	14.	B
5.	A	15.	C
6.	C	16.	A
7.	D	17.	E
8.	A	18.	D
9.	A	19.	B
10.	B	20.	B

21. A
22. C
23. D
24. D
25. C

PREPARING WRITTEN MATERIAL

PARAGRAPH REARRANGEMENT
COMMENTARY

The sentences which follow are in scrambled order. You are to rearrange them in proper order and indicate the letter choice containing the correct answer at the space at the right.

Each group of sentences in this section is actually a paragraph presented in scrambled order. Each sentence in the group has a place in that paragraph; no sentence is to be left out. You are to read each group of sentences and decide upon the best order in which to put the sentences so as to form as well-organized paragraph.

The questions in this section measure the ability to solve a problem when all the facts relevant to its solution are not given.

More specifically, certain positions of responsibility and authority require the employee to discover connections between events sometimes, apparently, unrelated. In order to do this, the employee will find it necessary to correctly infer that unspecified events have probably occurred or are likely to occur. This ability becomes especially important when action must be taken on incomplete information.

Accordingly, these questions require competitors to choose among several suggested alternatives, each of which presents a different sequential arrangement of the events. Competitors must choose the MOST logical of the suggested sequences.

In order to do so, they may be required to draw on general knowledge to infer missing concepts or events that are essential to sequencing the given events. Competitors should be careful to infer only what is essential to the sequence. The plausibility of the wrong alternatives will always require the inclusion of unlikely events or of additional chains of events which are NOT essential to sequencing the given events.

It's very important to remember that you are looking for the best of the four possible choices, and that the best choice of all may not even be one of the answers you're given to choose from.

There is no one right way to these problems. Many people have found it helpful to first write out the order of the sentences, as they would have arranged them, on their scrap paper before looking at the possible answers. If their optimum answer is there, this can save them some time. If it isn't, this method can still give insight into solving the problem. Others find it most helpful to just go through each of the possible choices, contrasting each as they go along. You should use whatever method feels comfortable, and works, for you.

While most of these types of questions are not that difficult, we've added a higher percentage of the difficult type, just to give you more practice. Usually there are only one or two questions on this section that contain such subtle distinctions that you're unable to answer confidently, and you then may find yourself stuck deciding between two possible choices, neither of which you're sure about.

Preparing Written Material

EXAMINATION SECTION
TEST 1

DIRECTIONS: The following groups of sentences need to be arranged in an order that makes sense. Select the letter preceding the sequence that represents the best sentence order. *PRINT THE LETTER OF THE CORRECT ANSWER IN THE SPACE AT THE RIGHT.*

Question 1

1. The ostrich egg shell's legendary toughness makes it an excellent substitute for certain types of dishes or dinnerware, and in parts of Africa ostrich shells are cut and decorated for use as containers for water.
2. Since prehistoric times, people have used the enormous egg of the ostrich as a part of their diet, a practice which has required much patience and hard work-to hard-boil an ostrich egg takes about four hours.
3. Opening the egg's shell, which is rock hard and nearly an inch thick, requires heavy tools, such as a saw or chisel; from inside, a baby ostrich must use a hornlike projection on its beak as a miniature pick-axe to escape from the egg.
4. The offspring of all higher-order animals originate from single egg cells that are carried by mothers, and most of these eggs are relatively small, often microscopic.
5. The egg of the African ostrich, however, weighs a massive thirty pounds, making it the largest single cell on earth, and a common object of human curiosity and wonder.

The best order is

A. 5 4 1 2 3
B. 1 4 5 3 2
C. 4 2 3 5 1
D. 4 5 2 3 1

1.____

Question 2

1. Typically only a few feet high on the open sea, individual tsunami have been known to circle the entire globe two or three times if their progress is not interrupted, but are not usually dangerous until they approach the shallow water that surrounds land masses.
2. Some of the most terrifying and damaging hazards caused by earthquakes are tsunami, which were once called "tidal waves"— a poorly chosen name, since these waves have nothing to do with tides.
3. Then a wave, slowed by the sudden drag on the lower part of its moving water column, will pile upon itself, sometimes reaching a height of over 100 feet.
4. Tsunami (Japanese for "great harbor wave") are seismic waves that are caused by earthquakes near oceanic trenches, and once triggered, can travel up to 600 miles an hour on the open ocean.
5. A land-shoaling tsunami is capable of extraordinary destruction; some tsunami have deposited large boats miles inland, washed out two-foot-thick seawalls, and scattered locomotive trains over long distances.

The best order is

A. 4 1 3 2 5
B. 1 3 4 2 5
C. 5 1 3 2 4
D. 2 4 1 3 5

2.____

Question 3

1. Soon, by the 1940's, jazz was the most popular type of music among American intellectuals and college students.
2. In the early days of jazz, it was considered "lowdown" music, or music that was played only in rough, disreputable bars and taverns.
3. However, jazz didn't take long to develop from early ragtime melodies into more complex, sophisticated forms, such as Charlie Parker's "bebop" style of jazz.
4. After charismatic band leaders such as Duke Ellington and Count Basic brought jazz to a larger audience, and jazz continued to evolve into more complicated forms, white audiences began to accept and even to enjoy the new American art form.
5. Many white Americans, who then dictated the tastes of society, were wary of music that was played almost exclusively in black clubs in the poorer sections of cities and towns.

The best order is

- A. 5 4 3 2 1
- B. 2 5 3 4 1
- C. 4 5 3 1 2
- D. 1 2 4 3 5

Question 4

1. Then, hanging in a windless place, the magnetized end of the needle would always point to the south.
2. The needle could then be balanced on the rim of a cup, or the edge of a fingernail, but this balancing act was hard to maintain, and the needle often fell off.
3. Other needles would point to the north, and it was important for any traveler finding his way with a compass to remember which kind of magnetized needle he was carrying.
4. To make some of the earliest compasses in recorded history, ancient Chinese "magicians" would rub a needle with a piece of magnetized iron called a lodestone.
5. A more effective method of keeping the needle free to swing with its magnetic pull was to attach a strand of silk to the center of the needle with a tiny piece of wax.

The best order is

- A. 4 2 5 1 3
- B. 4 3 5 2 1
- C. 4 5 2 1 3
- D. 4 1 3 5 2

Question 5

1. The now-famous first mate of the *HMS Bounty*, Fletcher Christian, founded one of the world's most peculiar civilizations in 1790.
2. The men knew they had just committed a crime for which they could be hanged, so they set sail for Pitcairn, a remote, abandoned island in the far eastern region of the Polynesian archipelago, accompanied by twelve Polynesian women and six men.
3. In a mutiny that has become legendary, Christian and the others forced Captain Bligh into a lifeboat and set him adrift off the coast of Tonga in April of 1789.
4. In early 1790, the *Bounty* landed at Pitcairn Island, where the men lived out the rest of their lives and founded an isolated community which to this day includes direct descendants of Christian and the other crewmen.
5. The *Bounty*, commanded by Captain William Bligh, was in the middle of a global voyage, and Christian and his shipmates had come to the conclusion that Bligh was a reckless madman who would lead them to their deaths unless they took the ship from him.

The best order is

A. 4 5 3 2 1
B. 1 3 5 2 4
C. 1 5 3 2 4
D. 3 1 5 4 2

Question 6

1. But once the vines had been led to make orchids, the flowers had to be carefully hand-pollinated, because unpollinated orchids usually lasted less than a day, wilting and dropping off the vine before it had even become dark.
2. The Totonac farmers discovered that looping a vine back around once it reached a five-foot height on its host tree would cause the vine to flower.
3. Though they knew how to process the fruit pods and extract vanilla's flavoring agent, the Totonacs also knew that a wild vanilla vine did not produce abundant flowers or fruit.
4. Wild vines climbed along the trunks and canopies of trees, and this constant upward growth diverted most of the vine's energy to making leaves instead of the orchid flowers that, once pollinated, would produce the flavorful pods.
5. Hundreds of years before vanilla became a prized food flavoring in Europe and the Western World, the Totonac Indians of the Mexican Gulf Coast were skilled cultivators of the vanilla vine, whose fruit they literally worshipped as a goddess.

The best order is

A. 2 3 4 1 5
B. 2 4 3 1 5
C. 5 3 4 2 1
D. 3 4 1 2 5

Question 7

1. Once airborne, the spider is at the mercy of the air currents—usually the spider takes a brief journey, traveling close to the ground, but some have been found in air samples collected as high as 10,000 feet, or been reported landing on ships far out at sea.
2. Once a young spider has hatched, it must leave the environment into which it was born as quickly as possible, in order to avoid competing with its hundreds of brothers and sisters for food.
3. The silk rises into warm air currents, and as soon as the pull feels adequate the spider lets go and drifts up into the air, suspended from the silk strand in the same way that a person might parasail.
4. To help young spiders do this, many species have adapted a practice known as "aerial dispersal," or, in common speech, "ballooning."
5. A spider that wants to leave its surroundings quickly will climb to the top of a grass stem or twig, face into the wind, and aim its back end into the air, releasing a long stream of silk from the glands near the tip of its abdomen.

The best order is

- A. 5 4 2 3 1
- B. 5 2 4 1 3
- C. 2 5 4 3 1
- D. 2 4 5 3 1

Question 8

1. For about a year, Tycho worked at a castle in Prague with a scientist named Johannes Kepler, but their association was cut short by another argument that drove Kepler out of the castle, to later develop, on his own, the theory of planetary orbits.
2. Tycho found life without a nose embarrassing, so he made a new nose for himself out of silver, which reportedly remained glued to his face for the rest of his life.
3. Tycho Brahe, the 17th-century Danish astronomer, is today more famous for his odd and arrogant personality than for any contribution he has made to our knowledge of the stars and planets.
4. Early in his career, as a student at Rostock University, Tycho got into an argument with the another student about who was the better mathematician, and the two became so angry that the argument turned into a sword fight, during which Tycho's nose was sliced off.
5. Later in his life, Tycho's arrogance may have kept him from playing a part in one of the greatest astronomical discoveries in history: the elliptical orbits of the solar system's planets.

The best order is

- A. 1 4 2 3 5
- B. 4 2 3 5 1
- C. 4 2 1 3 5
- D. 3 4 2 5 1

Question 9

1. The processionaries are so used to this routine that if a person picks up the end of a silk line and brings it back to the origin—creating a closed circle—the caterpillars may travel around and around for days, sometimes starving ar freezing, without changing course.
2. Rather than relying on sight or sound, the other caterpillars, who are lined up end-to-end behind the leader, travel to and from their nests by walking on this silk line, and each will reinforce it by laying down its own marking line as it passes over.
3. In order to insure the safety of individuals, the processionary caterpillar nests in a tree with dozens of other caterpillars, and at night, when it is safest, they all leave together in search of food.
4. The processionary caterpillar of the European continent is a perfect illustration of how much some insect species rely on instinct in their daily routines.
5. As they leave their nests, the processionaries form a single-file line behind a leader who spins and lays out a silk line to mark the chosen path.

The best order is

A. 4 3 5 2 1
B. 3 5 4 2 1
C. 3 5 2 1 4
D. 4 5 3 1 2

Question 10

1. Often, the child is also given a handcrafted walker or push cart, to provide support for its first upright explorations.
2. In traditional Indian families, a child's first steps are celebrated as a ceremonial event, rooted in ancient myth.
3. These carts are often intricately designed to resemble the chariot of Krishna, an important figure in Indian mythology.
4. The sound of these anklet bells is intended to mimic the footsteps of the legendary child Rama, who is celebrated in devotional songs throughout India.
5. When the child's parents see that the child is ready to begin walking, they will fit it with specially designed ankle bracelets, adorned with gently ringing bells.

The best order is

A. 2 3 4 1 5
B. 2 5 3 1 4
C. 5 4 1 3 2
D. 5 3 2 1 4

Question 11

1. The settlers planted Osage orange all across Middle America, and today long lines and rectangles of Osage orange trees can still be seen on the prairies, running along the former boundaries of farms that no longer exist.
2. After trying sod walls and water-filled ditches with no success, American farmers began to look for a plant that was adaptable to prairie weather, and that could be trimmed into a hedge that was "pig-tight, horse-high, and bull-strong."
3. The tree, so named because it bore a large (but inedible) fruit the size of an orange, was among the sturdiest and hardiest of American trees, and was prized among Native Americans for the strength and flexibility of bows which were made from its wood.
4. The first people to practice agriculture on the American flatlands were faced with an important problem: what would they use to fence their land in a place that was almost entirely without trees or rocks?
5. Finally, an Illinois farmer brought the settlers a tree that was native to the land between the Red and Arkansas rivers, a tree called the Osage orange.

The best order is

A. 2 1 5 3 4
B. 1 2 3 4 5
C. 4 2 5 3 1
D. 4 2 1 3 5

Question 12

1. After about ten minutes of such spirited and complicated activity, the head dancer is free to make up his or her own movements while maintaining the interest of the New Year's crowd.
2. The dancer will then perform a series of leg kicks, while at the same time operating the lion's mouth with his own hand and moving the ears and eyes by means of a string which is attached to the dancer's own mouth.
3. The most difficult role of this dance belongs to the one who controls the lion's head; this person must lead all the other "parts" of the lion through the choreographed segments of the dance.
4. The head dancer begins with a complex series of steps, alternately stepping forward with the head raised, and then retreating a few steps while lowering the head, a movement that is intended to create the impression that the lion is keeping a watchful eye for anything evil.
5. When performing a traditional Chinese New Year's lion dance, several performers must fit themselves inside a large lion costume and work together to enact different parts of the dance.

The best order is

A. 5 3 4 2 1
B. 3 4 2 5 1
C. 3 1 5 4 2
D. 4 2 3 5 1

Question 13   13._____

1. For many years the shell of the chambered nautilus was treasured in Europe for its beauty and intricacy, but collectors were unaware that they were in possession of the structure that marked a "missing link" in the evolution of marine mollusks.
2. The nautilus, however, evolved a series of enclosed chambers in its shell, and invented a new use for the structure: the shell began to serve as a buoyancy device.
3. Equipped with this new flotation device, the nautilus did not need the single, muscular foot of its predecessors, but instead developed flaps, tentacles, and a gentle form of jet propulsion that transformed it into the first mollusk able to take command of its own destiny and explore a three-dimensional world.
4. By pumping and adjusting air pressure into the chambers, the nautilus could spend the day resting on the bottom, and then rise toward the surface at night in search of food.
5. The nautilus shell looks like a large snail shell, similar to those of its ancestors, who used their shells as protective coverings while they were anchored to the sea floor.

The best order is

A. 5 2 4 1 3
B. 5 1 2 3 4
C. 1 2 5 3 4
D. 1 5 2 4 3

Question 14   14._____

1. While France and England battled for control of the region, the Acadiens prospered on the fertile farmland, which was finally secured by England in 1713.
2. Early in the 17th century, settlers from western France founded a colony called Acadie in what is now the Canadian province of Nova Scotia.
3. At this time, English officials feared the presence of spies among the Acadiens who might be loyal to their French homeland, and the Acadiens were deported to spots along the Atlantic and Caribbean shores of America.
4. The French settlers remained on this land, under English rule, for around forty years, until the beginning of the French and Indian War, another conflict between France and England.
5. As the Acadien refugees drifted toward a final home in southern Louisiana, neighbors shortened their name to "Cadien," and finally "Cajun," the name which the descendants of early Acadiens still call themselves.

The best order is

A. 1 4 2 3 5
B. 2 1 3 5 4
C. 2 1 4 3 5
D. 5 2 3 4 1

Question 15

1. Traditional households in the Eastern and Western regions of Africa serve two meals a day-one at around noon, and the other in the evening.
2. The starch is then used in the way that Americans might use a spoon, to scoop up a portion of the main dish on the person's plate.
3. The reason for the starch's inclusion in every meal has to do with taste as well as nutrition; African food can be very spicy, and the starch is known to cool the burning effect of the main dish.
4. When serving these meals, the main dish is usually served on individual plates, and the starch is served on a communal plate, from which diners break off a piece of bread or scoop rice or fufu in their fingers.
5. The typical meals usually consist of a thick stew or soup as the main course, and an accompanying starch—either bread, rice, *or fufu, a* starchy grain paste similar in consistency to mashed potatoes.

The best order is

A. 5 2 3 4 1
B. 5 1 4 3 2
C. 1 4 5 3 2
D. 1 5 4 2 3

Question 16

1. In the early days of the American Midwest, Indiana settlers sometimes came together to hold an event called an apple peeling, where neighboring settlers gathered at the homestead of a host family to help prepare the hosts' apple crop for cooking, canning, and making apple butter.
2. At the beginning of the event, each peeler sat down in front of a ten- or twenty-gallon stone jar and was given a crock of apples and a paring knife.
3. Once a peeler had finished with a crock, another was placed next to him; if the peeler was an unmarried man, he kept a strict count of the number of apples he had peeled, because the winner was allowed to kiss the girl of his choice.
4. The peeling usually ended by 9:30 in the evening, when the neighbors gathered in the host family's parlor for a dance social.
5. The apples were peeled, cored, and quartered, and then placed into the jar.

The best order is

A. 1 5 3 4 2
B. 2 5 3 4 1
C. 1 2 5 3 4
D. 2 1 5 4 3

Question 17

1. If your pet turtle is a land turtle and is native to temperate climates, it will stop eating some time in October, which should be your cue to prepare the turtle for hibernation.
2. The box should then be covered with a wire screen, which will protect the turtle from any rodents or predators that might want to take advantage of a motionless and helpless animal.
3. When your turtle hasn't eaten for a while and appears ready to hibernate, it should be moved to its winter quarters, most likely a cellar or garage, where the temperature should range between 40° and 45° F.
4. Instead of feeding the turtle, you should bathe it every day in warm water, to encourage the turtle to empty its intestines in preparation for its long winter sleep.
5. Here the turtle should be placed in a well-ventilated box whose bottom is covered with a moisture-absorbing layer of clay beads, and then filled three-fourths full with almost dry peat moss or wood chips, into which the turtle will burrow and sleep for several months.

The best order is

A. 1 4 3 5 2
B. 3 4 2 5 1
C. 3 2 4 1 5
D. 4 5 2 3 1

Question 18

1. Once he has reached the nest, the hunter uses two sturdy bamboo poles like huge chopsticks to pull the nest away from the mountainside, into a large basket that will be lowered to people waiting below.
2. The world's largest honeybees colonize the Nepalese mountainsides, building honeycombs as large as a person on sheer rock faces that are often hundreds of feet high.
3. In the remote mountain country of Nepal, a small band of "honey hunters" carry out a tradition so ancient that 10,000 year-old drawings of the practice have been found in the caves of Nepal.
4. To harvest the honey and beeswax from these combs, a honey hunter climbs above the nests, lowers a long bamboo-fiber ladder over the cliff, and then climbs down.
5. Throughout this dangerous practice, the hunter is stung repeatedly, and only the veterans, with skin that has been toughened over the years, are able to return from a hunt without the painful swelling caused by stings.

The best order is

A. 2 4 3 5 1
B. 2 4 1 5 3
C. 5 3 2 4 1
D. 3 2 4 1 5

Question 19

1. After the Romans left Britain, there were relentless attacks on the islands from the barbarian tribes of northern Germany–the Angles, Saxons, and Jutes.
2. As the empire weakened, Roman soldiers withdrew from Britain, leaving behind a country that continued to practice the Christian religion that had been introduced by the Romans.
3. Early Latin writings tell of a Christian warrior named Arturius (Arthur, in English) who led the British citizens to defeat these barbarian invaders, and brought an extended period of peace to the lands of Britain.
4. Long ago, the British Isles were part of the far-flung Roman Empire that extended across most of Europe and into Africa and Asia.
5. The romantic legend of King Arthur and his knights of the Round Table, one of the most popular and widespread stories of all time, appears to have some foundation in history.

The best order is

A. 5 4 3 2 1
B. 5 4 2 1 3
C. 4 5 2 3 1
D. 4 3 2 1 5

19.___

Question 20

1. The cylinder was allowed to cool until it sould stand on its own, and then it was cut from the tube and split down the side with a single straight cut.
2. Nineteenth-century glassmakers, who had not yet discovered the glazier's modern techniques for making panes of glass, had to create a method for converting their blown glass into flat sheets.
3. The bubble was then pierced at the end to make a hole that opened up while the glassmaker gently spun it, creating a cylinder of glass.
4. Turned on its side and laid on a conveyor belt, the cylinder was strengthened, or tempered, by being heated again and cooled very slowly, eventually flattening out into a single rectangular piece of glass.
5. To do this, the glassmaker dipped the end of a long tube into melted glass and blew into the other end of the tube, creating an expanding bubble of glass.

The best order is

A. 2 5 3 4 1
B. 2 4 5 3 1
C. 3 5 2 4 1
D. 3 1 4 5 2

20.___

Question 21

21.____

1. The splints are almost always hidden, but horses are occasionally born whose splinted toes project from the leg on either side, just above the hoof.
2. The second and fourth toes remained, but shrank to thin splints of bone that fused invisibly to the horse's leg bone.
3. Horses are unique among mammals, having evolved feet that each end in what is essentially a single toe, capped by a large, sturdy hoof.
4. Julius Caesar, an emperor of ancient Rome, was said to have owned one of these three-toed horses, and considered it so special that he would not permit anyone else to ride it.
5. Though the horse's earlier ancestors possessed the traditional mammalian set of five toes on each foot, the horse has retained only its third toe; its first and fifth toes disappeared completely as the horse evolved.

The best order is

A. 3 5 2 1 4
B. 5 3 2 4 1
C. 3 2 5 1 4
D. 5 2 3 1 4

Question 22

22.____

1. The new building materials—some of which are twenty feet long, and weigh nearly six tons—were transported to Pohnpei on rafts, and were brought into their present position by using hibiscus fiber ropes and leverage to move the stone columns upward along the inclined trunks of coconut palm trees.
2. The ancestors built great fires to heat the stone, and then poured cool seawater on the columns, which caused the stone to contract and split along natural fracture lines.
3. The now-abandoned enclave of Nan Madol, a group of 92 man-made islands off the shore of the Micronesian island of Pohnpei, is estimated to have been built around the year 500 A.D.
4. The islanders say their ancestors quarried stone columns from a nearby island, where large basalt columns were formed by the cooling of molten lava.
5. The structures of Nan Madol are remarkable for the sheer size of some of the stone "logs" or columns that were used to create the walls of the offshore community, and today anthropologists can only rely on the information of existing local people for clues about how Nan Madol was built.

The best order is

A. 5 4 3 2 1
B. 5 3 1 4 2
C. 3 5 4 2 1
D. 3 1 4 2 5

Question 23

1. One of the most easily manipulated substances on earth, glass can be made into ceramic tiles that are composed of over 90% air.
2. NASA's space shuttles are the first spacecraft ever designed to leave and re-enter the earth's atmosphere while remaining intact.
3. These ceramic tiles are such effective insulators that when a tile emerges from the oven in which it was fired, it can be held safely in a person's hand by the edges while its interior still glows at a temperature well over 2000° F.
4. Eventually, the engineers were led to a material that is as old as our most ancient civilizationsglass.
5. Because the temperature during atmospheric re-entry is so incredibly hot, it took NASA's engineers some time to find a substance capable of protecting the shuttles.

The best order is

A. 5 2 1 3 4
B. 2 5 4 1 3
C. 2 3 1 2 5
D. 5 4 3 1 2

Question 24

1. The secret to teaching any parakeet to talk is patience, and the understanding that when a bird "talks," it is simply imitating what it hears, rather than putting ideas into words.
2. You should stay just out of sight of the bird and repeat the phrase you want it to learn, for at least fifteen minutes every morning and evening.
3. It is important to leave the bird without any words of encouragement or farewell; otherwise it might combine stray remarks or phrases, such as "Good night," with the phrase you are trying to teach it.
4. For this reason, to train your bird to imitate your words you should keep it free of any distractions, especially other noises, while you are giving it "lessons."
5. After your repetition, you should quietly leave the bird alone for a while, to think over what it has just heard.

The best order is

A. 1 4 2 5 3
B. 1 2 4 3 5
C. 3 2 1 5 4
D. 3 1 5 4 2

Question 25

25. _____

1. As a school approaches, fishermen from neighboring communities join their fishing boats together as a fleet, and string their gill nets together to make a huge fence that is held up by cork floats.
2. At a signal from the party leaders, or *nakura,* the family members pound the sides of the boats or beat the water with long poles, creating a sudden and deafening noise.
3. The fishermen work together to drag the trap into a half-circle that may reach 300 yards in diameter, and then the families move their boats to form the other half of the circle around the school of fish.
4. The school of fish flee from the commotion into the awaiting trap, where a final wall of net is thrown over the open end of the half-circle, securing the day's haul.
5. Indonesian people from the area around the Sulu islands live on the sea, in floating villages made of lashed-together or stilted homes, and make much of their living by fishing their home waters for migrating schools of snapper, scad, and other fish.

The best order is

A. 1 5 3 4 2
B. 1 2 4 3 5
C. 5 1 2 3 4
D. 5 1 3 2 4

KEY (CORRECT ANSWERS)

1.	D	11.	C
2.	D	12.	A
3.	B	13.	D
4.	A	14.	C
5.	C	15.	D
6.	C	16.	C
7.	D	17.	A
8.	D	18.	D
9.	A	19.	B
10.	B	20.	A

21. A
22. C
23. B
24. A
25. D

PREPARING WRITTEN MATERIAL

EXAMINATION SECTION
TEST 1

DIRECTIONS: Each question consists of a sentence which may or may not be an example of good English usage. Examine each sentence, considering grammar, punctuation, spelling, capitalization, and awkwardness. Then choose the correct statement about it from the four choices below it. If the English usage in the sentence given is better than any of the changes suggested in choices B, C, or D, pick choice A. (Do not pick a choice that will change the meaning of the sentence.)

1. We attended a staff conference on Wednesday the new safety and fire rules were discussed.

    A. This is an example of acceptable writing.
    B. The words "safety," "fire" and "rules" should begin with capital letters.
    C. There should be a comma after the word "Wednesday."
    D. There should be a period after the word "Wednesday" and the word "the" should begin with a capital letter

2. Neither the dictionary or the telephone directory could be found in the office library.

    A. This is an example of acceptable writing.
    B. The word "or" should be changed to "nor."
    C. The word "library" should be spelled "libery."
    D. The word "neither" should be changed to "either."

3. The report would have been typed correctly if the typist could read the draft.

    A. This is an example of acceptable writing.
    B. The word "would" should be removed.
    C. The word "have" should be inserted after the word "could."
    D. The word "correctly" should be changed to "correct."

4. The supervisor brought the reports and forms to an employees desk.

    A. This is an example of acceptable writing.
    B. The word "brought" should be changed to "took."
    C. There should be a comma after the word "reports" and a comma after the word "forms."
    D. The word "employees" should be spelled "employee's."

5. It's important for all the office personnel to submit their vacation schedules on time.

    A. This is an example of acceptable writing.
    B. The word "It's" should be spelled "Its."
    C. The word "their" should be spelled "they're."
    D. The word "personnel" should be spelled "personal."

6. The report, along with the accompanying documents, were submitted for review. 6.__

    A. This is an example of acceptable writing.
    B. The words "were submitted" should be changed to "was submitted."
    C. The word "accompanying" should be spelled "accompaning."
    D. The comma after the word "report" should be taken out.

7. If others must use your files, be certain that they understand how the system works, but 7.__
   insist that you do all the filing and refiling.

    A. This is an example of acceptable writing.
    B. There should be a period after the word "works," and the word "but" should start a new sentence
    C. The words "filing" and "refiling" should be spelled "fileing" and "refileing."
    D. There should be a comma after the word "but."

8. The appeal was not considered because of its late arrival. 8.__

    A. This is an example of acceptable writing.
    B. The word "its" should be changed to "it's."
    C. The word "its" should be changed to "the."
    D. The words "late arrival" should be changed to "arrival late."

9. The letter must be read carefuly to determine under which subject it should be filed. 9.__

    A. This is an example of acceptable writing.
    B. The word "under" should be changed to "at."
    C. The word "determine" should be spelled "determin."
    D. The word "carefuly" should be spelled "carefully."

10. He showed potential as an office manager, but he lacked skill in delegating work. 10.__

    A. This is an example of acceptable writing.
    B. The word "delegating" should be spelled "delagating."
    C. The word "potential" should be spelled "potencial."
    D. The words "he lacked" should be changed to "was lacking."

KEY (CORRECT ANSWERS)

1.	D		6.	B
2.	B		7.	A
3.	C		8.	A
4.	D		9.	D
5.	A		10.	A

TEST 2

DIRECTIONS: Each question consists of a sentence which may or may not be an example of good English usage. Examine each sentence, considering grammar, punctuation, spelling, capitalization, and awkwardness. Then choose the correct statement about it from the four choices below it. If the English usage in the sentence given is better than any of the changes suggested in choices B, C, or D, pick choice A. (Do not pick a choice that will change the meaning of the sentence.)

1. The supervisor wants that all staff members report to the office at 9:00 A.M. 1.____
    - A. This is an example of acceptable writing.
    - B. The word "that" should be removed and the word "to" should be inserted after the word "members."
    - C. There should be a comma after the word "wants" and a comma after the word "office."
    - D. The word "wants" should be changed to "want" and the word "shall" should be inserted after the word "members."

2. Every morning the clerk opens the office mail and distributes it . 2.____
    - A. This is an example of acceptable writing.
    - B. The word "opens" should be changed to "open."
    - C. The word "mail" should be changed to "letters."
    - D. The word "it" should be changed to "them."

3. The secretary typed more fast on a desktop computer than on a laptop computer. 3.____
    - A. This is an example of acceptable writing.
    - B. The words "more fast" should be changed to "faster."
    - C. There should be a comma after the words "desktop computer."
    - D. The word "than" should be changed to "then."

4. The new stenographer needed a desk a computer, a chair and a blotter. 4.____
    - A. This is an example of acceptable writing.
    - B. The word "blotter" should be spelled "blodder."
    - C. The word "stenographer" should begin with a capital letter.
    - D. There should be a comma after the word "desk."

5. The recruiting officer said, "There are many different goverment jobs available." 5.____
    - A. This is an example of acceptable writing.
    - B. The word "There" should not be capitalized.
    - C. The word "goverment" should be spelled "government".
    - D. The comma after the word "said" should be removed.

6. He can recommend a mechanic whose work is reliable. 6.____
    - A. This is an example of acceptable writing.
    - B. The word "reliable" should be spelled "relyable."
    - C. The word "whose" should be spelled "who's."
    - D. The word "mechanic" should be spelled "mecanic."

7. She typed quickly; like someone who had not a moment to lose. 7.___
    A. This is an example of acceptable writing.
    B. The word "not" should be removed.
    C. The semicolon should be changed to a comma.
    D. The word "quickly" should be placed before instead of after the word "typed."

8. She insisted that she had to much work to do. 8.___
    A. This is an example of acceptable writing.
    B. The word "insisted" should be spelled "incisted."
    C. The word "to" used in front of "much" should be spelled "too."
    D. The word "do" should be changed to "be done."

9. He excepted praise from his supervisor for a job well done. 9.___
    A. This is an example of acceptable writing.
    B. The word "excepted" should be spelled "accepted."
    C. The order of the words "well done" should be changed to "done well."
    D. There should be a comma after the word "supervisor."

10. What appears to be intentional errors in grammar occur several times in the passage. 10.___
    A. This is an example of acceptable writing.
    B. The word "occur" should be spelled "occurr."
    C. The word "appears" should be changed to "appear."
    D. The phrase "several times" should be changed to "from time to time."

KEY (CORRECT ANSWERS)

1.	B	6.	A
2.	A	7.	C
3.	B	8.	C
4.	D	9.	B
5.	C	10.	C

TEST 3

Questions 1-5.

DIRECTIONS: Same as for Tests 1 and 2.

1. The clerk could have completed the assignment on time if he knows where these materials were located.

    A. This is an example of acceptable writing.
    B. The word "knows" should be replaced by "had known."
    C. The word "were" should be replaced by "had been."
    D. The words "where these materials were located" should be replaced by "the location of these materials."

    1.____

2. All employees should be given safety training. Not just those who have accidents.

    A. This is an example of acceptable writing.
    B. The period after the word "training" should be changed to a colon.
    C. The period after the word "training" should be changed to a semicolon, and the first letter of the word "Not" should be changed to a small "n."
    D. The period after the word "training" should be changed to a comma, and the first letter of the word "Not" should be changed to a small "n."

    2.____

3. This proposal is designed to promote employee awareness of the suggestion program, to encourage employee participation in the program, and to increase the number of suggestions submitted.

    A. This is an example of acceptable writing.
    B. The word "proposal" should be spelled "preposal."
    C. The words "to increase the number of suggestions submitted" should be changed to "an increase in the number of suggestions is expected."
    D. The word "promote" should be changed to "enhance" and the word "increase" should be changed to "add to."

    3.____

4. The introduction of inovative managerial techniques should be preceded by careful analysis of the specific circumstances and conditions in each department.

    A. This is an example of acceptable writing.
    B. The word "techniques" should be spelled "techneques."
    C. The word "inovative" should be spelled "innovative."
    D. A comma should be placed after the word "circumstances" and after the word "conditions."

    4.____

5. This occurrence indicates that such criticism embarrasses him.

    A. This is an example of acceptable writing.
    B. The word "occurrence" should be spelled "occurence."
    C. The word "criticism" should be spelled "critisism."
    D. The word "embarrasses" should be spelled "embarasses."

    5.____

KEY (CORRECT ANSWERS)

1. B
2. D
3. A
4. C
5. A

EXAMINATION SECTION
TEST 1

DIRECTIONS: Each question or incomplete statement is followed by several suggested answers or completions. Select the one that BEST answers the question or completes the statement. *PRINT THE LETTER OF THE CORRECT ANSWER IN THE SPACE AT THE RIGHT.*

1. It is GENERALLY accepted that, of the following, the MOST important medium for developing integration and continuity in learning on the job is

    A. day-to-day experience on the job
    B. the supervisory conference
    C. the staff meeting
    D. the professional seminar

2. Assume that you find that one of your workers is over-identifying with a particular client. Of the following, the MOST appropriate step for you to take FIRST in dealing with this situation is to

    A. transfer the case to another worker
    B. inform the worker that he cannot give satisfactory service if he overidentifies with a client
    C. interview the client yourself to determine his feelings about his relationship with the worker
    D. arrange a conference with the worker to discuss the reasons for her overidentification with this client

3. The one of the following which is the MOST likely reason why a newly-appointed supervisor would have a tendency to interfere actively in a relationship between one of his workers and a client is that the supervisor

    A. has unresolved feelings about relinquishing the role of worker, and has not yet accepted his role as supervisor
    B. must give direct assistance in the situation because the worker cannot handle it
    C. is attempting to share with his worker the knowledge and skill which he has developed in direct practice
    D. has not realized that immediate responsibility for work with clients has been delegated to others

4. A worker who has a tendency to resist authority and supervision can be helped MOST effectively if, of the following, the supervisor

    A. behaves in a strict and impersonal manner so that the worker will accept his authority as a supervisor
    B. modifies the relationship so that he will be less authoritarian and threatening to the worker
    C. gives the worker a simple, matter-of-fact interpretation of the supervisory relationship and has an understanding acceptance of the worker's response
    D. temporarily establishes a peer relationship with the worker in order to overcome his resistance

5. Before interviewing a newly-appointed worker for the first time, of the following, it is DESIRABLE for the supervisor to

   A. learn as much as he can about the worker's background and interests in order to eliminate the routine of asking questions and eliciting answers
   B. review the job information to be covered in order to make it easier to be impersonal and keep to the business at hand
   C. send the worker orientation material about the agency and the job and ask him to study it before the interview
   D. review available information about the worker in order to find an area of shared experience to serve as a *taking off* point for getting acquainted

6. In interviewing a new worker, of the following, it is IMPORTANT for the supervisor to

   A. give direction to the progress of the interview and maintain a leadership role throughout
   B. allow the worker to take the initiative in order to give him full scope for freedom of expression
   C. maintain a non-directional approach so that the worker will reveal his true attitudes and feelings
   D. avoid interrupting the worker, even though he seems to want to do all the talking

7. When a new worker, during his first few days, shows such symptoms of insecurity as *stage fright,* helpless immobility, or extreme talkativeness, of the following, it would be MOST helpful for the supervisor to

   A. start the worker out on some activity in which he is relatively secure
   B. ignore the symptoms and allow the worker to *sink or swim* on his own
   C. have a conference with the worker and interpret to him the reasons for his feelings of insecurity
   D. consider the probability that this worker may not be suited for a profession which requires skill in interpersonal relationships

8. Of the following, the MOST desirable method of minimizing workers' dependence on the supervisor and encouraging self-dependence is to

   A. hold group instead of individual supervisory conferences at regular intervals
   B. schedule individual supervisory conferences only in response to the workers' obvious need for guidance
   C. plan for progressive exposure to other opportunities for learning afforded by the agency and the community
   D. allow workers to learn by trial and error rather than by direct supervisory guidance

9. Of the following, it would NOT be appropriate for the supervisor to use early supervisory conferences with the new worker as a means of

   A. giving him direct practical help in order to get going on the job
   B. estimating the level of his native abilities, professional skills and experience
   C. getting clues as to his characteristic ways of learning in a new situation
   D. assessing his potential for future supervisory responsibility

10. Without careful planning by the supervisor for orientation of the new worker, an informal system of orientation by co-workers inevitably develops.
Such an informal system of orientation is USUALLY

    A. *beneficial*, because many new workers learn more readily when instructed by their peers
    B. *harmful*, because informal orientation by an undesig-nated co-worker can lead a new worker astray instead of helping him
    C. *beneficial*, because assumption by subordinates of responsibility for orientation will free the supervisor for other urgent work
    D. *harmful*, because such informal orientation by a co-worker will tend to destroy the authority of the supervisor

10.____

11. Of the following, the BEST way for a supervisor to assist a subordinate who has unusual work pressures is to

    A. relieve him of some of his cases until the pressures subside
    B. help him to decide which cases should be given the most attention during the period of pressure, and how to provide coverage for less urgent cases
    C. inform him that he must learn to tolerate and adjust to such pressures
    D. point out that he should learn to understand the causes of the pressures, which probably resulted from his own deficiencies

11.____

12. Many supervisors have a tendency to use case records mainly for the purpose of analysis of the workers' skill or evaluation of their performance.
Of the following, a PROBABLE result of this practice is that

    A. workers are likely to tie-in recording with supervisory evaluation of their work, without giving proper emphasis to their importance in improving service to clients
    B. the worker is likely to devote an inordinate amount of time to case records at the expense of his clients
    C. the records are likely to be too lengthy and detailed, limiting their value for other important purposes
    D. the records are likely to be of little value for administrative and research purposes

12.____

13. A common obstacle to adequate recording in a large social work agency is the fact that many workers consider recording to be a time-consuming chore.
In order to obtain the cooperation of staff in keeping proper records, of the following, it is MOST important for an agency to provide

    A. indisputable evidence of the intelligent use of records as tools in formulating policy and improving service
    B. a system of checks and controls to assure that workers are preparing adequate and timely records
    C. adequate clerical services and mechanical equipment for recording
    D. sufficient time for recording in the organization of every job

13.____

14. The one of the following which is NOT a purpose of keeping case records in an agency is

    A. planning   B. research
    C. training   D. job classification

14.____

15. When a supervisor is reviewing the records of a worker, of the following, he should plan to read

    A. records of new cases only, following up each interview selectively
    B. the total caseload, in order to determine which aspects of the worker's performance should be examined
    C. those records which the worker has brought to the supervisor's attention because of the need for help
    D. a block of records selected according to the worker's need for help, and some records selected at random

16. The one of the following which is the PRIMARY purpose of the regular staff meeting in an agency is

    A. initiation of action in order to get the agency's work done
    B. staff training and development
    C. program and policy determination
    D. communication of new policies and procedures

17. Of the following, group supervision in an agency is intended as a means of

    A. strengthening the total supervisory process
    B. shifting the focus of supervision from the individual to the group
    C. saving costs in terms of time and manpower
    D. influencing policy through group interaction

18. The supervisor's job brings him closer to such limiting factors in the operation of an agency as faulty administrative structure, shortage of funds and lack of facilities, inadequacies in personnel practices, community pressures, and excessive workload.
    For the supervisor to make a practice of communicating to his subordinates his feelings of frustration about such limitations in the work setting would be

    A. *appropriate,* because the worker will be more understanding of the supervisor's burdens and frustrations
    B. *inappropriate,* because the climate created will block rather than further the purposes of supervision
    C. *appropriate,* because such communication will create a more democratic climate between the worker and the supervisor
    D. *inappropriate,* because the supervisor must support and condone agency policies and practices in the presence of subordinates

19. A suggestion has been made that the teaching and administrative functions of supervision should be separated, so that the supervisor responsible for teaching would not be responsible for evaluation of the same workers.
    The one of the following which is the MOST important reason for this point of view is that

    A. elements that confer on the supervisor a position of authority and power unduly threaten the learning situation
    B. teaching skill and administrative ability do aot usually go together
    C. a supervisor who has been responsible for training a worker is likely to be prejudiced in his favor
    D. performance evaluation and total job accountability should be two separate functions

20. In reviewing a worker's cases in preparation for a periodic evaluation, you note that she has done a uniformly good job with certain types of cases and poor work with other types of cases.
Of the following, the BEST approach for you to take in this situation is to

    A. bring this to the worker's attention, find out why she favors certain types of clients, and discuss ways in which she can improve her service to all clients
    B. bring this to the worker's attention and suggest that she may need professional counselling, as she seems to be blocked in working with certain types of cases
    C. assign to her mainly those cases which she handles best and transfer the types of cases which she handles poorly to another worker
    D. accept the fact that a worker cannot be expected to give uniformly good service to all clients, and take no further action

20.____

KEY (CORRECT ANSWERS)

1.	B	11.	B
2.	D	12.	A
3.	A	13.	A
4.	C	14.	D
5.	D	15.	D
6.	A	16.	A
7.	A	17.	A
8.	C	18.	B
9.	D	19.	A
10.	B	20.	A

TEST 2

DIRECTIONS: Each question or incomplete statement is followed by several suggested answers or completions. Select the one that BEST answers the question or completes the statement. *PRINT THE LETTER OF THE CORRECT ANSWER IN THE SPACE AT THE RIGHT.*

1. Of the following, the choice of method to be used in the supervisory process should be influenced MOST by the

    A. number and type of cases carried by each worker
    B. emotional maturity of the worker
    C. number of workers supervised and their past experience
    D. subject matter to be learned and the long range goals of supervision

2. In an evaluation conference with a worker, the BEST approach for the supervisor to take is to

    A. help the worker to identify his strengths as a basis for working on his weaknesses
    B. identify the worker's weaknesses and help him overcome them
    C. allow the worker to identify his weaknesses first and then suggest ways of overcoming them
    D. discuss the worker's weaknesses but emphasize his strengths

3. Assume that a worker is discouraged about the progress of his work and feels that it is futile to attempt to cope with many of his cases.
   Of the following, it would be BEST for the supervisor to

    A. suggest to the worker that such feelings are inappropriate for a professional worker
    B. tell the worker that he must seek professional help in order to overcome these feelings
    C. reduce the worker's caseload and give him cases that are less complex
    D. review with the worker several of his cases in which there were obvious accomplishments

4. The supervisor is responsible for providing the worker with the following means of support, with the EXCEPTION of

    A. interest and advice on his personal problems
    B. instruction on community resources
    C. inspiration for carrying out the work of the agency
    D. understanding his strengths and limitations

5. When a worker frequently takes the initiative in asking questions and discussing problems during a supervisory conference, this is PROBABLY an indication that the

    A. supervisor is not sufficiently interested in the work
    B. conference is a positive learning experience for the worker
    C. worker is hostile and resists supervision
    D. supervisor's position of authority is in question

6. When a supervisor finds that one of his workers cannot accept criticism, of the following, it would be BEST for the supervisor to

   A. have the worker transferred to another supervisor
   B. warn the worker of disciplinary proceedings unless his attitude changes
   C. have the worker suspended after explaining the reason
   D. explore with the worker his attitude toward authority

7. Of the following, the condition which the inexperienced worker is LEAST likely to be aware of, without the guidance of the supervisor, is

   A. when he is successful in helping a client
   B. when he is not making progress in helping a client
   C. that he has a personal bias toward certain clients
   D. that he feels insecure because of lack of experience

8. The supervisor should provide an inexperienced worker with controls as well as freedom MAINLY because controls will

   A. enable him to set up his own controls sooner
   B. put him in a situation which is closer to the realities of life
   C. help him to use authority in handling a casework problem
   D. give him a feeling of security and lay the foundation for future self-direction

9. A result of the use of summarized case recording by the worker is that it

   A. gives the supervisor more responsibility for selecting cases to discuss in conference
   B. makes more time available for other activities
   C. lowers the morale of many workers
   D. decreases discussion of cases by the worker and the supervisor

10. The distinction between the role of professional workers and the role of auxiliary or sub-professional workers in an agency is based upon the

    A. position within the agency hierarchy
    B. amount of close supervision given
    C. emergent nature of tasks assigned
    D. functions performed

11. Of the following, the MOST important source of learning for the worker should be

    A. departmental directives and professional literature
    B. his co-workers in the agency
    C. the content of in-service training courses
    D. the clients in his caseload

12. A client is MOST likely to feel that he is receiving acceptance and understanding if the social worker

    A. gets detailed information about the client's problem
    B. demonstrates that he realistically understands the client's problem
    C. has an intellectual understanding of the client's problem
    D. offers the client assurance of assistance

13. A client will be MORE encouraged to speak freely about his problems if the worker

    A. avoids asking too many questions
    B. asks leading rather than pointed questions
    C. suggests possible answers
    D. identifies with the client

14. A client would be MOST likely to be able to accept help in a time of crisis and need if the worker

    A. explains agency policy to him
    B. responds immediately to the client's need
    C. explains why help cannot be given immediately
    D. reaches out to help the client establish his rightful claim for assistance

15. It is a generally accepted principle that the worker should interpret for himself what the client is saying, but usually should not pass his interpretation on to the client because the client

    A. will become hostile to the worker
    B. should arrive at his own conclusions at his own pace
    C. must request the interpretation first
    D. usually wants facts, rather than the worker's interpretation

16. In evaluating the client's capacity to cope with his problems, it is MOST important for the worker to assess his ability to

    A. form close relationships
    B. ask for help
    C. express his hostility
    D. verbalize his difficulties

17. When a worker finds that he disagrees strongly with an agency policy, it is DESIRABLE for him to

    A. share his feelings about the policy with his client
    B. understand fully why he has such strong feelings about the policy
    C. refer cases involving the policy to his supervisor
    D. refuse to give help in cases involving the policy

18. Which of the following practices is BEST for a supervisor to use when assigning work to his staff?

    A. Give workers with seniority the most difficult jobs
    B. Assign all unimportant work to the slower workers
    C. Permit each employee to pick the job he prefers
    D. Make assignments based on the workers' abilities

19. In which of the following instances is a supervisor MOST justified in giving commands to people under his supervision?
    When

    A. they delay in following instructions which have been given to them clearly
    B. they become relaxed and slow about work, and he wants to speed up their production
    C. he must direct them in an emergency situation
    D. he is instructing them on jobs that are unfamiliar to them

20. Which of the following supervisory actions or attitudes is MOST likely to result in getting subordinates to try to do as much work as possible for a supervisor?
    He

    A. shows that his most important interest is in schedules and production goals
    B. consistently pressures his staff to get the work out
    C. never fails to let them know he is in charge
    D. considers their abilities and needs while requiring that production goals be met

---

KEY (CORRECT ANSWERS)

1.	D	11.	D
2.	A	12.	B
3.	D	13.	D
4.	A	14.	D
5.	B	15.	B
6.	D	16.	A
7.	C	17.	B
8.	D	18.	D
9.	B	19.	C
10.	D	20.	D

TEST 3

DIRECTIONS: Each question or incomplete statement is followed by several suggested answers or completions. Select the one that BEST answers the question or completes the statement. *PRINT THE LETTER OF THE CORRECT ANSWER IN THE SPACE AT THE RIGHT.*

1. One of your workers comes to you and complains in an angry manner about your having chosen him for some particular assignment. In your opinion, the subject of the complaint is trivial and unimportant, but it seems to be quite important to your worker.
   The BEST of the following actions for you to take in this situation is to

   A. allow the worker to continue talking until he has calmed down and then explain the reasons for your having chosen him for that particular assignment
   B. warn the worker to moderate his tone of voice at once because he is bordering on insubordination
   C. tell the worker in a friendly tone that he is making a tremendous fuss over an extremely minor matter
   D. point out to the worker that you are his immediate supervisor and that you are running the unit in accordance with official policy

1. _____

2. The one of the following which is the LEAST desirable action for an assistant supervisor to take in disciplining a subordinate for an infraction of the rules is to

   A. caution him against repetition of the infraction, even if it is minor
   B. point out his progress in applying the rules at the same time that you reprimand him
   C. be as specific as possible in reprimanding him for rule infractions
   D. allow a cooling-off period to elapse before reprimanding him

2. _____

3. A training program for workers assigned to the intake section should include actual practice in simulated interviews under simulated conditions.
   The one of the following educational principles which is the CHIEF justification for this statement is that

   A. the workers will remember what they see better and longer than what they read or hear
   B. the workers will learn more effectively by actually doing the act themselves than they would learn from watching others do it
   C. the conduct of simulated interviews once or twice will enable them to cope with the real situation with little difficulty
   D. a training program must employ methods of a practical nature if the workers are to find anything of lasting value in it

3. _____

4. In order for a supervisor to employ the system of democratic leadership in his supervision, it would *generally* be BEST for him to

   A. allow his subordinates to assist in deciding on methods of work performance and job assignments but only in those areas where decisions have not been made on higher administrative levels

4. _____

B. allow his subordinates to decide how to do the required work, interposing his authority when work is not completed on schedule or is improperly completed
C. attempt to make assignments of work to individuals only of the type which they enjoy doing
D. maintain control over job assignment and work production, but allow the subordinates to select methods of work and internal conditions of work at democratically conducted staff conferences

5. In a unit in which supervision has been considered quite effective, it has become necessary to press for above-normal production for a limited period to achieve a required goal. The one of the following which is a LEAST likely result of this pressure is that

   A. there will be more *griping* by employees
   B. some workers will do both more and better work than has been normal for them
   C. there will be an enhanced feeling of group unity
   D. there will be increased absenteeism

6. For a supervisor to encourage competitive feelings among his staff is

   A. *advisable,* chiefly because the workers will perform more efficiently when they have proper motivation
   B. *inadvisable,* chiefly because the workers will not perform well under the pressure of competition
   C. *advisable,* chiefly because the workers will have a greater incentive to perform their job properly
   D. *inadvisable,* chiefly because the workers may focus their attention on areas where they excel and neglect other essential aspects of the job

7. In selecting jobs to be assigned to a new worker, the supervisor should assign those jobs which

   A. give the worker the greatest variety of experience
   B. offer the worker the greatest opportunity to achieve concrete results
   C. present the worker with the greatest stimulation because of their interesting nature
   D. require the least amount of contact with outside agencies

8. A supervisor should avoid a detailed discussion of a worker-client interview with a new worker before the worker has fully recorded the interview CHIEFLY because such a discussion might

   A. cover matters which are already fully covered and explained in the written record
   B. make the worker forget some important detail learned during the interview
   C. color the recording according to the worker's reaction to his supervisor's opinions
   D. minimize the worker's feeling of having reached a decision independently

9. Some supervisors encourage their workers to submit a list of their questions about specific jobs or their comments about problems they wish to discuss in advance of the worker-supervisor conference. This practice is

   A. *desirable,* chiefly because it helps to stimulate and focus the worker's thinking about his caseload
   B. *undesirable,* chiefly because it will stifle the worker's free expression of his problems and attitudes

C. *desirable,* chiefly because it will allow the conference to move along more smoothly and quickly
D. *undesirable,* chiefly because it will restrict the scope of the conference and the variety of jobs discussed

10. An alert supervisor hears a worker apparently giving the wrong information to a client and immediately reprimands him severely.
For the supervisor to reprimand the worker at this point is poor CHIEFLY because

   A. instruction must precede correct performance
   B. oral reprimands are less effective than written reprimands
   C. the worker was given no opportunity to explain his reasons for what he did
   D. more effective training can be obtained by discussing the errors with a group of workers

11. The one of the following circumstances when it would generally be MOST proper for a supervisor to do a job himself rather than to train a subordinate to do the job is when it is

   A. a job which the supervisor enjoys doing and does well
   B. not a very time-consuming job but an important one
   C. difficult to train another to do the job, yet is not difficult for the supervisor to do
   D. unlikely that this or any similar job will have to be done again at any future time

12. Effective training of subordinates requires that the supervisor understand certain facts about learning and forgetting processes.
Among these is the fact that people GENERALLY

   A. forget what they learned at a much greater rate during the first day than during subsequent periods
   B. both learn and forget at a relatively constant rate and this rate is dependent upon their general intellectual capacity
   C. learn at a relatively constant rate except for periods of assimilation when the quantity of retained learning decreases while information is becoming firmly fixed in the mind
   D. learn very slowly at first when introduced to a new topic, after which there is a great increase in the rate of learning

13. It has been suggested that a subordinate who likes his supervisor will tend to do better work than one who does not.
According to the MOST widely held current theories of supervision, this suggestion is a

   A. *bad* one, since personal relationships tend to interfere with proper professional relationships
   B. *bad* one, since the strongest motivating factors are fear and uncertainty
   C. *good* one, since liking one's supervisor is a motivating factor for good work performance
   D. *good* one, since liking one's supervisor is the most important factor in employee performance

14. One factor which might be given consideration in deciding upon the optimum span of control of a supervisor over his immediate subordinates is the position of the supervisor in the hierarchy of the organization.
It is *generally* considered PROPER that the number of subordinates immediately supervised by a higher, upper echelon supervisor _____ the number supervised by lower level supervisors.

    A. is unrelated to and tends to form no pattern with
    B. should be about the same as
    C. should be larger than
    D. should be smaller than

15. The one of the following instances when it is MOST important for an upper level supervisor to follow the chain of command is when he is

    A. communicating decisions
    B. communicating information
    C. receiving suggestions
    D. seeking information

16. At the end of his probationary period, a supervisor should be considered potentially valuable in his position if he shows

    A. awareness of his areas of strength and weakness, identification with the administration of the department, and ability to learn under supervision
    B. skill in work, supervision, and administration, and a friendly, democratic approach to the staff
    C. knowledge of departmental policies and procedures and ability to carry them out, ability to use authority, and ability to direct the work of the staff
    D. an identification with the department, acceptance of responsibility, and ability to give help to the individuals who are to be supervised

17. Good supervision is selective because

    A. it is not necessary to direct all the activities of the person
    B. a supervisor would never have time to know the whole caseload of a worker
    C. workers resent too much help from a supervisor
    D. too much reading is a waste of valuable time

18. An important administrative problem is how precisely to define the limits of authority that is delegated to subordinate supervisors.
Such definition of limits of authority should be

    A. as precise as possible and practicable in all areas
    B. as precise as possible and practicable in areas of function, but should allow considerable flexibility in the area of personnel management
    C. as precise as possible and practicable in the area
    D. of personnel management, but should allow considerable flexibility in the areas of function
    E. in general terms so as to allow considerable flexibility both in the areas of function and in the areas of personnel management

19. Experts in the field of personnel relations feel that it is generally a bad practice for subordinate employees to become aware of pending or contemplated changes in policy or organizational set-up via the *grapevine* CHIEFLY because

    A. evidence that one or more responsible officials have proved untrustworthy will undermine confidence in the agency
    B. the information disseminated by this method is seldom entirely accurate and generally spreads needless unrest among the subordinate staff
    C. the subordinate staff may conclude that the administration feels the staff cannot be trusted with the true information
    D. the subordinate staff may conclude that the administration lacks the courage to make an unpopular announcement through official channels

20. Supervision is subject to many interpretations, depending on the area in which it functions.
    Of the following, the statement which represents the MOST appropriate meaning of supervision as it is known in social work practice is that it

    A. is a leadership process for the development of new leaders
    B. is an educational and administrative process aimed at teaching personnel the goal of improved service to the client
    C. is an activity aimed chiefly at insuring that workers will adhere to all agency directives
    D. provides the opportunity for administration to secure staff reaction to agency policies

21. A supervisor may utilize various methods in the supervisory process.
    The one of the following upon which sound supervisory practice rests in the selection of supervisory techniques is

    A. an estimate of the worker arrived at through current and past evaluation of performance as well as through worker's participation
    B. the previous supervisor's evaluation and recommendation
    C. the worker's expression of his personal preference for certain types of experience
    D. the amount of time available to supervisor and supervisee

22. It is the practice of some supervisors, when they believe that it would be desirable for a subordinate to take a particular action in a case, to inform the subordinate of this in the form of a suggestion rather than in the form of a direct order.
    In general, this method of getting a subordinate to take the desired action is

    A. *inadvisable;* it may create in the mind of the subordinate the impression that the supervisor is uncertain about the efficacy of her plan and is trying to avoid whatever responsibility she may have in resolving the case
    B. *advisable;* it provides the subordinate with the maximum opportunity to use her own judgment in handling the case
    C. *inadvisable;* it provides the subordinate with no clear-cut direction and, therefore, is likely to leave her with a feeling of uncertainty and frustration
    D. *advisable;* it presents the supervisor's view in a manner which will be most likely to evoke the subordinate's cooperation

23. A veteran supervisor noticed that one of her workers of average ability had begun developing some bad work habits, becoming especially careless in her recordkeeping. After reprimand from the supervisor, the investigator corrected her errors and has been doing satisfactory work since then.
For the supervisor to keep referring to this period of poor work during her weekly conferences with this employee would *generally* be considered poor personnel practice CHIEFLY because

    A. praise rather than criticism is generally the best method to use in improving the work of an unsatisfactory worker
    B. the supervisor cannot know whether the employee's errors will follow an established pattern
    C. the fault which evoked the original negative criticism no longer exists
    D. this would tend to frustrate the worker by making her strive overly hard to reach a level of productivity which is beyond her ability to achieve

23._____

24. Assume that you are now a supervisor in a specific unit. Two experienced investigators in your unit, both of whom do above average work, have for some time not gotten along with each other for personal reasons. Their attitude toward one another has suddenly become hostile and noisy disagreement has taken place in the office.
The BEST action for you to take FIRST in this situation is to

    A. transfer one of the two investigators to another unit where contact with the other investigator will be unnecessary
    B. discuss the problem with the two investigators together, insisting that they confide in you and tell you the cause of their mutual antagonism
    C. confer with the two investigators separately, pointing out to each the need to adopt an adult professional attitude with respect to their on-the-job relations
    D. advise the two investigators that should the situation grow worse, disciplinary action will be considered

24._____

25. It has long been recognized that relationships exist between worker morale and working conditions. The one of the following which BEST clarifies these existing relationships is that morale is

    A. affected for better or for worse in direct relationship to the magnitude of the changes in working conditions for better or worse
    B. better when working conditions are better
    C. little affected by working conditions so long as the working conditions do not approach the intolerable
    D. more affected by the degree of interest shown in providing good working conditions than by the actual conditions and may, perversely, be highest when working conditions are worst

25._____

KEY (CORRECT ANSWERS)

1.	A	11.	D
2.	D	12.	A
3.	B	13.	C
4.	A	14.	D
5.	D	15.	A
6.	D	16.	D
7.	B	17.	A
8.	C	18.	A
9.	A	19.	B
10.	C	20.	B

21. A
22. D
23. C
24. C
25. D

EXAMINATION SECTION
TEST 1

DIRECTIONS: Each question or incomplete statement is followed by several suggested answers or completions. Select the one that BEST answers the question or completes the statement. *PRINT THE LETTER OF THE CORRECT ANSWER IN THE SPACE AT THE RIGHT.*

1. Assume that you are a supervisor recently assigned to a new unit. You notice that, for the past few days, one of the employees in your unit whose work is about average has been stopping work at about four o'clock and has been spending the rest of the afternoon relaxing at his desk. The BEST of the following actions for you to take in this situation is to
   A. assign more work to this employee since it is apparent that he does not have enough work to keep his busy
   B. observe the employee's conduct more closely for about ten days before taking any more positive action
   C. discuss the matter with the employee, pointing out to him how he can use the extra hour daily to raise the level of his job performance
   D. question the previous supervisor in charge of the unit in order to determine whether he had sanctioned such conduct when he supervised that unit

1.___

2. A supervisor, newly assigned in charge of a small project, discovers that the previous supervisor and one of the employees supervised by him put all their business communications with each other in written form. The newly assigned supervisor finds that the employee is continuing to put his communications in writing and has requested that the supervisor do the same in order to prevent misunderstandings.
It would generally be BEST for the supervisor to
   A. accede to the request since the likelihood of misunderstandings will be reduced and since, as a newly assigned supervisor, he should not make changes until he is well established and accepted
   B. allow the employee to communicate with him in the way in which he chooses but refuse to communicate with the employee in writing except in cases where he would generally consider written communications to be desirable, on the grounds that too much of the supervisor's time would be wasted thereby
   C. inform the employee that neither one of them is to use written communications excessively in order to reduce the time consumed by communication but with the understanding that the employee may resort to writing in cases where he has serious reason to fear a misunderstanding

2.___

D. instruct the employee to cease the use of written communications in excess of the use of them by the other employees and refuse to accede to his request since the result would be excessive waste of time

3. A policy of direct crosswise communication on a project between a member of the management staff and a member of the maintenance staff of equal or superior status rather than following the chain of command upward through the manager and down through the top maintenance supervisor is a policy to be
   A. *discouraged*, primarily because it places responsibility where it does not belong and makes the quality of communication erratic and undependable
   B. *discouraged*, primarily because the manager and upper level supervisors will fail to receive the full information they need to make policy and administrative decisions
   C. *encouraged*, primarily because it results in decision making at the lowest practical level
   D. *encouraged*, primarily because it shortens the communication time and improves the quality of communication

4. A supervisor in a large department should be thoroughly familiar with modern methods of personnel administration. This statement is
   A. *true*; because this familiarity will help him in performing the normal functions of his office
   B. *false*; because in a large city personnel administration is not a departmental matter, but is centralized in a civil service commission
   C. *true*; because this knowledge will insure the elimination of personnel problems in a department
   D. *false*; because the departmental problems of a minor character are handled by the personnel representative, while major problems are the responsibility of the commissioner

5. The LEAST true of the following is that a supervisor in a large department
   A. executes the policy laid down by the commissioner or his deputies
   B. in the main, carries out the policies of the commissioner but with some leeway where his own frame of reference is determinative
   C. is never required to formulate policy
   D. is responsible for the successful accomplishment of a section of the department's program

6. In the supervision of young inexperienced investigators, the MOST important training task for the supervisor is to
   A. encourage investigators to make their own decisions about case problems
   B. give experience-based answers to various problems that arise in cases
   C. teach investigators how to analyze and assess important facts in order to make decisions about case problems
   D. teach investigators how to recognize evidence of mental breakdown

7. The supervisor is responsible for the accuracy of the work performed by his subordinates.
   Of the following procedures which he might adopt to insure the accurate copying of long reports from rough draft originals, the MOST effective one is to
   A. examine the rough draft for errors in grammar, punctuation, and spelling before assigning it to a typist to copy
   B. glance through each typed report before it leaves his bureau to detect any obvious errors made by the typist
   C. have another employee read the rough draft original to the typist who typed the report, and have the typist make whatever corrections are necessary
   D. rotate assignments involving the typing of long reports equally among all the typists in the unit

8. In the course of your duties, you receive a letter which, you believe, should be called to the attention of your superior.
   Of the following, the BEST reason for attaching previous correspondence to this letter before giving it to your superior is that
   A. there is less danger, if such a procedure is followed, of misplacing important letters
   B. this letter can probably be better understood in the light of previous correspondence
   C. your supervisor is probably in a better position to understand the letter than you
   D. this letter will have to be filed eventually so there is no additional work involved

9. The most successful supervisor wins his victories through preventive rather than through curative action.
   The one of the following which is the MOST accurate statement on the basis of this counsel is that
   A. success in supervision may be measured more accurately in terms of errors corrected than in terms of errors prevented
   B. anticipating problems makes for better supervision than waiting until these problems arise

C. difficulties that cannot be prevented by the supervisor cannot be overcome
D. the solution of problems in supervision is best achieved by scientific methods

10. Suppose that a stenographer recently appointed to your bureau submits a memorandum suggesting a change in office procedure that has been tried before and has been found unsuccessful.
Of the following, the BEST action for you to take is to
A. send the stenographer a note acknowledging receipt of the suggestion, but do not attempt to carry out the suggestion
B. point out that suggestions should come from her supervisor, who has a better knowledge of the problems of the office
C. try out the suggested change a second time, lest the stenographer lose interest in her work
D. call the stenographer in, explain the change is not practicable, and compliment her for her interest and alertness

11. Suppose that you are assistant to one of the important administrators in your department. You receive a note from the head of the department asking your superior to assist with a pressing problem that has arisen by making an immediate recommendation. Your superior is out of town on official business for a few days and cannot be reached. The head of the department, evidently, is not aware of his absence.
Of the following, the BEST action for you to take is
A. send the note back to the head of the department without comment so as not to incriminate your supervisor
B. forward the note to one of the administrators in another division of the department
C. wait until your supervisor returns and bring the note to his attention immediately
D. get in touch with the head of the department immediately and inform him that your superior is out of town

12. One of your duties may be to estimate the budget of your unit for the next fiscal year. Suppose that you expect no important changes in the work of your unit during the next year.
Of the following, the MOST appropriate basis for estimating next year's budget is the
A. average budget of your unit for the last five years
B. budget of your unit for the current year plus fifty percent to allow for possible expansion
C. average current budget of units in your department
D. budget of your unit for the current fiscal year

13. Suppose that you are acting as supervisor to an important administrator in your department.
Of the following, the BEST reason for keeping a separate *pending* file of letters to which answers are expected very soon is that
   A. important correspondence should be placed in a separate, readily accessible file
   B. a periodic check of the *pending* file will indicate the possible need for follow-up letters
   C. correspondence is never final, so provision should be made for keeping files open
   D. there is seldom sufficient room in the permanent files to permit filing all letters

14. In order to be BEST able to teach a newly appointed employee who must learn to do a type of work which is unfamiliar to him, his supervisor should realize that during the first stage in the learning process the subordinate is generally characterized by
   A. acute consciousness of self
   B. acute consciousness of subject matter, with little interest in persons or personalities
   C. inertness or passive acceptance of assigned role
   D. understanding of problems without understanding of the means of solving them

15. The MOST accurate of the following principles of education and learning for a supervisor to keep in mind when planning a training program for the employees under his supervision is that
   A. his employees, like all other individuals, vary in the rate at which they learn new material and in the degree to which they can retain what they do learn
   B. experienced employees who have the same basic college education and agency experience will be able to learn new material at approximately the same rate of speed
   C. the speed with which employees can learn new material after the age of forty is half as rapid as at ages twenty to thirty
   D. with regard to any specific task, it is easier and takes less time to break an experienced employee of old, unsatisfactory work habits than it is to teach him new, acceptable ones

16. A supervisor has been transferred from supervision of one group of units to another group of units in the same center. He spends the first three weeks in his new assignment in getting acquainted with his new subordinates, their caseload problems, and their work. In this process, he notices that some of the case records and forms which are submitted to him by two of the assistant supervisors are carelessly or improperly prepared.
The BEST of the following actions for the supervisor to take in this situation is to

A. carefully check the work submitted by these assistant supervisors during an additional three weeks before taking any more positive action
B. confer with these offending workers and show each one where his work needs improvement and how to go about achieving it
C. institute an in-service training program specifically designed to solve such a problem and instruct the entire subordinate staff in proper work methods
D. make a note of these errors for documentary use in preparing the annual service rating reports and advise the workers involved to prepare their work more carefully

17. A supervisor, who was promoted to this position a year ago, has supervised a certain assistant supervisor for this one year. The work of the assistant supervisor has been very poor because he has done a minimum of work, refused to take sufficient responsibility, been difficult to handle, and required very close supervision. Apparently due to the increasing insistency by his supervisor that he improve the caliber of his work, the assistant supervisor tenders his resignation, stating that the demands of the job are too much for him. The opinion of the previous supervisor, who had supervised this assistant supervisor for two years, agrees substantially with that of the new supervisor.
Under such circumstances, the BEST of the following actions the supervisor can take in general is to
A. recommend that the resignation be accepted and that he be rehired should he later apply when he feels able to do the job
B. recommend that the resignation be accepted and that he not be rehired should he later so apply
C. refuse to accept the resignation but try to persuade the assistant supervisor to accept psychiatric help
D. refuse to accept the resignation, promising the assistant supervisor that he will be less closely supervised in the future since he is now so experienced

17.___

18. Rumors have arisen to the effect that one of the social investigators under your supervision has been attending classes at a local university during afternoon hours when he is supposed to be making field visits.
The BEST of the following ways for you to approach this problem is to
A. disregard the rumors since, like most rumors, they probably have no actual foundation in fact
B. have a discreet investigation made in order to determine the actual facts prior to taking any other action
C. inform the investigator that you know what he has been doing and that such behavior is overt dereliction of duty and is punishable by dismissal

18.___

D. review the investigator's work record; spot check his cases and take no further action unless the quality of his work is below average for the unit

19. The one of the following instances when it is MOST important for an upper level supervisor to follow the chain of command is when he is
    A. communicating decisions
    B. communicating information
    C. receiving suggestions
    D. seeking information

19.___

20. In order to maintain a proper relationship with a worker who is assigned to staff rather than line functions, a line supervisor should
    A. accept all recommendations of the staff worker
    B. include the staff worker in the conferences called by the supervisor for his subordinates
    C. keep the staff worker informed of developments in the area of his staff assignment
    D. require that the staff worker's recommendations be communicated to the supervisor through the supervisor's own superior

20.___

21. Of the following, the GREATEST disadvantage of placing a worker in a staff position under the direct supervision of the supervisor whom he advises is the possibility that the
    A. staff worker will tend to be insubordinate because of a feeling of superiority over the supervisor
    B. staff worker will tend to give advice of the type which the supervisor wants to hear or finds acceptable
    C. supervisor will tend to be mistrustful of the advice of a worker of subordinate rank
    D. supervisor will tend to derive little benefit from the advice because to supervise properly he should know at least as much as his subordinate

21.___

22. One factor which might be given consideration in deciding upon the optimum span of control of a supervisor over his immediate subordinates is the position of the supervisor in the hierarchy of the organization.
    It is generally considered proper that the number of subordinates immediately supervised by a higher, upper echelon supervisor
    A. is unrelated to and tends to form no pattern with the number supervised by lower level supervisors
    B. should be about the same as the number supervised by a lower level supervisor
    C. should be larger than the number supervised by a lower level supervisor
    D. should be smaller than the number supervised by a lower level supervisor

22.___

23. An important administrative problem is how precisely to define the limits on authority that are delegated to subordinate supervisors.
Such definition of limits of authority should be
   A. as precise as possible and practicable in all areas
   B. as precise as possible and practicable in areas of function, but should allow considerable flexibility in the area of personnel management
   C. as precise as possible and practicable in the area of personnel management, but should allow considerable flexibility both in the areas of function and in the areas of personnel management
   D. in general terms so as to allow considerable flexibility both in the areas of function and in the areas of personnel management

24. The one of the following causes of clerical error which is usually considered to be LEAST attributable to faulty supervision or inefficient management is
   A. inability to carry out instructions
   B. too much work to do
   C. an inappropriate record-keeping system
   D. continual interruptions

25. Assume that you are the supervisor of a clerical unit in a large agency. One of your subordinates violates a rule of the agency, a violation which requires that the employee be suspended from his work for one day. The violated rule is one that you have found to be unduly strict and you have recommended to the management of the agency that the rule be changed or abolished. The management has been considering your recommendation but has not yet reached a decision on the matter.
In these circumstances, you should
   A. not initiate disciplinary action, but, instead, explain to the employee that the rule may be changed shortly
   B. delay disciplinary action on the violation until the management has reached a decision on changing the rule
   C. modify the disciplinary action by reprimanding the employee and informing him that further action may be taken when the management has reached a decision on changing the rule
   D. initiate the prescribed disciplinary action without commenting on the strictness of the rule or on your recommendation

KEY (CORRECT ANSWERS)

1. C
2. C
3. D
4. A
5. C

6. C
7. C
8. B
9. B
10. D

11. D
12. D
13. B
14. A
15. A

16. B
17. B
18. B
19. A
20. C

21. B
22. D
23. A
24. A
25. D

TEST 2

DIRECTIONS: Each question or incomplete statement is followed by several suggested answers or completions. Select the one that BEST answers the question or completes the statement. *PRINT THE LETTER OF THE CORRECT ANSWER IN THE SPACE AT THE RIGHT.*

1. As a supervisor, assume that a newly appointed employee is assigned to your unit.
   The one of the following which is likely to have the LEAST value in motivating the new employee when he first reports to you is
   A. an explanation of disciplinary measures which may be taken against employees
   B. indication by you that he can always come to you for help
   C. the first impression he gets of you and his fellow employees
   D. your emphasis on the importance of the work when interviewing him

   1.___

2. Assume that you are in charge of a unit of employees. A new appointee reports to you for the first time.
   Of the following, the MOST advisable action for you to take FIRST is to
   A. attempt to evaluate his attitude toward the work he will be required to perform
   B. discuss with him the general nature of the duties he is to perform
   C. explain the opportunities he will have for promotion within the department
   D. have him read over any available material pertaining to departmental rules and regulations for employees

   2.___

3. Your department conducts a formal training course for new appointees.
   Under these circumstances, a supervisor should assume that
   A. he can safely delegate all responsibility for any additional training required to one of his experienced men who will work with the new appointee in the field
   B. he is thus relieved of the effort required to train new appointees who may be assigned to his unit
   C. he will still be responsible for supplementary training of new appointees assigned to his unit
   D. his responsibility for training should be limited to making suggestions for improving the formal training program based on his observation of the work of new appointees

   3.___

4. In the development of an on-the-job training program, the FIRST step should be
   A. consideration of the cost of such a program
   B. consideration of the problem of interesting the workers in such a program
   C. determination of the training facilities which may be available
   D. determination of those areas in which training is required

5. Assume that a recent appointee has completed whatever basic training was provided for him. It becomes necessary to give him a special assignment for which he has not been specifically trained. He is given this assignment without any instructions as to how it should be carried out.
   This should be considered as
   A. *advisable* because a worker has to feel his own way on special assignments
   B. *advisable* because there comes a time when a worker should be encouraged to exercise his own initiative
   C. *inadvisable* because a worker needs guidance on any aspect of the job with which he is unfamiliar
   D. *inadvisable* because various superior officials of the department may have different ideas concerning the methods to be used in special assignments

6. Assume that you are holding a conference with the workers in your unit. During the conference, one of the employees, in an offensive manner, challenges a statement you make. You are reasonably sure but not certain that what you have said is correct.
   The MOST advisable action for you to take at the conference is to
   A. admit that you may be in error but reprimand the man for his manner of speaking
   B. avail yourself of the opportunity to point out to the group what constitutes bad manners
   C. ignore the man's manner but make sure that the group feels your statement is correct
   D. say that you will determine the correct facts as soon as possible and inform the staff

7. Suppose that a new inspectional procedure has been ordered by the chief of your bureau. You think that it may meet with some objection by your staff.
   As a unit supervisor, the MOST advisable action for you to take in order to minimize such resistance is to
   A. appoint a committee from your staff to study the procedure and report on its advantages and disadvantages
   B. discuss, at a staff conference, the intent of the new procedure and the means of carrying it out

C. inform the staff that this is an order coming from a higher authority and it must be carried out regardless of personal feelings
D. issue detailed instructions concerning the new procedure to each member of your staff

8. Suppose that at conferences with your staff, you find that, usually, only one of the men participates in the discussion.
Under these circumstances, the MOST advisable action for you to take is to
   A. speak to him privately and ask him to refrain from speaking so much at staff conferences
   B. stimulate the other men by asking them direct questions at staff conferences
   C. tell him directly, at conferences, that you would prefer to hear from the other men for a change
   D. use the technique of not looking at this man when asking questions in order to prevent him from *getting the floor*

9. Which of the following do you consider to be the MOST important factor to be considered in evaluating the work of an employee?
His
   A. ability to maintain good personal relationships with his supervisor, his fellow workers, and the community
   B. effectiveness in helping to carry out the objectives of the program
   C. observance of departmental rules and regulations governing employees
   D. personal awareness of the significance of his work to the welfare of the community

10. Of the following, the MOST valid statement concerning the supervisor and the probationary period is:
    A. Proper personnel selection methods should make it unnecessary for supervisory personnel to be concerned with evaluation of probationers
    B. Requiring an immediate supervisor to report on the capability of a candidate at the end of his probationary period is inadvisable since he usually has had no part in the initial selection of personnel
    C. The probationary period should be considered as an integral part of the personnel selection process and thus should be an active concern of immediate supervisors
    D. The value of a probationary period is likely to be greater when the supervisor is required to report only when he considers a candidate not suitable for permanent appointment rather when he is required to certify that a candidate is suitable

11. An employee under your supervision complains to you about   11.___
    the fact that you recommended him for a performance
    rating indicating merely satisfactory work. He feels
    that he deserves a higher rating, while you are convinced
    that your recommendation was justified.
    Of the following, the MOST advisable action for you to
    take is to
    A. advise him of his right to appeal the rating given
       and the required procedure for making such an appeal
    B. explain to him that, as a supervisor, your experience
       and your opportunity to evaluate his work against
       that of other employees enable you to give him a
       fair and just rating
    C. give him your specific reasons for considering his
       performance average or satisfactory and not qualify-
       ing for a higher rating
    D. point out to him that relatively few persons receive
       an above-average rating and that there is always
       opportunity for a higher rating in the future

12. Assume that your superior has assigned to your unit a   12.___
    special investigation which is to be completed by a
    certain date. Considering the regular work load, you
    feel that the investigation cannot be completed in the
    allotted time. You point this out to him but he insists
    that you handle the assignment without any increase in
    staff.
    Of the following, the MOST advisable course of action for
    you to take is to
    A. agree to undertake the assignment but insist upon
       some assurance that this situation will not be
       repeated
    B. be as noncommittal as possible with the determination
       to secure evidence to show that you should not be
       given the assignment
    C. take the matter up with higher authority but inform
       him that you have done so
    D. undertake the assignment with the intention to keep
       him closely informed concerning the progress of the
       work

13. Assume that, as a supervisor, you have received somewhat   13.___
    conflicting orders from two superiors not of equal rank.
    Of the following, the MOST advisable course of action for
    you to follow is to
    A. attempt to carry out the orders of each superior as
       far as you can
    B. carry out the orders of the person higher in rank
    C. consult your immediate superior concerning the situa-
       tion
    D. use your own judgment and follow those orders which
       seem more reasonable

14. Assume that you are a supervisor. Your immediate superior frequently gives assignments to your subordinates without your knowledge.
    Of the following, the MOST advisable way for you to handle this situation is to
    A. discuss it with your immediate superior
    B. instruct your staff that they are to accept assignments only from you
    C. keep a record of such instances and forward a memorandum concerning them to higher authority in the department
    D. realize and accept the fact that, as your superior, he has authority over you

15. Of the following, the one which would LEAST likely aid a supervisor in long range planning is
    A. a practical attitude of not worrying about possible problems until they arise
    B. estimating future needs on the basis of past experience
    C. obtaining early knowledge of contemplated changes
    D. staff conferences with the employees under his supervision

16. Of the following, the one that is likely to be of LEAST value as a direct source of help for a supervisor is
    A. a compilation of departmental rules and regulations
    B. a manual of standard operating procedures
    C. civil service rules and regulations
    D. the personnel officer of the department

17. Assume that you suspect that a field worker under your supervision goes home early in the afternoon. In spot checking one of his daily reports, you find that he has indicated that his last inspection was made at a certain establishment at 4 P.M. The owner of the establishment states that the inspection was made at 1 P.M.
    Of the following, the MOST advisable course of action for you to take FIRST is to
    A. attempt to determine whether any animosity exists between the owner of this establishment and the employee
    B. check with owners of establishments listed on the report as having been visited before the establishment in question was visited
    C. confront the employee with the information you have obtained from the owner of the establishment
    D. send a report of these circumstances to your immediate superior

18. Assume that one of the employees under your supervision is frequently absent. Although you have discussed the matter with him several times, his attendance record remains unsatisfactory.

The MOST advisable course of action for you to take NEXT is to
- A. discuss the problem again with the employee to see if any new factors have arisen which cause his continued absence
- B. give him another chance
- C. recommend that appropriate penalties be applied since the problem has already been discussed with him
- D. advise him to seek expert counsel concerning his personal problems

19. Assume that you are a supervisor. One of the men you supervise angrily demands an interview with you to discuss his dissatisfaction with his work assignment.
Of the following, the course of action you should take FIRST in this situation is to
- A. advise him to take the matter up with your superior
- B. arrange for a private interview as soon as possible to discuss his grievance
- C. explain to the employee that all assignments are made by you only after consideration of what is best for satisfactory accomplishment of the work of the unit
- D. promise the employee that you will review the work assignments in your unit to determine whether any changes are warranted

20. Of the following, the one which would likely aid a supervisor MOST in maintaining morale among his staff is
- A. ignoring any rumors that are transmitted through the organization's *grapevine*
- B. maintenance of an aloof attitude in his contacts with the group under his supervision
- C. scrupulous care in not revealing any information which the administration requests him to treat as confidential
- D. seeking, through consultation with his own superior, to find a remedy if situations outside of his division threaten to upset his own group

21. Of the following, the one which a supervisor should try to avoid MOST is
- A. consideration that rumors in the organization may contain some elements of truth
- B. handling of grievances which are voiced by his entire staff, as opposed to individual grievances
- C. offering personal counsel when it is requested of him by subordinates
- D. use of disciplinary measures to secure proper conduct of subordinates

22. Suppose that you are a supervisor. At a social function which you attend, unfavorable remarks concerning certain activities of your department are made in the course of conversation. You happen to be in agreement with what is being said.
    Under these circumstances, you should consider that
    A. it is best to be noncommittal in such situations
    B. it is necessary for you to convince the others of the value of these activities
    C. it would be advisable for you to suggest that those interested write a group letter of complaint to the department
    D. you are a private citizen as well as a public employee and therefore are free to express your personal opinion at a social function

23. Assume that you are a supervisor in charge of an inspectional unit. A merchant whose weighing and measuring devices were tested by one of the inspectors under your supervision takes the trouble to write a letter of complaint to the Commissioner of the department. In this letter he states that the manner in which the inspection was conducted gave customers in the store the impression that improper devices were being used although no violations were found. The letter is referred to you for appropriate action.
    Of the following, the MOST advisable action for you to take FIRST is to
    A. arrange for an inspector not known by the accused inspector to observe him in the field and report his findings to you
    B. call a staff meeting at which you will discuss proper procedures to be used when making inspections
    C. interview the inspector involved to get his version of the incident
    D. make personal observations, in the field, of the manner in which inspections are being conducted

24. In attempting to protect consumers against various types of fraud, the law states that, in certain instances, possession of a certain substance by a dealer is presumptive evidence of his intent to use it to defraud.
    From the point of view of the enforcing agency, the PRINCIPAL value of such legislation is that
    A. it offers more protection of the rights of the consumer than it does of the rights of the dealer
    B. such evidence, by its very nature, is superior to direct evidence
    C. the agency is relieved of the difficulties involved in attempting to obtain direct evidence
    D. this constitutes a more comprehensive definition of the offense involved

25. Departments of municipal government frequently suggest the enactment of legislation in fields in which they are interested.
Such suggestions are
   A. *advisable* because basic legislation is already available
   B. *advisable* because the departments have the best knowledge of their problems and needs
   C. *inadvisable* because the city already has a Law Department
   D. *inadvisable* because departments have biased viewpoints

25.____

KEY (CORRECT ANSWERS)

1. A
2. B
3. C
4. D
5. C

6. D
7. B
8. B
9. B
10. C

11. C
12. D
13. C
14. A
15. A

16. C
17. B
18. C
19. B
20. D

21. D
22. A
23. C
24. C
25. B

MENTAL DISORDERS AND TREATMENT PRACTICES

This section reviews eight areas that are usually tested on examinations:

- The Characteristics of Various Psychiatric Disorders
- The Needs of Special Groups (Children, Geriatrics)
- The Influences of Environment, Society, and Family on Psychiatric Disorders
- Psychotropic Drugs (Reactions and Uses)
- The Assessment and Evaluation of Patients
- The Functions and Purposes of the Treatment Team
- The Development and Implementation of the Treatment Plan
- Methods for Handling People with Various Emotional or Psychiatric Disorders

THE CHARACTERISTICS OF VARIOUS PSYCHIATRIC DISORDERS

It is often difficult to assign labels to human behavior with any large degree of accuracy. Behavior sometimes changes rapidly, and the interpretation of what behavior a label actually represents can vary greatly from one person to the next. One can often learn a great deal more about a person by observing their behavior than by reading a diagnostic label about that person. Regardless, diagnostic labels can be helpful to members of a treatment team as a shorthand method of describing a group of behaviors one might expect from certain individuals. They are also required for many insurance forms. A diagnosis may be useful as long as one views the diagnosis as an ongoing process, and can continue to look at the patient with *new eyes.*

The Difference Between Neurosis and Psychosis

People suffering from a neurosis are usually able to manage with the concerns of daily life, although there is often some distortion in their concept of reality. Those suffering from a neurosis may feel inferior, unloved, or have a long-term feeling of fear or dread. They may have obsessions, compulsions or phobias, but they are rarely dangerous to themselves or others. They usually have some insight into their problems, and except in severe cases, don't require hospitalization. Many go through life without obtaining any help for their problems. Those who experience a psychosis, however, are out of touch with reality and live in an imaginary world. They may hear voices, feel that they are being persecuted, or experience very deep depressions. There is a very definite split between the reality of those suffering from psychoses and the reality of the world. Unlike those suffering from neuroses, those suffering from psychoses often lose track of time, person, and place, and they have little insight into the nature of their behavior. They usually require hospitalization and their behavior is sometimes injurious to other people or themselves, although they may insist that there is nothing wrong with them.

Categories of Neurosis

It is important to keep in mind that rarely will all of a patient's symptoms fall into any one category, and that symptoms may change over time from one category to another. *Anxiety Neuroses* constitute approximately 35% of all neurotic disorders. Those suffering from anxiety neuroses have a tendency to view the world as hostile and cruel, and may frequently restrict daily activities in order to feel safer in their environment. They often feel tense, worried, and anxious, but are unable to articulate exactly why they feel this way. Many anxious individuals are very uncertain of themselves in even minor stress producing situations, and they may have real difficulties in concentrating because of their high anxiety levels.

Other symptoms may include strong anxiety reactions with difficulty catching one's breath, perspiration, increased heart beat, dizziness, and feeling that they are dying. They may come to the Emergency Room of a hospital complaining of a heart attack or heart troubles. It is important to keep in mind that many elements of the anxiety reaction are seen in patients with other neurotic disorders.

Conversion Reactions or *Hysteria* involve the loss of ability to perform some physical function that the person could previously perform, which is psychogenic in origin. This reaction is an attempt by the individual to defend herself or himself from some anxiety producing situation by developing physical symptoms that have no organic or physical cause. These reactions are not common, and constitute less than five percent of neurotic disorders. The lost function is often symbolically related to a situation which has produced stress or anxiety, and is often an attempt to escape from that situation. The person may lose the ability to hear or speak, have unusual bodily sensations, or lose control of some motor function. Since there is no physical cause of dysfunction, some people assume that the pain or paralysis is not real, or that this type of person is faking. *Dissociative Reactions* also serve to protect the individual from particularly stressful situations. Amnesia, fugue, and multiple personalities are the major categories of dissociative reactions. Despite the prevalence of *amnesia* on soap operas, dissociative reactions account for less than five percent of all neurotic disorders. Amnesiacs usually forget specific information for a specified but variable period of time. The patient does not, however, forget his or her basic lifestyle or habits. In *fugue,* the person combines the amnesia with flight, and leaves the area where the stressful situation is. Usually the person is unaware of where he or she has been, or where he or she is going. There are very few cases of *multiple personalities.* In this disorder, the person shows different ways of responding to the environment. Each individual personality within the person is a complete personality system, and may dominate the person's reactions to his or her environment, depending upon the situation.

Obsessive-Compulsive Reactions involve either the inability to stop thinking about something the person does not want to think about, or the obligatory performance of a repetitive act. People experiencing these reactions often recognize they are irrational, but are unable to stop doing them. They often attempt to rearrange their environment, which they may perceive as threatening, in an attempt to impose control and structure, so they can control their environment and feel safer. Those suffering from compulsive reactions feel a strong need to perform or repeat certain behaviors, often in order to prevent something terrible from happening to them. (This might involve pre-determined ways to enter a room, brush their teeth, get into bed, begin conversations, etc.) Of course, many people may exhibit aspects of this behavior. Observing some professional baseball players before they pitch or take a pitch can certainly demonstrate this point. There is little cause for concern if the patterns are relatively temporary and help the person in some way obtain their goal. When the behaviors begin to unduly restrict a person's activities, then the situation becomes more serious. People exhibiting this behavior are often unable to make decisions effectively, are often perfectionists, have a strong need for structure, and are fairly rigid. Those who are obsessed with unwanted thoughts may have quite a variety of areas that they think about. The most common areas, however, concern religion, ethical concerns (something being absolutely right or wrong), bodily functions, and suicide.

Phobic Reactions involve a strong, persistent irrational fear of an object, condition, or place. It is believed that phobias usually involve a displacement of anxiety from the original cause to the phobic object. The phobia serves to assist the individual in avoiding the anxiety-causing situation. Some of the most common phobias include fear of crowds, being alone, darkness, thunderstorms, and high places. It is often very difficult to discover the symbolic significance of a particular phobia.

Neurotic Depressive Reactions involve an intensification of normal grief reactions. Research has indicated that those suffering from this reaction are unable to *bounce back* from upsetting or discouraging events. People who suffer from this reaction tend to have a poor self-concept, exaggerated dependency needs, a tendency to feel guilty about almost anything, and to turn those guilt feelings against themselves in a highly punitive way. The possibility of suicide should be kept in mind when working with these patients.

Categories of Psychosis

Psychoses are generally divided into two categories, *functional psychoses* and *organic psychoses*. Functional psychoses are caused by psychological stress, while organic psychoses are caused by a disorder of the brain for which physical pathology can be demonstrated. A third category, *toxic psychoses,* is sometimes used to refer to psychotic reactions caused by toxic substances such as drugs or poisons.

Schizophrenia accounts for approximately 25 percent of all first admissions to mental institutions, and is the largest single diagnostic group of psychotic patients. The *paranoid schizophrenic* shows a great deal of suspiciousness and hostility, and may be very aggressive. The *simple type schizophrenic* is shy and withdrawn, and shows interest in his or her environment. The *hebephrenic schizophrenic* often has bizarre mannerisms and may appear quite manic. He or she may laugh and giggle inappropriately, and become preoccupied with unimportant matters. The *catatonic schizophrenic* may remain motionless for days or hours, and may refuse to eat. The two phases of catatonia are the *stuporous phase* where the person is motionless and *catatonic excitement* where the person is over-active and appears manic. While the catatonic schizophrenic may alternate between these two phases, most show a preference for just one. Someone suffering from *schizoaffective schizophrenia* will have significant thought disorders and mood variations. They may initially appear to be depressed or manic, but a basic personality disorganization also exists. These are the major categories of schizophrenia you should need for the exam. Since the exam announcement states basic knowledge is required, it is very possible some of the above categories may be too specific. We have included them just in case, however.

The general symptoms of schizophrenia include an inability to deal with reality, the presence of hallucinations or delusions, inappropriate emotions, autism and various other unusual behaviors. There is often a very noticeable inability to organize thoughts. Schizophrenic reactions that occur suddenly are referred to as *acute* schizophrenic reactions, while those that develop slowly over a rather lengthy period are called *chronic* schizophrenic reactions.

Paranoid Reactions in people account for less than one percent of psychiatric admissions. Those with this behavior usually mistrust the motives of everyone, are very resentful, and often hostile. They may show signs of grandiosity or persecution. The person often believes that whatever happens is related to him or her. The major difference between paranoid patients and paranoid schizophrenics is that the paranoid patient usually has better control of his or her thought processes, and is able to make more appropriate responses to situations. They are usually more reality-oriented, and able to state their feelings more effectively.

Affective Reactions are those that represent a change in the normal affect, or mood, of a person. There are two major categories of affective disorders: *manic-depressive reactions* and *involutional psychotic reactions.* In the manic-depressive reaction, the manic and depressive states alternate. In the manic phase, the person may be extremely talkative, agitated or elated, and demonstrate a great deal of physical and verbal activity. They may also exhibit some grandiosity. In the depressive phase, the person is joyless, quiet, and inhibited. The manic reactions are often divided into three degress of severity, each category representing a more severe degree of manic reaction. *Hypomania* is the least severe, *acute mania* is the next, and *delirious mania* is the most severe state. The term *involutional psychosis is* usually related to a patient's age. For women, the involutional age is considered to be somewhere between 40 and 55, and the involutional period for men is somewhere between 50 and 65. It seems that stresses are greater for men and women during these periods, and that these stresses may trigger psychotic reactions which are generally transient. These people generally have a long history of feeling guilty and very anxious, have little diversity of activity, and few sources of satisfaction in their lives.

<u>Selected Personality Disorders</u>

This category includes behavior which is maladaptive, but neither psychotic nor neurotic. This group includes *antisocial reactions,* the *abuse of alchol and other drugs,* and *sexual deviations.* The *antisocial* or *sociopathic* personality type fails to develop a concern for others and uses relationships to get what he or she wants. There is little or no concern about what effect their behavior might have on others, and they seldom feel remorse or guilt. They are often likable, friendly, intelligent people. Their relationships with others tend to be superficial, however, because they lack the capacity for deep emotional responses. The sociopath is often impulsive and seeks immediate gratification of his or her wants. He or she often is unreliable, untruthful, undependable and insincere. A large number of people have sociopathic traits which, as with most other characteristics, vary in severity and number. Sociopaths are found in all professions, although many are able to control their acting out behaviors or channel them in more socially acceptable ways. They avoid acting out not because of internal values, but because they do not wish to get caught. Sociopaths usually have a low frustration tolerance, are easily bored, and continually seek excitement. The sociopath most frequently comes to treatment because he or she has been *caught* doing something or been required to seek help by an employer or family member.

Sexual Deviations occur in those who fail to develop what their society considers appropriate sexual behavior. The major sexual deviations include child molestation, rape, sadism, masochism, voyeurism, fetishism, transvestism, exhibitionism, pedophilia, and incest. As you can see, some of these behaviors are much more harmful to other people than others are.

PSYCHOTROPIC DRUGS (REACTIONS AND USES)

The two major classifications of the psychotropic drugs are the tranquilizers, which are further divided into major (or anti-psychotic) and minor (or antianxiety) groups, and the antidepressants. Other drugs used include anticonvulsants, sedatives, hypnotics, and antiparkinsons.

Tranquilizers are meant to calm disturbed patients, and free them from agitation or disturbance. Drugs designed as *antipsychotic,* or *major tranquilizers,* also help to reduce the frequency of hallucinations, delusions, thought disorders, and the type of withdrawal seen in catatonic schizophrenia. It may take several days of drug therapy before the symptoms begin to subside, but during this time the patient becomes less fearful, hostile and upset by his disturbed sensory perceptions. The *phenothiazine derivatives* are the largest group of antipsychotic drugs. All the drugs in this group have essentially the same type of action on the body, but vary according to strength and the type and severity of their side effects. These drugs include:

Thorazine	Trilafon	Taractan
Mellaril	Compazine	Navane
Stelazine	Dartal	Sordinal
Prolixin	Proketazine	Haldol
Sparine	Tindal	Loxitane
Vesprin	Repoise	Moban

Serious side effects are very important to watch for. For these drugs, the phenothiazine derivatives, there are three major types of extrapyramidal symptoms (EPS): (1) akinesia - inability to sit still, complaints of fatigue and weakness, and continuous movement of the hands, mouth, and body; (2) pseudoparkinsonism -restlessness, mask-like facial expressions, drooling, and tremors; (3) tardive dyskenesia - lack of control over voluntary movements. Symptoms may include involuntary grimacing, sucking and chewing movements, pursing of the tongue and mouth, jerking of the hands, feet and neck, and drooping head. Immediate action must be taken to combat these side effects. The administration of antiparkinson drugs usually produces a dramatic reduction in symptoms. Unless spotted and treated early, however, these can become permanent.

Other side effects may include muscle spasms, shuffling gait, skin rash, eye problems, trembling hands and fingers, fainting, wormlike tongue movements, sore throat and fever, yellowing of skin or eyes, dry mouth, constipation, excessive weight gain, edema, a drop in blood pressure when moving from a lying to standing position, decreased sexual interest, sensitivity to light and prone to sunburn and visual problems, blurred vision, drowsiness, and increased perspiration. Just about any physical symptom or behavior could be caused by a reaction to a drug.

Special Considerations: Patients receiving a high dose of a phenothiazine drug should have their blood pressure checked regularly. Long exposures of skin to sunlight should be avoided (a wide-brimmed hat and long-sleeved clothing can also help). If a patient receiving phenothiazines is lethargic and wants to sleep a great deal, the dose of the drug may be too high and need adjustment. Patients on phenothiazines should not drive or use dangerous equipment. These drugs greatly increase the effects of alcohol. In the first three to five days, a person may feel drowsy and dizzy upon standing. Antipsychotic drugs tend to mask the symptoms of diseases and dictate that patients receiving them undergo thorough physical examinations every six months.

The *Minor Tranquilizers,* or *antianxiety drugs,* reduce anxiety and muscle tension associated with it. They are useful primarily with psychoneurotic and psychosomatic disorders. When given in small doses, they are relatively safe and have few side effects. Unlike the antipsychotic drugs, some of the antianxiety drugs tend to be habit-forming. If the drug is discontinued, the person may experience severe withdrawal symptoms, such as convulsions or delirium. These drugs include:

Librium	Milpath	Frienquel
Azene	Deprol	Phobex
Tranxene	Milprem	Softran
Valium	Miltown	Atarax
Ativan	Robaxin	Vistaril
Serax	Solacen	Trancopal

Side effects may include rashes, chills, fever, nausea, headaches, poor muscle coordination, some inability to concentrate, and dizziness. Excessive amounts of these drugs may lead to coma and death; however, death is less likely with an overdose of minor tranquilizers than with an overdose of barbituates. Patients taking these should be cautioned against driving or performing tasks that require careful attention to detail and mental alertness.

Antidepressants, such as the *Tricyclic Antidepressants,* are used to elevate the patient's mood, and increase appetite and mental and physical alertness. Drugs in this group tend to take one to four weeks of use before significant changes occur in the patient's outlook. Since these drugs sometimes excite patients instead of sedating them, patients must be observed closely for reactions. These drugs include:

Elavil	Sinequan
Endep	Tofranil
Asendine	Aventyl
Morpramin	Vivactil
Adapin	Marplan
Presamine	Janimine

Common side effects include dry mouth, fatigue, weakness, nausea, increased appetite, increased perspiration, heartburn, and sensitivity to sunlight. *Serious side effects* include blurred vision, constipation, irregular heartbeat, problems urinating, headache, eye pain, fainting, hallucination, vomiting, unusually slow pulse, seizures, skin rash, sore throat and fever, and yellowing of eyes and skin.

Serious side effects include blurred vision, constipation, irregular heartbeat, problems urinating, headache, eye pain, fainting, hallucination, vomiting, unusually slow pulse, seizures, skin rash, sore throat and fever, and yellowing of eyes and skin.

Monoamineoxidose Inhibitors (MAO Inhibitors) are sometimes used for depression, but can have *very* serious side effects, and can also lead to serious hypertensive crisis. Their use must be very closely monitored. Their use with some over-the-counter drugs can be very serious. Foods containing Typtophen or Tyramine (some examples: caffeine, chocolate, herring, beans, chicken liver, cheese, beer, pickles, wine) should be avoided also. *Side effects* to watch for include severe headaches, stiff neck, nausea, vomiting, dilated pupils, and cold, clammy skin. A hypertensive crisis requires *immediate* treatment. These drugs include: Marplan, Nardil, Parnate, and Ludiomil.

In addition to the above psychotropic drugs, sedatives, hypnotics, anticonvulsants, and antiparkinsons drugs are also used. Since the exam announcement includes uses and reactions of only the psychotropic drugs, we will not review the non-psychotropic drugs. We will mention, however, the use and reactions of *Lithium Carbonate* (also known as Eskolith, Lithane,

Lithobid, and Lithonate). This drug is primarily used in the treatment of manic depressive psychoses since it is effective in decreasing excessive motor activity, talking, and unstable behavior by acting on the brain's metabolism. It also decreases swings in mood. The correct dose is close to the overdose level for this drug, so it is important to watch closely for symptoms and to report them immediately. *Common side effects* include dry mouth, metal taste, slightly increased urination, hand tremors, increased appetite, and fatigue. *Serious side effects* include greatly increased urination, nausea, vomiting, diarrhea, loss of muscle coordination, muscle cramps or weakness, irritability, confusion, slurred speech, blackout spells, and coma. These side effects require medical attention. *Special Considerations:* This drug must sometimes be taken from one to several weeks before the resident feels better. Hot weather, hot baths, and too much exercise can be dangerous, as too much perspiring can lead to an overdose. The person should drink two to three quarts of fluid a day, but should not drink large quantities of caffeine-containing beverages like coffee, tea, or colas.

GLOSSARY OF TERMS
IN
MENTAL HEALTH, ALCOHOL ABUSE,
DRUG ABUSE, AND MENTAL RETARDATION

CONTENTS

	Page
A La Carte Rate .... Behavior Modification	1
Block .... Clinical or Counseling Psychologist	2
Clinical Research .... Death	3
Degree of Improvement .... Face-To-Face Group Interaction Contact	4
Face-To-Face Individual Contact .... General	5
Generalizable Research .... In-Service Education	6
Interaction Intensity .... Milieu Therapy	7
Mission .... Orientation Programs	8
Output Units .... Procedure	9
Program .... Psychological Evaluation and Testing	10
Psychological Technician .... Rehabilitation, Restoration, Habilitation Services	11
Research Or Program Analyst... .... Special Education And Tutoring Service	12
Rehabilitation, Restoration, Habilitation Services...... Socio-epidemiological research	13
Somatic Treatment .... Supply Officer	14
Support Transactions, Other .... United States	15
Unrelated Meetings, Conferences, Workshops .... Zip Code Area Or Zip Area	16

GLOSSARY OF TERMS
IN
MENTAL HEALTH, ALCOHOL ABUSE, DRUG ABUSE, AND MENTAL RETARDATION

A LA CARTE RATE: A rate based on a specific itemization of services received by arecipient (even though the cost value of such services may be based on the average).

ACCOUNTANT (fiscal officer): A person who works with or is in charge of accountingactivities.

ACCOUNTING: The systematic recording and summarizing of business and financial transactions and analyzing, verifying and reporting results. Includes patient accounts.

ACTIVE RECIPIENT: A recipient currently under, the status of receiving direct services in the first through fourth order of interaction.

ADJUSTMENTS TO REVENUE: Both positive and negative adjustments to revenues such as donated service discounts, contractual adjustments, administrative adjustments and allowance for bad debts.

ADULT ACTIVITY SERVICE: A service designed to involve patients and participants inpursuing hobbies, playing games, serving, cooking, etc. The distinction between this and vocational rehabilitation is that none of the skills acquired would qualify the patient for paid employment.

ADMINISTERING AGENCY: The individual, group or corporation appointed, elected or otherwise designated in which ultimate responsibility and authority are vested for the conduct of the program, organization or organizational unit.

ADMINISTRATIVE ASSISTANT: A person who assists an administrator or is assigned certain routine administrative tasks which assist the administrator.

ADMINISTRATIVE OFFICER, CHIEF: A person appointed by the administering authority who has responsibility for directing a program and managing the resources for it.

ADMINISTRATIVE RESEARCH: Systematic observations or studies of the operations of organizations or their parts in relation to specific categories of interest (models of decision-making, flow of information, human stress and organizational change).

ADMINISTRATIVE STAFF: Staff members who provide the intraorganizational services (functions or support services) to clinical staff and to the organization itself,

AFFILIATION: Working relationships between organizations which are developed through contracts or agreements (usually written) for exchange or provision of services, training of staff, scientific advancement, professional counsel or administrative support.

ALCOHOL OR DRUG ADDICTION COUNSELOR: An individual often having had personal experiences in alcohol or drug addiction who works in a variety of counseling capacities with alcohol or drug abuse programs.

AUTHORITY: The explicit official or legal power or sanction which furnishes the grounds or justifies the provider organization's program.

BASIC RESEARCH: Systematic observations or experiments regarding throught, emotion or behavior in general or in relation to specific categories of disability (i.e., schizophrenia, mental retardation).

BASIC PROFESSIONAL EDUCATION: Experiences provided as practicum, field experiences, internships, residency training, etc. as part of the basic formal education leading to a degree.

BEHAVIOR MODIFICATION: The modification of individual behavior through systematic application of learning theory and principles. Includes application of operant conditioning techniques--the Skinner-Lindsley principles of systematically strengthening certain responses and weakening others--and of behavior shaping through differential reinforcement.

BLOCK: A well-defined piece of land bounded by streets or roads, railroad tracks, streams, other features on a map, or by invisible political boundaries.

BLOCK GROUP: Combination of blocks, approximately equal in area, which do not cut across census tract lines.

BLOCKFACE: A boundary segment of a block. A city block has a blockface on each side, usually with a range of house or building numbers.

BOARD CERTIFIED PSYCHIATRIST: A fully trained psychiatrist who is certified by the American Board of Psychiatry and Neurology, Inc.

BOARD ELIGIBLE PSYCHIATRIST: A psychiatrist who is fully trained and experienced, but has not yet been certified by American Board of Psychiatry and Neurology, Inc.

BUDGETING: Planning and allocation of fiscal resources to own organizational units, services and activities.

BUILDING AND LAND: The land, off-site capital utility improvements, roads, sidewalks, on-site, capital improvement, and buildings which are available for use by the organisation for its activities, functions and program.

BUILDING EXPENSES: Building rental, repairs, depreciation, light, heat, water and related building and land operating expenses.

BUSINESS OFFICER: A person who directs the supportive and fiscal services for a mental health program. This includes budget preparation and paying and accounting, purchasing, supply and inventory control, etc. It often also includes supervising food preparation, housekeeping and maintenance operations.

CARE SERVICES: Services related to providing for generic human needs for shelter, food, income, transportation and supervision.

CASE REVIEW: Staff conferences and case discussions of review to determine the assignment or reassignment of cases and appropriateness of treatment. Includes formal utilization review.

CASE-ORIENTED CONSULTATION: Consultation, the purpose of which is to assist the con-sul- tee in providing services to a specific client (individual, family group or therapy group) of the consultee.

CATCHMENT AREA: Geographical division from which recipients are admitted to a specified mental health organization for services. This usually refers to an area served by an organization.

CENSUS TRACT: Small permanent areas into which large cities and adjacent areas have been divided for the purpose of showing comparable small-area statistics. <u>Census tract boundaries are determined by a local committee and approved by the Census Bureau.</u> Census tracts conform to county lines and are designed to be relatively homogeneous in population characteristics, economic status and living conditions. The average tract has about 4,000 inhabitants.

CHAPLAIN OR PASTORAL COUNSELOR: A clergyman with special training in counseling parsons with emotional problems.

CHARACTERISTICS OF RECIPIENTS OF INDIVIDUAL-ORIENTED SERVICES: The descriptive qualifiers which further classify the recipient or, which singly or in combination, will uniquely identify or describe him, or which show his relation to the organization at a specific time.

CHEMOTHERAPY: Treatment by the use of medications. Includes tranquilizers, anti-depressants, anticonvulsants, sedatives, etc.

CLINICAL PROGRAM ADMINISTRATOR: A person who has responsibility for directing a clinical program or unit. (Medical director, clinical director, unit director)

CLINICAL OR COUNSELING PSYCHOLOGIST: A practitioner trained in psychological techniques including personality, aptitude, intelligence or memory testing, therapy, counseling, behavior modification and research.

CLINICAL RESEARCH: Systematic experiments to determine the causes, treatments and rehabilitation of various disabilities.

COLLATERAL TREATMENT OR COUNSELING: Treatment of the patient through interviews beyond the diagnostic level with collateral persons, such interviews centering around the patient's problems without the patient himself necessarily seen. Includes treatment of a child by working with the parents or the treatment of an oldster by working through family members.

COMMUNITY CARETAKERS: Individuals such as clergymen, lawyers, or family physicians who enroll in educational activities provided by a mental health program.

COMMUNITY-ORIENTED SERVICES: Services provided to representatives of other organizations, individual practitioners or to the general public, related to alcohol abuse, drug abuse, mental retardation, mental health in general or to related aspects of their recipients or programs.

COMMUNITY-ORIENTED SERVICE RECIPIENTS: Individuals or agents to whom community-oriented services are provided. (Synonym: indirect service recipient) The recipients above may further be classified according to whether they are facilities/ agencies, organization/ groups or private practitioners, and may be identified by additional words specifying exactly which agency, group or individual in the community is referred to.

COMMUNITY PLANNING AND DEVELOPMENT: Participation as a representative of an alcohol, drug abuse, mental retardation or mental health organization with community leaders, organizations and citizen groups, to plan for the enhancement and enrichment of the community and develop solutions for community problems.

CONSULTATION: A process of interaction between a staff of the organization (consultant) and representative(s) of another organization or individual practitioner (consultee) to assist the consultee, to impart behavioral science knowledge, skills or attitudes, and to aid the consultee in carrying out his mission(s).

CONTINUING EDUCATION: Short courses, workshops, etc., to update or enhance the clinical competencies of staff.

CONTRACTUAL ADJUSTMENT: An adjustment based on the uncollectable value of service rendered to a recipient which represents the difference between the full established rates for individual services and lower contractual rates.

CONTRACTUAL EXPENSES: Services purchased from another organization.

COST-FINDING: A system or method of allocating and reallocating costs from a point of data collection or original expenditure into different sets or subsets of costs, to charge all relevant costsdirect, indirect, or unassignedto other organizational units or final producing cost centers.

COUNSELING PSYCHOLOGIST: A psychologist whose special competence is in counseling clients, testing the interests of and giving professional guidance to individuals.

COUNTY: A primary political and administrative division of a state. In Louisiana these divisions are called parishes. In Alaska there are no counties and census statistics are shown for its election districts which are equivalent to counties.

COUNTY-CITY-LOCAL FUND REVENUE: Revenue received as authorized by any act of county, city or multi-level boards; legislative or executive branches of such governments other than fees in payment for specific services rendered.

COUPLE THERAPY: Treatment of intimate partners but excluding other significant family members, children or siblings. Includes married and "unmarried" couples.

DATA MANAGEMENT: Information collection, analysis and use of data and information designed to monitor and assess the functioning of the program, including routine statistical reporting or recipient characteristics, costs, efficiency, community characteristics, service loads and program efforts.

DEATH: (Specify level at time of death.) A change by the fact of a person's dying while in a recipient-status.

DEGREE OF IMPROVEMENT: A judgment of the degree of change in the recipient's condition. This is the traditional way of classifying recipient's results.

DEPARTMENT: Organizational unit whose purpose is to provide administrative and supportive services tp the organization itself.

DETOXIFICATION: Treatment by use of medication, rest, fluids and nursing care to restore physiological function after it has been upset by toxic agents such as alcohol or barbiturates.

DIDACTIC: Formal teaching in context of lectures, seminars, case conferences.

DIRECT COSTS: The costs that are charged directly to the organizational unit originally making the expenditure, regardless of their later reallocation (if any) to other organizational units or final producing cost centers.

DISCONTINUATION: (Specify level or combination of levels recipient is leaving). A "discontinuation" refers to the change of a person, other than by death, by removal from, leaving or discontinuing a recipient-status directly or through another person acting for him, in a specified level in a mental health system.

DIVISION: Organizational unit whose primary purpose is to recipients other than the organization itself.

DOMICILIARY SERVICES: A supervised residential program to provide an individual with total living care.

DONATED SERVICE DISCOUNT: An adjustment based on the uncollectable value of servicerendered to recipients who are financially unable to pay full established rates.

DONATIONS: "Revenue" which represents free contributions from individuals, corporations, charitable organizations, united community chests, foundations and others, other than above.

DOWN TIME: Activities which are not productive of individual-oriented, community-oriented, intraorganization-oriented, or manpower training and education services.

DUAL RATE: A rate which explicitly includes both 1) a fixed inclusive rate element unique to the type of service or program and 2) an a la carte rate element specific to the amount of time or specifically prescribed procedures or transactionr provided the recipient.

DUAL RESOURCE AFFILIATIONS: a) Contractee pays salaries or operating expenses of affiliate's organization for work or use at the affiliate's site; b) contractee's own staff, equipment, or materials are authorized for work or use at the affiliate's site.

EDUCATION AND VOCATIONAL EVALUATION: Evaluation to determine an individual's academic or vocational interests, aptitude, achievements.

ENUMERATION DISTRICT (ED): An area with small population (averaging 700) defined by the Census Bureau and used for the collection and tabulation of population and housing census data.

EQUIPMENT: The fixed, major movable or minor machinery, fixtures, articles, vehicles,apparatus, "things" and furniture which have a relatively long useful life and are not consumed in the course of a program.

EQUIPMENT EXPENSES: Equipment used, rental, repairs and depreciation expenses.

EVALUATIVE RESEARCH: Utilization of scientific research methods and techniques or the purpose of evaluating a program.

EXPENSES: The amount of resources, expressed in money, consumed in producing a service or carrying on an activity. (The service potential of the resources has been released and transformed into an expense.)

FACE-TO-FACE CONGREGATE COMMUNITY SESSION: Contact through continuous face-to-face group life or group living in a structured community setting.

FACE-TO-FACE GROUP INTERACTION CONTACT: Contact through face-to-face interaction, in person, with two or more people in which group interaction is one of the primary outcomes planned.

FACE-TO-FACE INDIVIDUAL CONTACT: Contact through face-to-face interaction with individuals and small groups (two, three or four people) where group interaction is not planned.

FACE-TO-FACE PRESENTATION TO GROUPS: Contact through lecture, speech or presentation to groups, where group interaction is not necessarily or primarily intended.

FACILITY: The plant, including buildings, grounds, supplies and equipment which are used or occupied by the organization or one of its units.

FACILITY MANAGEMENT: Day-to-day operations of the buildings, offices and grounds, including the maintenance, housekeeping, feeding, logistics, supply and related activities.

FAMILY TREATMENT OR COUNSELING: Treatment applied to the family as a unit. (All or significant members of the family are considered as recipients. This excludes groups of families and/or groups of married couples.)

FEDERAL FUND REVENUE: Revenue received as authorized by any act of Congress or the Executive Branch of the federal government, other than fees in payment for specific services rendered.

FEE: The net charge, expressed in money, which represents that portion of the set rate (9-E), plus or minus adjustments, if any, which ip billed to the recipient or third party payer.

FEE-FOR-SERVICE AFFILIATIONS: a) Affiliate directly bills the recipient or third party payer but receives no payments from the contractee; b) affiliate bills contractee, who in turn may or may not bill recipient or third party payer.

FEES FOR SERVICE: Revenue earned from charges made to recipients of services of the organization, including that portion paid by third party payers such as Medicare, Medicaid, compensation insurance, commercial insurance and other payers. This includes contract fees.

FIFTH ORDER INTERACTION: Intermittent delivery of services to a recipient on suspended, postponed or inactive status. Includes persons on waiting list, long term leave, provisional discharge or in a prepayment program status.

FIRST ADDITION: (Specify level or combination of levels coming into.) A "first addition" refers to the change of a person from Having had no prior recipient-status in a specified level in a mental health system to having current recipient status.

FIRST ORDER INTERACTION: Continuous delivery of services to a recipient pn a 24-hour basis in the service setting. Includes inpatient and resident care status.

FIXED COSTS: The costs which remain constant in total amount regardless of the level or fluctuation in the volume of program activity.

FIXED FEE AFFILIATIONS: a) Affiliate bills contractee at a <u>fixed fee</u> per calendar period regardless of services provided to recipient; b) affiliate-bills contractee at a <u>fixed rate</u> or <u>per cent</u> per calendar period, based on a variable such as staff hours expended, per cent bed occupancy, or other indirect indicator; c) contractee pays affiliate a <u>lump-sum</u> one-time payment for the performance of services.

FOURTH ORDER INTERACTION: Intermittent or brief services to a recipient on an unscheduled or casual contact basis. Includes walk-in contacts, unscheduled consultations and telephone calls status.

FULL RATE: The full established cost value, expressed in dollars, of the services rendered to recipients.

FUND RAISING: Promoting or lobbying for allocation of funds for own programs.

FUND REVENUE, OTHER: Revenue, other than donations, received from any other source than fees, federal, state, or local government sources, including gains on sale of assets, interest earned and miscellaneous other income, other than fees in payment for specific services rendered.

GENERAL (and special): "General" refers to facilities that provide treatment and care to persons who have a variety of medical conditions (e.g., a general hospital); "special" refers to facilities that provide treatment and care to persons who have specified medical conditions (e.g., a psychiatric hospital).

GENERALIZABLE RESEARCH: The study activities performed by staff of the organization for the production of scientific knowledge through testing of theories where it is the intent to follow scientific principles so that finding may be generalized beyond the immediate data or situation, or where the findings may be so general as to be only remotely germane to the immediate situation.

GEOGRAPHIC AREA RESIDENTS: The inhabitants of the total or subdivisions of the country who can be specified as living within identifiable boundaries.

GOAL (objective): A reality-constrained, time-specific, problem-oriented statement which specifies the desired change or end-state which an organization seeks to bring about. (Example: To educate all Portage County residents arrested for driving while under the influence of alcohol)

GOAL ATTAINMENT: Goals are set for each individual or community. Goals may be set in various terms such as "resolution of problems," "full employment," "independent social living," "reduced incidence of truancy." The extent to which the goal has been attained is then rated.

GROUP TREATMENT OR COUNSELING: Treatment by the use of group dynamics or group interaction. Includes group psychotherapy, group psychoanalysis, group play therapy, psychodrama, groups of families and/or groups of married couples, but excludes family therapy and group orientation, group intake or group diagnostic procedures.

HEARING EVALUATION: An evaluation to determine the cause and extent of hearing disorders and need for corrective work.

INACTIVE RECIPIENT: Individual for whom the organization has a defined responsibility by virtue of;contract or charge (HMO, group-insurance, welfare, clients, etc.) but who is not currently active or receiving services.

INCLUSIVE RATE: A periodic uniform rate, with variation for major type of service or program, established without regard to the specific level of utilization and without specific itemization of services received by a recipient.

INCOME MAINTENANCE: A service designed to provide the recipient with sufficient money or in-kind income to maintain a reasonable standard of living.

INDIGENOUS WORKER: A person whose primary qualification is his personal experience in the culture of the persons he serves, who works in a variety of counseling and behavior changing techniques in mental health programs or as an advocate for the clients of such programs.

INDIRECT COSTS: The costs that are reallocated from the organizational unit originally making the expenditure to another organizational unit which controls or influences the cost.

INDIVIDUAL TREATMENT OR COUNSELING: Treatment by individual interview. Includes supportive psychotherapy, relationship therapy, uncovering or insight psychoanalysis, counseling, play therapy, hypnotherapy (with or without the use of drugs) and casework treatment.

INDIVIDUAL-ORIENTED SERVICES: Services provided directly to a specific client (individual, collateral, family group or therapy group) in relation to their own positive mental health or to their own alcohol abuse, drug abuse, mental retardation or mental disorder problem.

INDIVIDUAL-ORIENTED SERVICE RECIPIENTS: Individuals for whom help is sought, families, collateral persons, therapy groups.

INFORMATION: Services which provide information about availability of services. Such services include crisis and information centers, 24-hour emergency (non face-to-face services and similar activities.

INFORMATION, SCREENING, REFERRAL: Services related to the availability, linkage, recipient's eligibility or suitability for own or other's programs.

IN-SERVICE EDUCATION: A systematic preparation of staff for the basic work they will perform in the agency.

INTERACTION INTENSITY: Degree of involvement and continuity between the recipient and provider of service.

INTERSTATE AREA: Combination of areas from two or more states such as Mid-Atlantic, East South Central, etc.

INTRAORGANIZATION SUPPORT FUNCTIONS: The activities or functions performed by or for the organization in which the direct recipient is the organization itself, and directed toward the support, maintenance and development of the organization itself.

INTRASTATE PLANNING AREA: A region within a given state usually comprising one or more counties with the division such that natural boundaries such as rivers or mountain ranges tend to give a certain economic or geographic homogeneity.

LAW: A statute enacted by a legislative branch, including the body of common law developed from judicial branch decisions, which expresses the binding custom, practice, conduct or action of an authority.

LEGAL STATUS: The legal authority, if any, by which a recipient enters and is held in a service-receiving status; there is considerable variation from state to state by differing statues. (Synonym: type of commitment)

LICENSED PRACTICAL OR LICENSED VOCATIONAL NURSE: A licensed nurse who has one year of practical nursing training.

LONG-TERM FACILITY: A long-term facility is defined as one in which over 50 percent of all patients admitted stay more than 30 days. However, in facilities such as residential drug units, different time durations may constitute long-term.

MANPOWER TRAINING ORIENTED SERVICES: A structured educational process of imparting job-related knowledge, skills and attitudes to individual practitioners and members of your own or of other organization (regular staff, volunteers, students or indigenous workers), to directly increase the recipient(s) knowledge, skills, attitudes or work effectiveness.

MANUAL, PHYSICAL AND RELATED TRANSACTIONS: Physical operation of equipment, machines, tools or appliances or physical handling of materials, supplies and other objects.

MEAL SERVICE: A service designed to provide the necessary food and nutritional requirements of the recipient in prepared meal.

MEDICAL SPECIALIST, OTHER: A physician who is specially trained or certified in one of the various specialties—radiologist, internist, pathologist, etc.

MEDICAL-SURGICAL SERVICE, OTHER: Other medical, dental or surgical procedures directed to general physical health.

MENTAL HEALTH AIDE OR ASSISTANT: A New Careers level mental health worker with only in-service education or technical school education who works in a community mental health program under the supervision of professionals.

MENTAL HEALTH MANPOWER TRAINING RECIPIENTS: Individuals, groups or organizations who receive the educational and training services of a program.

MENTAL HEALTH NURSE: A registered nurse who specializes in working with communities about the public health aspects of persons with emotional problems or about the prevention of such problems.

MENTAL HEALTH TECHNICIAN (mental health associate): A person with 1 or 2 years of formal training (perhaps an associate degree) who carries out a range of individual and community-oriented services in mental health programs.

MENTAL HEALTH WORKER: A paraprofessional worker with an associate degree or other training or experience in mental health who performs a variety of techniques on behalf of patients and their families either in institutions or in communities. These persons work in an organized system under the general supervision of other mental health professionals.

MILIEU THERAPY: Treatment by a structured total physical, psychological and social environment to meet the needs of the individual or group of recipients.

MISSION: A general group of program objectives which have one or more characteristics in common. (Example: alcohol preventive mission)

MONEY: Cash, investments, receivables, and budgeted-to-be-received operating funds which are available for use by the organization for its activities, functions andprogram.

MOVEMENT CHANGES OF RECIPIENT OF INDIVIDUAL-ORIENTED SERVICE: The progress of an individual in or out of a system, from one recipient category to another, or from one program, organizational unit, site or interaction intensity status to another.

MUTUAL INTEREST AFFILIATIONS: a) Contractee and affiliate, in consortium, receive operating or capital construction monies from a common funding agency based on agreement to cooperate in their mutual use; b) contractee and affiliate share salaries and other operating or capital expenses to perform work of benefit to each or to mutual recipients; c) eachthe contractee and affiliatebears own expenses with no exchange of monies, but agree to the free flow of recipients between them, the sharing of records and information, and the continuance of staff responsibility for recipients regardless of location.

NEUROLOGICAL EVALUATION: A complete examination of the central, peripheral and sympathetic nervous system, noting observations and findings supplemented by diagnosis, if indicated.

NEUROLOGIST: A physician who is specially trained in the diagnosis and treatment of diseases of the nervous system.

NEWSPAPERS, MAGAZINES: Contact through mass media messages in newspapers, magazines,journals, newsletters and other regular or special news publications.

NON-WORK ACTIVITIES: Activities that do not directly relate to the staff's^ responsibilities or the organization's programs, objectives or goals.

NURSE: A practitioner of nursing who is registered or licensed in nursing by state law.

NURSE, REGISTERED: A nurse who is registered to practice nursing by a state board of nurse registration.

OBJECTIVE (goal): A concise description of a desired end state sought at a specified future point in time, related to a human need. (Example: reduce alcohol-related motor vehicle deaths 20% by 1975.)

OCCUPATIONAL THERAPIST:, A practitioner trained in occupational therapy who uses arts and crafts techniques in the treatment and rehabilitation of patients.

OFF DUTY OR DOWN TIME ACTIVITIES: Sick leave, vacation, compensatory time off, mealor break time activities, waiting and other personal non-work activities.

ON CALL: Prearranged waiting, holding oneself available for potential demands or requests for services.

ON LEAVE: Time spent away from work while on vacation, sick leave, compensatory time, administrative leave, military leave, jury duty and miscellaneous absences or tardinesses.

OPERATING EXPENSES, OTHER: Printing, publications, subscriptions, dues, fees, licenses and other related expenses.

OPERATING SUPPLIES: Supplies, articles and materials used and related expenses.

ORGANIZATION: An administrative and functional structure and a grouping of persons within that structural entity defined by law, charter, license, contract and agreement to carry out enunciated purposes or missions.

ORGANIZATIONAL UNIT: A component of the organization established for the delivery of services to which specific resources are assigned.

ORGANIZING: Establishing conceptual relationships among component staff and units of the organization, services and resources, as a necessary precedent to action.

ORIENTATION PROGRAMS: Orientation to the objectives and procedures of the agency.

OUTPUT UNITS: Amounts of services provided expressed in terms of adopted units of services reflecting the costs of resources expended.
PERSON HOURS: Hours and minutes of staff time expended.
PERSONAL: Activities related to coffee, lunch and rest breaks.
PERSONAL ADJUSTMENT TRAINING: Provision of training in self-help and motor skills, habit training, self-care training, toilet training, activities of daily living and social development preliminary to special education or other placement.
PERSONAL CARE: A service designed to assist a recipient perform the routine tasks of daily living such as bathing, hair care, mouth care, feeding, personal hygiene, toileting, shaving, dressing, grooming and escorting on foot.
PERSONNEL: The clinical and administrative staff employees, volunteers, consultants and residents/students-in-placement who are available to perform the activities and functions of a program.
PERSONNEL EXPENSES: Salaries and wages, employee benefits and consultant fee expenses.
PERSONNEL OFFICER: A person who recruits staff, prepares payrolls, maintains personnel records, manages grievance procedures and performs related personnel functions.
HYSICAL EVALUATION: A complete examination of the body noting observations and findings, supplemented by diagnosis, if indicated.
PHYSICIAN: An individual who is licensed to practice medicine.
PHYSICIAN, GENERAL: A physician who is licensed to practice general medicine.
PLANNING AND EVALUATION OFFICER: A person who estimates, projects and identifies trends and needs of the program and the community, initiates plans for program changes to meet.these needs and evaluates the degree of success in meeting needs.
POLICY: A statement of philosophy and direction which guides the conduct of the organization.
POTENTIAL RECIPIENT AT LARGE: Individual who has no relationship to the organization unless or until a situation arises for which services are required. (i.e., catchment area target population)
POTENTIAL RECIPIENT CONTACT: A recipient under the status of receiving information/screening/referral services. (Synonym: information-referral-screening recipient, inquirer, pre-patient.
PRACTICUM: Supervision and informal teaching of trainees in the course of their assigned experience with recipients (including rounds, team meetings).
PREPARATION FOR TRAINING: Course design, preparation for presentations, reading.
PRESENTING PROBLEM: This is typically presented from the viewpoint of the client rather than from in-depth psychopathological interpretation of staff: work, social relations, physical complaints, sexuality, suicide, anxiety/depression, alcohol drug abuse, psychopathologic symptoms, etc.
PROBLEM EVALUATION, EXAMINATION, ASSESSMENT: Services related to identifying the detailed nature and extent of the recipient's condition and formulating a plan for services.
PROBLEM EVALUATIONS, OTHER: Many other problem evaluations not unique to mental health are also provided (e.g., laboratory, dental, electroencephalogram, etc.).
PROBLEM RESOLUTION: The presenting problem of individuals or the community are categorized and rated as to whether the problems have been mitigated. (Example: less frequent bed wetting, decreased suicidal rate)
PROCEDURE: A particular series of operational steps to be followed in order to implement a policy.
PROGRAM: A set of related organizations, resources, and/or program transactions directed to the accomplishment of a defined jset of objectives for a specified target population or a specified geographic area.

PROGRAM AND ORGANIZATION DEVELOPMENT: Sessions for developing and implementing new program directions for the agency.

PROGRAM APPROPRIATENESS: The extent to which programs are directed toward those problems that are believed to have the greatest importance, based on the philosophy and the value systems of decision-makers.

PROGRAM CLINICAL STAFF AND TECHNOLOGISTS: Staff members who are licensed or otherwise qualified to provide individual-oriented, community-oriented, manpower development or research services of the program.

PROGRAM EFFICIENCY: The cost in resources of attaining objectives; the relationship between effort and effect, or input and output; evaluation in terms of cost (money, time, personnel, public convenience); a ratio between effort and achievement, the capacity of an individual, organization, facility, operation or activity to produce results in proportion to the effort expended.

PROGRAM EFFECTIVENESS: The extent to which pre-established program objectives are attained as a result of program activity; the results of effort relative to an immediate goal; the degree or extent to which success is achieved in resolving a' problem.

PROGRAM EFFORT: The quantity and quality of activity that takes place or of resources that are consumed.

PROGRAM EVALUATION: Determining the degree to which a program is meeting its objectives, the problems it is encountering and the side effects it is creating.

PROGRAM OUTCOME: The effects achieved for a target population by a program.

PROGRAM PLANNING: The process of designing and adjusting the organization's program activities and services to its program purposes, objectives, goals and priorities.

PROGRAM PURPOSE: A general statement of intent about a range of human needs or problems of a target population to which an organization addresses its services.

PROGRAM SIDE EFFECTS: All effects of program operation other than attainment of objectives. These side effects may be desirable or undesirable and may be anticipated or unanticipated.

PROGRAM-ORIENTED CONSULTATION: Consultation, the purpose of which is to assist the consultee in planning and developing his program or in solving his own program system problems.

PSYCHIATRIC AIDE, PSYCHIATRIC TECHNICIAN OR ATTENDANT: A worker who provides ward level psychiatric care and treatment to mental patients often under supervision of a nurse after a period of inservice training.

PSYCHIATRIC EVALUATION: The psychodiagnostic process, including a medical history and mental status, which notes the attitudes, behavior, estimate of intellectual functioning, memory functioning, orientation and an inventory of the patient's assets in a descriptive (but not an interpretative) fashion; impressions and recommendations.

PSYCHIATRIC NURSE: A registered nurse who specializes in working with psychiatric patients.

PSYCHIATRIC RESIDENT: A physician still in specialty training to become a psychiatrist.

PSYCHIATRIC SOCIAL WORKER: A social worker who specializes in work with mental patients and their families.

PSYCHIATRIST: A physician who is trained in the diagnosis and treatment of mentaldisorders.

PSYCHOANALYST: A psychiatrist who has special training in and uses the technique of psychoanalysis with his clients.

PSYCHOLOGICAL EVALUATION AND TESTING: The evaluation of cognitive processes and emotions and problems of adjustment in individuals or in groups, through interpretation of tests of mental abilities, aptitudes, interests, attitudes, emotions, motivation and personality characteristics, including the interpretation of psychological tests of individuals.

PSYCHOLOGICAL TECHNICIAN: A person trained in psychology who performs limited psychological functions under rather close supervision.

PSYCHOMETRIST: A psychologist who specializes in tests of measurement such as intelligence tests.

PSYCHOSOCIAL EVALUATION: The determination and examination of the social situation of the individual related to family background, family interaction, living arrangements, psycho-/or socioeconomic problems, treatment evaluation and statement of future goals and plans.

PUBLIC INFORMATION AND PUBLIC EDUCATION: A one-way educational process of imparting knowledge to and changing attitudes of the general public, segments of the population or special target groups to increase understanding of positive mental health and mental disorder and availability of resources.

PUBLIC INFORMATION OFFICER: A person who prepares and disseminates information regarding the program for the public media, the general public and for special publics. He may also have public relations responsibilities for assuring an accurate image of the program.

PUBLIC RELATIONS: Activities for developing reciprocal understanding and goodwill between the organization and the public, other organizations, and other alcohol, drug abuse, mental retardation and mental health programs.

PURCHASING AGENT: A person who purchases supplies and equipment.

READDITION: (Specify level or combination of levels coming into.) A "readdition" refers to the change of a person (who has had prior recipient-status on a specified level in a mental health system) from no immediate prior recipient-status to having current recipient-status.

RECIPIENT: A person, family, collateral person, group, organization or general public who receives or is eligible for the services of a specified organization by virtue of membership in the largest population.

RECIPIENT DAYS (patient days): Days (or fractions) of recipient (patient) time expended.

RECIPIENT OF MANPOWER TRAINING: Students from institutions of higher education, staff of own agency, community caretakers, other agency's staff.

RECIPIENT REIMBURSEMENT STATUS: The source from which an organization is reimbursed for services provided to a recipient. (Synonym: pay status)

RECIPIENT SATISFACTION: Reports by individuals or community recipients regarding their degree of satisfaction or improvement.

RECORD-KEEPING, OTHER: Preparation, updating, filing, retrieval, and use of records related to office communications, work flow, scheduling and facility operations.

RECORDS MANAGEMENT: Patient-client clinical records: Preparation and updating of health and other records necessary for the provision of individual-oriented services, including scoring and report writing related to psychological tests. Includes notating in clinical records by staff.

RECORDS OFFICER, CLINICAL: A person responsible for the organization and maintenance of clinical records of recipients. (Medical record administrator in hospital unit)

RECREATION THERAPIST: A practitioner who uses recreational skills and techniques in the treatment and rehabilitation of patients.

REFERRAL: Services which direct, guide or link the recipient to other appropriate community resources.

REFERRAL SOURCE: The individual, agency or group who recommended service to recipient or recipient to service.

REGULATION: A rule or order having the force of law issued by an executive branch of government to control custom, practice or conduct.

REHABILITATION, RESTORATION, HABILITATION SERVICES: Services related to preparing or training a person to function within the limits of the original or residual disability by the acquisition, return or accommodation to loss of skills, knowledge.

RESEARCH OR PROGRAM ANALYST: A person who plans, organizes, performs studies and prepares reports about the program's effectiveness and efficiency or does independent research studies.

RESOURCES: The personnel, equipment, supplies, physical structures and money, owned or controlled, which are the source of supply or support of the operation of an organization.

REVENUES: The amount of all potential income, at the program's full established rates, of all services rendered to recipients, regardless of the amounts actually paid by or on behalf of the recipient, including both fee and fund revenues.

ROOM AND SHELTER: A service designed to provide the necessary sleeping and living space to the recipient.

RURAL PLACE: That portion of some area which is not classified as urban.

SCREENING: Activities which determine the type and extent of the problem of the individual seeking help, conducted by persons competent to make such judgements.

SECOND ORDER INTERACTION: Continuous delivery of services to a recipient for a substantial portion of a 24-hour period in the service setting. Includes day, night, weekend, half-way, quarter-way, millieu and therapeutic communities, classes and conferences, etc...status and may be subclassified accordingly.

SERVICE MISSION: One or more related activities or transactions between the recipient and provider, or on behalf of the recipient or a third party, which is intended to produce a defined outcome.

SESSION: Face-to-face staff-to-group. (See Part 6-B.)

SET RATE: The established charge which to varying degrees reflects the cost value of the services provided to recipients.

SHELTERED WORK: A service in which the handicapped may receive 1) work evaluation; 2) social and personal adjustment training; 3) vocational skill training; 4) extended employment either in transition to outside employment or as a terminal work adjustment (may be reported separately).

SHORT-TERM FACILITIES: A short-term facility is one in which over 50 per cent of all patients admitted stay less than 30 days. However, in facilities such as residential drug units, different time durations may constitute short-term.

SITE: The local place or scene at which the provider staff are present at the time services are delivered.

SIXTH ORDER INTERACTION: Receiving no services of any kind but has the status of being a member of the target population.

SOCIAL REHABILITATION SERVICE: The process of helping an individual in his psycho-social adjustment by learning or relearning social skills. Includes occupational therapy, industrial therapy, recreational therapy, resocialization programs and music therapy.

SOCIAL WORK CASE AIDE OR TECHNICIAN: A practitioner who works under the supervision of a social worker to carry limited social work responsibilities.

SOCIAL WORKER: A practitioner specially trained in social and community techniques to help families and patients with their social problems and adjustment to community.

SOCIAL WORKER, GENERIC: A practitioner with an MSW or Bachelor's degree in social work, but not specialized.

SOCIO-EPIDEMIOLOGICAL RESEARCH: Studies to determine incidence and prevalence of various disabilities and problems related to socioeconomic and epidemiclogical factors.

SOMATIC TREATMENT: Treatment of mental disorder by the use of physical procedures other than chemotherapy or detoxification. Includes electroconvulsive therapy, insulin therapy, narcotherapy, hydrotherapy, etc.

SPECIAL EDUCATION AND TUTORING SERVICE: Training and teaching of the mentally retarded and emotionally disturbed to increase their social, academic and vocational skills.

REHABILITATION, RESTORATION, HABILITATION SERVICES: Services related to preparing or training a person to function within the limits of the original or residual disability by the acquisition, return or accommodation to loss of skills, knowledge.

RESEARCH OR PROGRAM ANALYST: A person who plans, organizes, performs studies and prepares reports about the program's effectiveness and efficiency or does independent research studies.

RESOURCES: The personnel, equipment, supplies, physical structures and money, owned or controlled, which are the source of supply or support of the operation of an organization.

REVENUES: The, .amount ,of all., potential income, at the program's full established rates, of all services rendered to recipients, regardless of the amounts actually paid by or on behalf of the recipient, including both fee and fund revenues.

ROOM AND SHELTER: A service designed to provide the necessary sleeping and living space to the recipient.

RURAL PLACE: That portion of some area which is not classified as urban.

SCREENING: Activities which determine the type and extent of the problem of the individual seeking help, conducted by persons competent to make such judgements.

SECOND ORDER INTERACTION: Continuous delivery of services to a recipient for a substantial portion of a 24-hour period in the service setting. Includes day, night, weekend, half-way, quarter-way, millieu and therapeutic communities, classes and conferences, etc...status and may be subclassified accordingly.

SERVICE MISSION: One or more related activities or transactions between the recipient and provider, or on behalf of the recipient or a third party, which is intended to produce a defined outcome.

SESSION: Face-to-face staff-to-group. (See Part 6-B.)

SET RATE: The established charge which to varying degrees reflects the cost value of the services provided to recipients.

SHELTERED WORK: A service in which the handicapped may receive 1) work evaluation; 2) social and personal adjustment training; 3) vocational skill training; 4) extended employment either in transition to outside employment or as a terminal work adjustment (may be reported separately).

SHORT-TERM FACILITIES: A short-term facility is one in which over 50 per cent of all patients admitted stay less than 30 days. However, in facilities such as residential drug units, different time durations may constitute short-term.

SITE: The local place or scene at which the provider staff are present at the time services are delivered.

SIXTH ORDER INTERACTION: Receiving no services of any kind but has the status of being a member of the target population.

SOCIAL REHABILITATION SERVICE: The process of helping an individual in his psycho-social adjustment by learning or relearning social skills. Includes occupational therapy, industrial therapy, recreational therapy, resocialization programs and music therapy.

SOCIAL WORK CASE AIDE OR TECHNICIAN: A practitioner who works under the supervision of a social worker to carry limited social work responsibilities.

SOCIAL WORKER: A practitioner specially trained in social and community techniques to help families and patients with their social problems and adjustment to community.

SOCIAL WORKER, GENERIC: A practitioner with an MSW or Bachelor's degree in social work, but not specialized.

SOCIO-EPIDEMIOLOGICAL RESEARCH: Studies to determine incidence and prevalence of various disabilities and problems related to socioeconomic and epidemiclogical factors.

SOMATIC TREATMENT: Treatment of mental disorder by the use of physical procedures other than chemotherapy or detoxification. Includes electroconvulsive therapy, insulin therapy, narcotherapy, hydrotherapy, etc.

SPECIAL EDUCATION AND TUTORING SERVICE: Training and teaching of the mentally retarded and emotionally disturbed to increase their social, academic and vocational skills.

SPECIAL TEACHER: A certified teacher with special preparation for working with the mentally retarded, emotionally disturbed or children with special learning disabilities.

SPECIAL THERAPISTS, OTHER: Practitioners who use specific skills and techniques in the treatment and rehabilitation of patients. (They may be classified by the technique such as art, music, drama, etc.)

SPEECH AND HEARING THERAPY: Corrective work for such disorders.

SPEECH EVALUATION: An evaluation to determine the cause and extent of speech disorders and need for corrective work.

STAFF: The personnel or combination of personnel who perform the activities and functions that comprise the services of a program.

STAFF ENHANCEMENT: Professional advancement or enrichment for the benefit of the recipients.

STAFF-ORIENTED CONSULTATION: Consultation, the purpose of which is to improve the knowledge, skills, attitudes or insights of the consultee himself, or to help him with crises associated with his emotional or related problems.

STAFFING-RECRUITING: The classifying, specifying, recruiting, selecting, placing and promoting of the organization's personnel.

STANDARD: A state or condition accepted as a minimal or exemplary condition, appearing in law, regulation or policy.

STANDARD METROPOLITAN STATISTICAL AREA (SMSA): Consists of a county or group of counties containing at least one city (or "twin cities") having 50,000 inhabitants or more (central city), plus adjacent counties that are metropolitan in character and are economically and socially integrated with the central city. The name of the central city is used as the name of the SMSA. In New England, SMSA's are defined in terms of cities and towns.

STATE: The major political units of the United States.

STATE FUND REVENUE: Revenue received as authorized by any act of state legislatures or executive branches of state governments other than fees in payment for specific services rendered.

STATISTICIAN: A person responsible for gathering, maintaining, analyzing, reporting and interpreting aggregate data about the recipients, staff and services of a program.

STEP-VARIABLE COSTS: The costs which vary over a wide range of program activity but do not fluctuate directly in proportion to some measure of program activity.

SUITABILITY DETERMINATION: Services intended to provide information about the availability or eligibility of a person for another organization's services.

SUPERVISED OBSERVATION: A service designed to provide the recipient with a protective, concerned observer, to gather information or to protect the recipient from harming himself, others or material goods.

SUPERVISING-DIRECTING: The assignment of tasks and review of performance to see that personnel perform appropriately.

SUPPLIES: The expendable articles and materials such as office, wearing apparel, Pharmaceuticals, housekeeping, dietary, fuel, audio-visual tapes, laboratory, testing, educational materials and supplies, etc.

SUPPLY OFFICER: A person who manages the inventories and stocks of supplies and equipment.

SUPPORT TRANSACTIONS, OTHER: Dictation, transcribing, case-recording, filing, typing, proof-reading, scheduling, billing, fee collection, drug dispensing, bookkeeping and related support transactions.

TARGET POPULATION: The population group or subgroup toward which the services of programs, organizations and organizational units are directed.

TEAM: Organizational units which consist of officially designated multi-disciplinary staff groups who coordinate and supplement their skills to provide services to recipients other than the organization itself, or the organization itself.

TEAM, EVALUATION: A team in which each specialist provides his specialty services as he feels they are indicated; evaluation decisions are made at team conferences.

TEAM, CLINICAL: A team of clinical staff and technologists officially designated who coordinate and supplement their skills to provide individual-oriented services to recipients other than the organization itself.

TEAM, CO-EQUAL: A team of workers in which there is no "captain," but each member is equal in making decisions. Roles of various team members may vary from day to day.

TEAM, MEDICAL (psychiatric) OR TREATMENT: A team of various professionals whose efforts are all directed by a physician or psychiatrist. This is the traditional treatment team.

TEAM, ONE-WORKER COORDINATED: A team in which the recipient has a single person, often a mental health worker, as his major coordinator for the decisions and activities of the team.

TEAM, REHABILITATION: A team of workers concerned primarily with the rehabilitation of the recipient and usually directed by a vocational counselor.

TECHNIQUES AND KNOWLEDGE: The sum of what is known and the technical methods for applying the body of knowledge, information and principles about mental illness, mental retardation, alcohol abuse, drug abuse and human behavior in general.

TELEPHONE INDIVIDUAL CONTACT: Contact by telephone with individuals and small groups to, from or about recipient.

TELEVISION, RADIO, MOTION PICTURE FILM OR AUDIO RECORDING: Contact through radio, television, film, or recording of lectures, panel discussion, interviews, demonstrations or documentary programs.

THERAPEUTIC COMMUNITY: Treatment by the use of continuous controlled congregate community living and manipulation of the community dynamics of the members of that community.

THIRD ORDER INTERACTION: Intermittent delivery of servcies to a recipient on a periodic scheduled short visit basis. Includes a scheduled outpatient service, regularly scheduled short training sessions and consultation status.

TRAINING OFFICER: A person who organizes and directs training functions such as orientation programs, in-service training, affiliate programs for professional students, continuing education and organizational development programs for staff.

TRANSACTION MODE: The generic method used by the provider staff in delivering services or performing support functions.

TRANSACTION UNITS: Simple count of the number of various services or steps carried out or completed.

TRANSPORTATION: A service designed to provide the recipient with the means to travel or to move about from place to place, by auto, bus or other conveyance.

TRAVEL: Physical movement from one location to another by auto, bus, rail or air transportation.

TREATMENT OR COUNSELING SERVICES: Services related to the reduction of disability or discomfort, amelioration of signs and symptoms and changes in specific physical, mental or social functioning.

UNITED STATES: Fifty states and the District of Columbia, excluding outlying areas of American Samoa, Canal Zone, Commonwealth of Puerto Rico.

UNRELATED MEETINGS, CONFERENCES, WORKSHOPS: Participation in such meetings, conferences or workshops that do not directly relate to the mission, objectives or goals of the organization.

URBAN PLACE: The term "place" refers to a concentration of population, regardless of legally prescribed units, powers or function. Urban places include all incorporated and unincorporated places of 2,500 or more and the towns, townships and counties classified as urban.

VARIABLE COSTS: The costs that are expected to fluctuate directly in proportion to some measure of program activity (such as the number of patients in beds; such as the number of patient-interviews).

VISITS: Face-to-face staff-to-others, individual contacts to include interviews and visits for the purpose of observation or visual inspection.

VOCATIONAL COUNSELOR: A practitioner trained in vocational testing and counseling who uses these techniques in the vocational and social rehabilitation of patients.

VOCATIONAL REHABILITATION, COUNSELING: Process to assist an individual in developing work skills, habits and attitudes and to assist him in job placement.

VOLUNTEER: A person who offers his services in a program free of charge. Most often these are part-time workers.

VOLUNTEER, GROUP: A person who provides his services as a member of a group (i.e., women's club, *a* fraternity, a church group). These services are often of a social or recreational kind.

VOLUNTEER, INDIVIDUAL: A person who offers his services as an individual (i.e., an art instructor, a foster grandparent).

VOLUNTEERS, DIRECTOR OF: A person who recruits, orients, assigns and assures the appropriate use of a volunteer staff. WAITING: Unarranged waiting for an activity to begin.

WRITTEN MESSAGE, INDIVIDUAL: Contact by individual letter, memorandum, telegram or other written message to, from or about recipient.

WRITTEN, OTHER: Contact through special pamphlet, poster, brochure, leaflets, flyers, textbooks, instructional material, etc.

WRITTEN TEST, INDIVIDUAL: Contact through administration of a written or mixed oral and written test, examination or observation test.

ZIP CODE AREA OR ZIP AREA: A numbered area for directing and sorting mail. Zip areas are established by the U.S. Post Office and may change according to postal requirements.

ANSWER SHEET

TEST NO. _____ PART _____ TITLE OF POSITION _____
(AS GIVEN IN EXAMINATION ANNOUNCEMENT - INCLUDE OPTION, IF ANY)

PLACE OF EXAMINATION _____ DATE _____
(CITY OR TOWN) (STATE)

RATING

USE THE SPECIAL PENCIL. MAKE GLOSSY BLACK MARKS.

	A	B	C	D	E		A	B	C	D	E		A	B	C	D	E		A	B	C	D	E		A	B	C	D	E
1						26						51						76						101					
2						27						52						77						102					
3						28						53						78						103					
4						29						54						79						104					
5						30						55						80						105					
6						31						56						81						106					
7						32						57						82						107					
8						33						58						83						108					
9						34						59						84						109					
10						35						60						85						110					

Make only ONE mark for each answer. Additional and stray marks may be counted as mistakes. In making corrections, erase errors COMPLETELY.

	A	B	C	D	E		A	B	C	D	E		A	B	C	D	E		A	B	C	D	E		A	B	C	D	E
11						36						61						86						111					
12						37						62						87						112					
13						38						63						88						113					
14						39						64						89						114					
15						40						65						90						115					
16						41						66						91						116					
17						42						67						92						117					
18						43						68						93						118					
19						44						69						94						119					
20						45						70						95						120					
21						46						71						96						121					
22						47						72						97						122					
23						48						73						98						123					
24						49						74						99						124					
25						50						75						100						125					

ANSWER SHEET

ST NO. _____ PART _____ TITLE OF POSITION _____
(AS GIVEN IN EXAMINATION ANNOUNCEMENT - INCLUDE OPTION, IF ANY)

PLACE OF EXAMINATION _____ DATE _____
(CITY OR TOWN)   (STATE)

RATING

USE THE SPECIAL PENCIL. MAKE GLOSSY BLACK MARKS.

	A	B	C	D	E		A	B	C	D	E		A	B	C	D	E		A	B	C	D	E		A	B	C	D	E
1						26						51						76						101					
2						27						52						77						102					
3						28						53						78						103					
4						29						54						79						104					
5						30						55						80						105					
6						31						56						81						106					
7						32						57						82						107					
8						33						58						83						108					
9						34						59						84						109					
10						35						60						85						110					

Make only ONE mark for each answer. Additional and stray marks may be counted as mistakes. In making corrections, erase errors COMPLETELY.

	A	B	C	D	E		A	B	C	D	E		A	B	C	D	E		A	B	C	D	E		A	B	C	D	E
11						36						61						86						111					
12						37						62						87						112					
13						38						63						88						113					
14						39						64						89						114					
15						40						65						90						115					
16						41						66						91						116					
17						42						67						92						117					
18						43						68						93						118					
19						44						69						94						119					
20						45						70						95						120					
21						46						71						96						121					
22						47						72						97						122					
23						48						73						98						123					
24						49						74						99						124					
25						50						75						100						125					